St.Helens Community Libraries

This book is due for return on or before the last date shown. Fines are charged on overdue books. Renewal may be made by personal application, post or telephone, quoting date, author, title and book number.

- 7 NOV 2013		
4 - DEC 2015		
2 2 MAR 2018		
2 7 NOV 2018		

Towns & Villages of Britain:

LANCASHIRE

Michael Smout

Series editor: Terry Marsh

Copyright © Michael Smout, 1999

All Rights Reserved. No part of this publication may be reproduced, stored in a retrieval system, or transmitted in any form or by any means – electronic, mechanical, photocopying, recording, or otherwise – without prior written permission from the publisher.

Published by Sigma Leisure – an imprint of
Sigma Press, 1 South Oak Lane, Wilmslow, Cheshire SK9 6AR, England.

British Library Cataloguing in Publication Data
A CIP record for this book is available from the British Library.

ISBN: 1-85058-644-6

Series Editor: Terry Marsh

Typesetting and Design by: Sigma Press, Wilmslow, Cheshire.

Cover Design: MFP Design & Print

Cover photographs: main picture – Halton village; smaller pictures, from top – Turton Tower, Turton; Downham; Cockersands Abbey, Cockerham.

Photographs: Micheal Smout (unless attributed otherwise)

Map: Morag Perrott

Printed by: MFP Design & Print

Preface

'Don't go yet,' shouted the old farmer, just outside Goosnargh. I had just taken a photograph of an old wayside cross he had pointed out to me. I went back along the road to see what he wanted me for. 'There's another cross just down the road,' he told me. 'Go past the house, turn left up the lane and you'll find it in the hedge.' He was typical of the many Lancastrians who have helped in the writing of this book. Wherever I went, the local post office and pub were always a ready source of information, as were the churchyard grass-cutter and the churchwarden. I'm not usually the asking sort, preferring to get well and truly lost before being humble enough to ask for directions, but everybody I met in my travels round the county - in town, village or farm - was invariably willing to be of help rather than to view me as a prospective burglar.

In researching the material, I visited many local libraries and county information centres. Again, all concerned went out of their way to be of assistance. County councils get beaten over the head for all sorts of things these days, so I am glad to be able to be unstinting in my praise.

One day I may write a book under some such title as *The Black Spots of Lancashire*. One of the black spots would be the number of churches that are closed to visitors. I quickly admit that the command 'Physician, heal thyself' comes to mind, since one of those guilty is my own church of St Michael, Aughton. I know that church insurers take a dim view of buildings that are left open, especially those in centres of population. Andrew Lloyd-Webber has helped to finance a small scheme to enable churches of particular interest to be open during the week. It would be good if this sort of scheme could be extended. Perhaps the lottery fund would be willing to extend its provision of money for church buildings to include financing supervision of open churches, particularly during the summer months.

Acknowledgements

My thanks are due to those who have helped in the labour of producing this volume. Terry Marsh, the series editor, has given advice and support beyond the call of duty. The fact that he is a Lancastrian living near Preston has been an additional bonus. I am grateful to Terry and Brian Wallington for allowing me to use some of their photographs. Graham Beech and the staff at Sigma Press have been their usual helpful selves. My wife Val, besides coming with me on some of my explorations, has stoically put up with the disappearance of the family car at often inconvenient times.

Michael Smout

LANCASHIRE

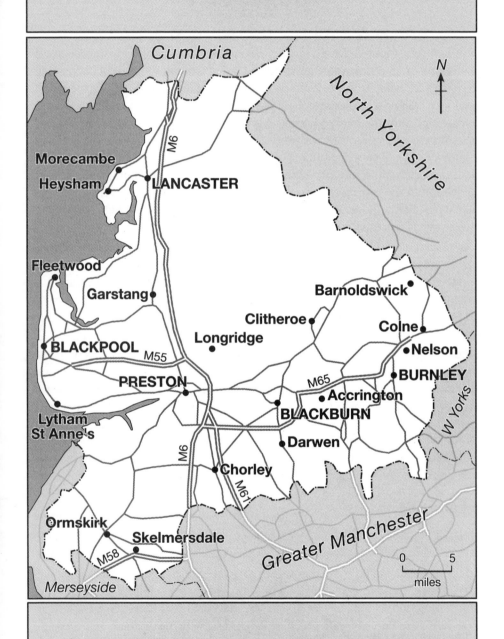

Contents

Introduction

Introduction to the Series

The 'Towns and Villages of Britain' is a series of titles detailing a county-by-county approach to the many delights and fascinations of our country's cities, towns, villages and hamlets. There is much of interest and value throughout our towns and villages, but not all of it is widely documented, and some of it, particularly local customs, folklore and traditions, is in danger of being lost forever. By bringing all this information together, county-by-county, it becomes possible to build a unique and substantially comprehensive library of knowledge.

All the books in the series are compiled to the same specification and in gazetteer format, and include information about the way or the reason a town or village evolved; references to anything associated with the preservation of the past, such as museums, heritage centres, historic or prehistoric sites, battle sites, places of worship and other locally or architecturally important buildings. Landscape features are also detailed, including important natural history sites, geological sites, water features, etc. as is information about important local people, and details of events or traditions, such as well-dressings and rush-bearing ceremonies. There are also notes about any significant present-day informal amenity/recreational features, like country parks, open access land, Areas of Outstanding Natural Beauty, nature reserves, and Sites of Special Scientific Interest. Finally, information is given on any significant Roman or prehistory context, and any anecdotal or endemic folklore references associated with the town or village which might illustrate a particular way of life or social development. The books are therefore eminently suitable for anyone interested in their own locality or in local history; students of history, folklore and related subjects; professional journalists wanting up-to-date and comprehensive information; public relations and similar businesses; photographers and artists, and, of course, the tourists and visitors to the counties.

Explanatory Notes

It has been suggested that to qualify as a village, a 'community' must possess a school, a pub, a post office and a church. Such a requirement, however, excludes a large number of places in Lancashire that are of immense interest, many having important historical associations, and which have played a vital part in the development of the county and its people. So, for the purposes of the books in this series, the criteria for inclusion have been kept deliberately simple: there must be something of interest about the place; or it must have associations with events and people of countywide or wider significance.

Often, the 'something of interest' will simply be the village church (its history, contents or architecture), or its green or a river bridge. In addition, the village may be important to the heritage of the county because it maintainsthe traditions, ways and beliefs of Lancashire culture, or has played a key role in the social, economic or political history of the county or the country as a whole.

Only occasionally, however, is the village pub of special interest in this context, and often the development of large supermarkets within easy travelling distance of the villages has, sadly, signalled the demise of the traditional village shop. Local schools have often been swallowed up by larger schools, and far too many post offices are proving difficult to sustain as viable concerns. So, while that 'classic' definition of a village has much to commend it, in reality it is today too restrictive.

Quite what makes a town is another, arguable, matter. But the precise definition is here not too important; it's the place and its people, not its status, that matters. As a very broad distinction, that no-one should take seriously, a 'hamlet' (a few of which appear in these books) is a distinct community, while a 'village' could be said to be a hamlet with a church, and a 'town' is a village with a market.

In many cases, the historical development of the community, whether a tiny village, a town or a city, is fascinating in itself, and so it is that each entry gradually builds up a picture of the county that is unique. That is what this book endeavours to portray, in a logical and easily accessible way, as well as being a source of reference.

Inevitably, there will be places that have been omitted that others might argue should have been included. But the value each community has to bring to a work of this nature has been carefully weighed; invariably, borderline cases have been given the benefit of the doubt and included.

It is equally clear that, taken to its logical conclusion, this book would be ten times larger, and there has had to be a considerable degree of selective editing to make it of manageable size. One day, perhaps, there could be one book that says everything there is to say about Lancashire . But could we afford to buy it?

Could we carry it? Would we want it, when part of the beauty of what does exist is the range of voices and shades of opinion so many different authors can bring?

Following the General Introduction, the book becomes a gazetteer, listing the towns and villages of the county in alphabetical order.

After each town or village name there appears, in square brackets, [ ], the name of the relevant district council (see below).

Next appears a two-letter, four-figure grid reference, which will pinpoint the settlement to within half a mile (one kilometre). This is followed by an approximate distance from some other, usually larger, settlement, together with an equally approximate direction indicator.

Those features or people 'of interest' directly associated with the settlement are highlighted in bold text, while an index lists other features or people only incidentally associated.

Where information is given about events, such as agricultural shows, or facilities, like museums, details of dates and hours of opening are available from any of the Tourist Information Centres listed at the end of this introductory section.

Lancashire

Memories of pre-1974 Lancashire linger long in the minds of those who, from that date, found themselves exiled to another area without having to move house. The population lost was disproportionately large for the amount of land. At the northern end, some of old Lancashire disappeared to help create the new county of Cumbria. At the other extreme, the cities of Manchester and Liverpool, and towns such as Southport, St Helens, Bolton and Wigan were swallowed up to form Greater Manchester and Merseyside. Warrington fell off the end into Cheshire. Even now, some are not reconciled to the situation. Southport, for instance, has a vocal group which advocates the return of the town to its Lancastrian roots. However, all was not loss all those years ago. Overnight, people who lived in parts of the West Riding of Yorkshire found that they were suddenly Lancastrians. All in all, the county became more rural than it had been, having been deprived of many of its large centres of population.

The thrill of new Lancashire is that it has a little bit of everything. To the east are the mill towns of the later Industrial Revolution – Blackburn (now a city), Burnley, Darwen and those strung along the Rossendale Valley. There are towns steeped in history – Lancaster being a prime example; seaside resorts such as Blackpool and Morecambe; and market centres such as Ormskirk and Kirkham. The railway town of Carnforth should also not be forgotten.

It is hard to find a village that has not had some connection with the hand-loom weaving industry. The estate villages of the likes of Downham, Bolton-by-Bowland and Singleton have an atmosphere all their own. The landscape moves from the often dour vistas of West Lancashire and the Fylde to the more rugged scenery of the Forest of Bowland, Pendle Hill and the West Pennine Moors. Rivers and streams abound, with the huge estuaries of the Ribble and the Wyre disgorging the waters of their many tributaries into the sea. Some of the water which does not make it to the sea is held in reservoirs, such as those at Rivington, to maintain the water supplies to populations often outside Lancashire. More finds a home in the two great arteries of the Lancaster and Leeds and the Liverpool canals.

The sad demolition of historic houses, particularly since the Second World War, has still left many with tales to tell. Gawthorpe, Samlesbury, and Towneley halls are but a few of those which encapsulate the histories of the landed gentry and lords of the manor. Ancient churches at Whalley, Barnoldswick, Great Mitton, Churchtown and elsewhere are a reminder of the role of the spiritual in the lives of every generation. The scant remains of Whalley, Sawley and Cockersand Abbeys point to an age when the recycling of material for use elsewhere was more important than a sense of history.

The Roman Conquest

A few Bronze Age and Iron Age circles are amongst the scant remains of those lengthy periods. The Bleasdale Circle represents the former, and the fort on Warton Crag the latter. The Romans were content simply to keep the area under control and left the population to get on with life and business undisturbed. Agricola established his fort at Ribchester in AD80. At Quernmore, the discovery of kilns for manufacturing tiles indicates that the Roman leaders lived in some style. The bathhouse at Lancaster reveals a little of the domestic life of those times.

The Norman Conquest

King William rewarded Roger de Poitou for his support during the conquest by giving him the land between the Ribble and the Mersey. In 1087, the area north of the Ribble was added to this. To establish his position at the main crossing point of the River Lune, Roger built a castle at Lancaster. The Domesday Survey of 1086, surveying all the lands south of the River Tyne, was a massive undertaking. The land that lies south of the Ribble in the modern county was described in the volume which covered land in Cheshire, while the rest of the county came under a general North-West heading.

The Dissolution of the Monasteries

The response of the Catholic North to the dissolution of the monasteries by Henry VIII was the revolt called the Pilgrimage of Grace. The monasteries had held great influence in terms of land, wealth and faith. Many had become corrupt and feeble. Henry took the opportunity to deprive them of their power and transfer their lands to his retainers. It is from this time that the histories of the great land-owning dynasties begin. The revolt of 1536-7, although strongest in Yorkshire and Durham, was supported by the abbots of the Lancashire monasteries, some of whom paid the price when the revolt was defeated. Although the main cause of the rising was ecclesiastical, there was also strong northern social discontent, which helped to encourage the rebellion. Henry responded by executing over 200 of his opponents.

The Civil War

From 1629, Charles I ruled the country without Parliament, proclaiming his belief in the divine right of kings. With the help of Archbishop Laud, the Star Chamber and other such means, he crushed the opposition of the Puritans, a body of Christians who wished to push the country further in a Protestant direction than the Reformation had done. A prominent opponent of the King's was Oliver Cromwell, a convinced Puritan, who founded the New Model Army, whose members were known as Ironsides. This army played a decisive part in the Parliamentary victories at Marston Moor in 1644 and Naseby in 1645. Until the restoration of the monarchy with Charles II in 1660, the Puritans were to be the dominant religious force in England.

In Lancashire, the Reformation had not penetrated very far. The leading families, such as the Blundells of Crosby, were nearly all Catholic, whereas Manchester was a Puritan stronghold. It follows that Catholic Lancashire supported the Royalists, and the Manchester part of it favoured the Parliamentarians. In 1643, the 7th Earl of Derby, with homes at Lathom and Knowsley, retrieved Preston, which had been taken by the Parliamentarians a few months previously. Whilst he was called away to his lands in the Isle of Man, the forces of Parliament retook Preston, plus Hornby and Thurland Castles. Lathom House, defended by the Earl of Derby's wife, Charlotte de Tremouille, in his absence, was placed under an unsuccessful siege. Help was lent to the Royalist cause in Lancashire by the arrival of Prince Rupert from the south. After some success at Bolton and Wigan, he was on the losing side at the Battle of Marston Moor, as he made his way towards York. Having made an alliance with Charles I, a Scottish army came south in 1648. It was met by Cromwell and his army around Preston and pursued, in some disorder, up to Walton Bridge. The remnant of the Scottish troops was chased onwards towards Warrington, with various local skirmishes taking place en route. The Earl of Derby paid for his support of the invasion, which was ended by the defeat at Worcester in 1651, by being executed at Bolton.

The restoration of the monarchy, in the shape of Charles II in 1660, led to severe restrictions on ministers who did not adhere to the liturgy and doctrine of the Church of England. The following year, Parliament passed the Clarendon Code. Two of its provisions had religious significance. The Act of Uniformity of 1662 restored the Book of Common Prayer in a slightly revised form. Two thousand ministers were ejected from the Church of England for refusing to assent to this. This led to the beginnings of Nonconformity. Three years later, the Five Mile Act prevented such ministers from coming within five miles of any city, town or parliamentary borough. Amongst the ministers who left their parishes at the time of the Great Ejection were Oliver Heywood of Ormskirk and Thomas Jollie of Altham.

The Age of Witchcraft

Along with Protestantism and Catholicism ran a third religious strand, that of superstition and witchcraft. King James I was a fervent believer in the evil power of witches and introduced harsh measures against witchcraft in 1604, a year after his accession to the throne of England. The word 'witches' means 'wise ones'. From the early centuries, they were simply the conductors of pagan nature rights. They were considered evil only from the 14th century, when their role was seen as opposed to the good of Christianity. This developed into a belief that witches had bad influences over people. The threat

they represented was taken so seriously that, in 1645, a 'Witchfinder General' was appointed to root them out. In Lancashire, the trial of the Pendle Witches in 1612 was the climax to the story of witchcraft in the county. See the entry for BARLEY.

The Quakers or Society of Friends

Within three years of George Fox founding the Quaker movement (see BARLEY entry), it had fifty thousand followers. From the 1650s, the term 'Quakers', became a nickname of the group, who *quaked* before the word of God. An interesting feature of Quaker graveyards is that few of the graves have any markings to identify the deceased.

The Jacobite Rebellions

After the death of Queen Anne in 1714, an invasion was made from Scotland in the following year, with the aim of placing James Edward, the son of James II, the Old Pretender, on the throne. The army, with support from John Dalton of Thurnham Hall, reached Lancaster, where James was proclaimed king. However, there was little local backing and the army was defeated at Preston. In 1745, Charles Edward, the Young Pretender, again rallied support in Scotland to replace George II as king. He and his troops took the same route through the north-west of England, passing through Preston and Manchester. At Derby, his officers refused to go any further and the long retreat started. Back in Scotland, Bonny Prince Charlie and his troops were comprehensively defeated at the Battle of Culloden.

The Industrial Revolution

By the middle of the 18th century, most of the cotton produced in England came from Lancashire, mainly in the form of fustian. But it was a slow process because of the weakness of the thread and the cumbersome process of manufacture. A number of inventions revolutionised the industry. In 1733, John Kay of Bury invented the flying-shuttle, which meant that there no longer needed to be a worker on either side of the loom. In 1764, James Hargreaves, from Standhill, produced his 'spinning jenny'. This enabled more threads to be spun on one machine. Five years later, James Arkwright of Preston unveiled the water frame. The extra strength of the warp enabled the looms to be driven by water power. Finally, in 1799 Samuel Crompton produced his 'mule', which produced a thread fine enough for muslin to be manufactured.

There were two main results of these advances in technology. Production started to move from the cottages and loom shops to custom-built mills near to good sources of water power. Arkwright himself built a mill at Birkacre in 1777 and Robert Peel, scion of a famous family, opened one in Bury. The invention of the steam engine by James Watt in 1761 led to the change from water to steam power in the mills. Work moved away from the smaller villages to mill towns such as Blackburn and Burnley. Along with this, fewer workers were needed for the production process. The consequent threat of unemployment led to riots such as the Plug Riot of 1842, when workers pulled the plugs out of mill boilers to disable them. More problems arose for the workers during the American Civil War when, in 1861, the southern ports were unable to export cotton because of the blockade imposed by the northern states. As workers in Lancashire were laid off, the consequence was much suffering and deprivation.

Vital to the success of the Industrial Revolution was the digging of the Leeds and Liverpool Canal. The Parliamentary bill was passed in 1770. Starting with construction in Halsall, the whole enterprise took 46 years to complete and cost £1.2 million. It was a huge engineering feat, which involved 100 locks in its 120 miles.

County Information Centres

Accrington – Town Hall, Accrington. Telephone 01254 872595

Blackburn – 15/17 Railway Road, Blackburn. Telephone 01254 681120

Blackpool – 1 Clifton Street, Blackpool. Telephone 01253 478222 (Seasonal: Promenade, Blackpool. Telephone 01253 478235)

Burnley – The Bus Station, Burnley. Telephone 01282 423125

Charnock Richard – M6 Motorway Service Area, Charnock Richard, Chorley. Telephone 01257 793773

Chorley – 55/57 Union Street, Chorley. Telephone 01257 241693

Clitheroe – 12/14 Market Place, Clitheroe. Telephone 01200 442226

Fleetwood – 15 North Albert Street, Fleetwood. Telephone 01253 772704

Lancaster – Bus Station, Lancaster. Telephone 01524 841656

Leyland – 116/118 Towngate, Leyland. Telephone 01772 621857

Lytham – 4 Clifton Square, Lytham. Telephone 01253 794405

Morecambe – Station Buildings, Central Promenade, Morecambe. Telephone 01524 582808

Nelson – Bus Station, Broadway, Nelson. Telephone 01282 698533

Ormskirk – Bus Station, Moor Street, Ormskirk. Telephone 01695 579062

Preston – Bus Station, Preston. Telephone 01772 556618

Rossendale – Kay Street, Rawtenstall. Telephone 01706 213677

Skelmersdale – Unit 59c, The Concourse, Skelmersdale. Telephone 01695 50463

The Towns & Villages

ABBEYSTEAD [Lancaster and Morecambe]

SD5654: 7 miles (11km) SE of Lancaster

Situated near the banks of the River Wyre, this small village of stone cottages was once part of Lord Sefton's estate, as were the surrounding farmsteads. At the centre of the village is the school, dating from 1674, and a water fountain in the wall of the 19th-century house opposite. To the west of the house is a round, stone-walled pinfold, where stray sheep used to be deposited. The name of the village is thought to refer to the **Abbey of Wyreside**, which was a Cistercian foundation from the mother abbey of Furness. The supposed site of the abbey is 100m/yds from the school. A local man, **William Cawthorne**, built and endowed the school. He was clerk to the governors of St Bartholomew's Hospital in London from 1661 to 1675. Tragedy struck the village in 1984, when sixteen people from St Michael's-on-Wyre, on a visit to a water scheme, were killed by an explosion of methane gas.

Known as the 'Shepherds' Church', the **church of Christ Church** is a mile (1.5km) west of the village, on the Dolphinholme road. It is called this because of the windows depicting sheep and shepherds. The words of Jesus on the lych-gate ('I am the door') continue this theme from Chapter 10 of St John's Gospel. The windows, and most of the rest of the building, date from the 1894 restoration. Of the previous structure, the only remains of significance are the 18th-century tower, the 1684 pulpit and a 1599 Geneva Bible. The church stands behind

a barn and war memorial, looking out over extensive views of valleys and hills.

Although Elizabethan in style, **Abbeystead House** was built as a hunting lodge by Lord Sefton in 1886. Known locally as 'The Mansion', it was constructed from local sandstone, brought from the quarry on Tarnbrook Fell. George V was a visitor in 1926. The 19 000 acre (7690 hectares) estate passed into the hands of the Duke of Westminster in 1990. The lodge is on the east side of the bridge and the house is approached along a long, private drive. However, it can be glimpsed from the footpath signposted off the lane by the bridge.

Jubilee Tower, by the roadside on High Cross Moor, 2½ miles (4km) north-west of the village, has fine views across to the coast. It was erected to commemorate the jubilee of Queen Victoria in 1887. When the car park was excavated in 1973, a 7th-century coffin, made from a tree, was found. The shroud was intact, but only the hair and finger nails of the body remained. These items are on show at Lancaster City Museum.

ABBEY VILLAGE [Chorley]

SD6423: 5 miles (8km) NE of Chorley

Close to the woods of Roddlesworth, until 1970 Abbey Village centred on its mill. Although it is now a residential area, the large mill building still dominates the community. The main road is lined with a row of cottages built for the millworkers. Since there was no abbey in the area, it is believed that the village is so named because it was a stopping place on an ancient route to Whalley Abbey,

Sheep pound, Abbeyfield

which started from a secret passage at Brinscall Hall.

ACCRINGTON [Hyndburn]

SD7629: 5 miles (8km) E of Blackburn

The principal town of the borough, the name 'Accrington' signifies a place of acorns. Its growth as a textile centre took place last century, along with a speciality in brick making. The distinctive red bricks are known as 'Accrington Bloods'. New roads, railways and the canal led to calico printing and then cotton weaving.

Today the centre is a conservation area, based on the market hall and traditional shops. The Italian-style architecture of the **Town Hall**, on Blackburn Road, is highlighted by the Corinthian columns supporting the porch over the entrance. It was formerly the Peel Institute, erected in 1858 in memory of the leading mill-owners in the town. At the rear of the Town Hall is the **Market Hall**, with its galleries, cast-iron roof and Roman-style entrance. Built in 1868, it still houses stallholders on market days. The **Carnegie Library**, in St James Street, dates from 1909, and contains busts of Shakespeare, Dante, Milton and others in the entrance hall. **Accrington Stanley football club**, known as 'The 'Owd Reds', was a founder member of the Football League in 1888. The team still plays at the Crown Ground.

The **'Accrington Pals' Regiment'** was one of the most renowned of Kitchener's First World War army. The colours of the Pals are laid up in the **church of St James**, in St James Street. Founded in 1546, the church was rebuilt in 1763 and extended in 1828. The sundial dates from 1718. Inside the church are memorials to the family of Sir Robert Peel, the nineteenth-century Prime Minister, and Sir James Hargreaves, the inventor of the spinning jenny. At the **church of St John the Evangelist**, in Addison Street, is a chapel dedicated to the Pals.

Set in extensive grounds with fine views across the valley, **Hollins Hall**, in Haworth Park, off the Manchester Road south of the centre, was given to the town in 1921. Built in 1909 but in the Tudor style, it was originally the residence of a leading cotton magnate and is now the home of the **Haworth Art Gallery**. The main attraction of the gallery is a collection of 146 items of Tiffany glass from the New York studios of Louis Tiffany. These were donated by a local man who had worked in the studios for 40 years. There is also an exhibition of water colours and 19th-century paintings.

The 19 arches of the stone **Accrington Viaduct** take the East Lancashire Railway high across the River Hyndburn in a spectacular curve.

ADLINGTON [Chorley]

SD6013: 3 miles (5km) SE of Chorley

The 'land of Eadwulf' is the possible Anglo-Saxon derivation of the name. Up to the 18th century, the lands changed in and out of the hands of the Adlington family. From that time, the hall and estates belonged to the Claytons. The only remains of the hall, which were demolished in the middle of the 19th century, are the two lodges and twin pillars on Chorley Lane. The pillars originally had a carved sphinx on top of each one. In the 18th century, some of the first muslins in the country were woven here, before it became a centre of the dyeing industry. Now mainly residential, but with civil engineering as a major industry, the village is well situated for the moors of Anglezarke and Winter Hill. The **church of Christ Church** was built as the parish church in 1839. The growth of the local population led to the erection of the **church of St Paul** in Railway Road in 1885. Approached through a small park, one of its windows was designed by Edward Burne-Jones. A tower was added in 1932 as a war memorial. Christ Church then became a chapel of ease. The building still remains on Church Street. Because of the High Church leanings of the vicar of St Paul's, a group from the congregation broke away to form St Philip's Protestant Reformed church. In 1934 this group reopened Christ Church, where services continued until 1975.

ALTCAR [West Lancashire]

SD3207: 5 miles (8km) W of Ormskirk

This straggling farming village was part of Lord Sefton's estate before it passed into the hands of Lord Leverhulme.

The **church of St Michael and All Angels**, by the sharp bend at the east end of the village, is a small, black and white, timbered church. It was built in the last century to replace an earlier building and remains of the latter (a font and holy water stoup) are found in the churchyard.

ALTHAM [Hyndburn]

SD7733: 2½ miles (5km) NE of Accrington

Disaster struck the village of Altham in 1883, when 68 men and boys were killed in an accident at Moorfield Colliery. The site is now part of the business park for small industries, but a plaque in the **church of St James** commemorates the sad event. The church stands on the A678, west of Altham bridge. Situated at the end of a long, tree-filled churchyard, it was built in Perpendicular style in 1512. The crenellated tower was added in the 19th century. There are traces of the previous Norman building in the tracery of the window at the east end of the north aisle and the piscina on the north wall of the chancel. The headstone of the doorway, built into the wall of the south chancel, is one of only three surviving in England. Also in the chancel are two 13th-century grave markers, which used to be in the churchyard. They have been known as 'Witch Stones', which suggests they may also have served the purpose of warding off evil spirits. In addition, the chancel contains a Jacobean gate-legged table and two 17th-century oak chairs. A priceless possession is one of only three pre-Reformation chalices known to have survived. When an octagonal font was given by Abbot Paslew of Whalley in the early 16th century, its Norman predecessor was relegated to the right corner of the porch. In the middle of the 19th century, the chancel was rebuilt and the gallery removed. A window, at the east end of the chancel, was installed in memory of John Hacking, the inventor of the carding machine. The records reveal a child marriage that was held in the church in 1526, between a nine-year-old girl and ten-year-old boy.

From 1649 to 1662, the Puritan vicar of Altham was **Thomas Jollie**. A strict disciplinarian, he once expelled a parishioner from church for using unchristian language to his mother-in-law. He was ejected when he refused to give assent to the Act of Uniformity. He then became the leader of local Nonconformity, holding secret meetings in the parish until moving to Wymondhouses. In 1930 it was discovered that there were a number of family vaults underneath the chancel, including that of the Whitakers who lived at Simonstone Hall from 1311 until the mid-19th century.

In the 12th century the manor was held by Hugh the Saxon, then by the de Altham family until 1371, and then, for three hundred years, by the Banastres.

Next to the church is the **Walton Arms,** which dates from Tudor times and was a coaching inn.

Altham Mill, adjacent to the Mill House and cottages, down a track off the main road at Altham Bridge, east of the church, was in operation between 1816 and 1880. There had been a mill on the site since the 12th century. Lydia Becker, one of the founders of the Suffragette Movement. lived at **Moorside House**. The house, built in 1830, is along the road off the main road, after the school.

APPLEY BRIDGE [West Lancashire]

SD5210: $3\frac{1}{2}$ miles (6km) N of Skelmersdale

The stone quarries surrounding Appley Bridge led to the growth of the village from an agricultural to an industrial community. The stone was transported by means of the Leeds and Liverpool Canal. As business expanded, so the community expanded up the hill from its original site by the bridge over the River Douglas.

At a crossroads called Dangerous Corner, at the corner of the A5209 and Appley Lane North, is the **Dicconson Arms**. Legend has it that the corner earned its name when the coffin of a farmer's wife fell off the hearse at there. The body came back to life again. When the woman eventually died again, measures were taken to prevent a reoccurrence of the previous happening. This time, as the hearse got to the corner, the farmer shouted to the driver, 'Slow down a bit, this is a dangerous corner.'

Another tale is that anyone removing the skull kept at **Skull House** will suffer the consequences. The house is not in Skull House Lane as might be expected, but in Beacon View opposite. By the bridge, **Basin Cottage** is built into the canal basin. Its café and stables were resting places for the bargees and their horses.

ARKHOLME [Lancaster and Morecambe]

SD5871: 5 miles (8km) E of Carnforth

Arkholme is a small village with stone cottages and cobbled footpaths, nestling in the Lune Valley. Basket-making was one of its traditional industries. Farming continues to be important. **Storrs Hall**, 1 mile (1.5km) south-west of the village on the B6254, was built in 1848 on the site of an earlier building for Francis Pearson, a Kirkby Lonsdale solicitor. At the rear is a mock pele tower.

The road opposite the Bayhorse Inn leads to the 16th-century **church of St John the Baptist**, on the banks of the River Lune. There has been a church on this site since the middle of the 15th century. A plaque on the west wall tells of improvements made in 1788, including the erection of the bellcot to house a 14th-century bell. There are two fonts at the west end, near a tiny model organ on one of the pillars. One is 18th century, the other is late 20th century and a memorial to the last village basket-maker. Above the choir stalls and a south side pillar are 15th-century carvings. On the west wall hangs a copy of the 1279 charter. In the churchyard are the remains of the village cross. The adjacent **Chapel Hill Motte** is a Saxon or Norman fortification.

AUGHTON [Lancaster and Morecambe]

SD5567: 6 miles (9km) NE of Lancaster

Pronounced 'afton', the village is little more than a group of stone cottages clustered around Aughton House. Near the River Claughton and surrounded by farmland, the isolated community is situated on a narrow lane at the bottom of a hill. The 1864 **church of St Saviour** is in another isolated position, on the Lancaster road at the top of the hill. Built of stone, the tiny building has a bellcot.

The hamlet was known as the home of the biggest pudding in the world. A pudding was made every 21 years in a boiler used by basket-makers to boil willows. The boiling process ensured that the willow could be used all the year round rather than only when the sap made it pliable. The pudding was mixed and boiled by the villagers and carried on a dray, which was driven by members of the Lunesdale Hunt. The last of these plum puddings regularly saw the light of day in 1887, although there was a revival of the custom in 1971.

AUGHTON [West Lancashire]

SD3905: 2 miles (3km) S of Ormskirk

Although the original village greens of Aughton (pronounced 'orton') near Ormskirk have been largely overwhelmed by suburban development, there is much of a rural air about the area away from the noise and bustle of the A59 trunk road. The one remaining green is **Holt Green**, at the eastern end of the village. The old cross was replaced in 1914 by a new one commemorating the coronation of King George V in 1911.

The base of the old Holt Green cross is now in the churchyard of the **church of St Michael**. Near it is a sundial that dates from 1736. It was reset in 1877, but still has the original Latin inscription, 'I only count the sunny hours.' The church has the remains of a Norman doorway behind a buttress in the south wall. East of the porch is a buttress across the doorway of the 11th-century church, of which only the lower part of the south wall remains. The tower and steeple were erected in the 14th century, four of the bells being cast in 1715. In the ground-floor bell chamber is a 14th-century font with hasp marks, indicating that it was locked in medieval times. This was to prevent the holy water being taken to cure boils and other illnesses. The five wooden angels by the font, bearing emblems of the Derby family, are some of those which were in the chancel until the restoration in 1876. The tower, unusually built into the north side of the building, contains four bells dating from 1714. The oak beams of the roof of the north aisle were put in place in 1545. There was a major restoration in 1912, mainly involving the removal of the white plaster which covered the inside walls. On Mill Lane, north of the A59, is the base of a wayside cross. It is situated by the entrance of the first house on the left.

Opposite the church, the **Stanley Arms** became a coaching inn when the turnpike road opened. It replaced the Ring o' Bells, which had been situated in the church grounds.

A back bedroom of **Aughton Old Hall** was called 'Cromwell's Room' because he was supposed to have slept there when he came to review the troops before the Battle of Aughton. After the battle of Marston Moor, the retreating Royalists were confronted by a large Roundhead battalion on Aughton Moor, in the area of the present Swanpool Lane. The Royalists suffered heavy losses and fled. The hall has Saxon foundations and was, until the 17th century, the home of the de Aughton family. For two centuries afterwards, the lords of the manor were the Plumbe-Tempest family. In front of the

hall are the remains of a Napoleonic pele tower.

Known as 'The Cathedral on the Hill', the **church of Christ Church** was a daughter church of St Michael's and was built in 1887 from local stone. Its prominent position at the top of Holborn Hill makes it a landmark for miles around.

Moor Hall, on Prescot Road, was built by the Stanley family in the 16th century. This was where Catholics held their worship in secret during times of persecution. Eventually, they found a permanent home with the erection in 1823 of St Mary's Church, further along Prescot Road. The hall remained in the hands of the Stanley family until 1840. Over the doorway were written the words, 'Pray ye for the good estate of Peter Stanley Esq. and Cecily his wife, with their children, who caused this work to be made in the year of our Lord 1566.'

The only remains of the first **Walsh Hall**, off Formby Lane, are part of the moat and a fireplace standing in the middle of a field. Demolished in 1891, this was the ancestral home of the Waleys family, who owned vast tracts of land in Lancashire.

BACUP [Rossendale]

SD8723: 3½ miles (6km) E of Rawtenstall

Moorland surrounds the town of Bacup, which still has some sandstone streets, at the eastern end of the Rossendale Valley. As well as being recognised as one of the best preserved mill towns in the country, it also boasts the shortest street in Britain. This is the 17ft (5.2m) long **Elgin Street**, with its one lone house, reached via Bankside Lane and Lord Street from the town centre.

Traditionally textiles were the main industry in Bacup. Although this is no longer so, the town has received recognition by English Heritage for the way in which the Victorian heritage has been conserved, particularly the Market Hall, the Maden Baths and various shops. **Nut dancing** is popular in the town. This involves groups of dancers dressed in outfits of black jumpers and clogs, kilts, white stockings and turbans. Every Easter Saturday, the Britannia coconutters, from the village 1 mile (1.5km) east of the town, still dance their way through the town. The name 'coconutters' derives from the husks of coconuts placed on the dancers' knees. It is thought that Cornish tin miners brought this essentially pagan tradition to the area in the late 19th century. The actual performance is a type of Morris or Moorish dance. The old town stocks, which were in use until 1850, are on the Todmorden Road.

The **church of St John the Evangelist**, on Bankside Street, was built in 1883. It has no tower, but a very wide aisle. There are relics of 19th-century home and mill life, a collection of butterflies and archaeological specimens at the **Natural History and Folk Museum** on Yorkshire Street. An outbuilding houses a display of industrial archaeology, including gas masks and miners' helmets.

At Moorlands Park, the **Pennine Aviation Museum** includes amongst its exhibits a De Havilland Vampire and a Canberra.

BAMBER BRIDGE [South Ribble]

SD5626: 2½ miles (4.km) SE of Preston

Bamber Bridge is a residential and industrial area, with its Walton Summit, Old Mill and Club Street estates. The main attraction is the Church Road conservation area, in which stands the thatched **Olde**

Hob Inn, which was built in 1616, the year of Shakespeare's death. The nearby Victorian **church of St Saviour** has a tower dating from 1837 and a chancel from 1887.

The **church of St Aidan** in Station Road has a yellow and red exterior. Built in 1895, it was extended in 1915.

The Pugins, father and son, designed the **church of the Blessed Virgin Mary** in Brown Edge Lane. It was built in 1892, although the tower dates from fifteen years earlier.

BALDERSTONE [Ribble Valley]

SD6332: 3½ miles (6km) NW of Blackburn

Near the Horseshoe Bend in the River Ribble, the village is set amongst rolling fields interspersed with woods and coppices. In the centre is the **church of St Leonard**, a sturdy, stone building of 1852, with small windows in the roof. Beech trees grow in the churchyard and small fir trees line the path to the entrance.

BANKS [West Lancashire]

SD3921: 4½ miles (7km) NE of Southport

Cockles, shrimps and fish were part of the village economy until thirty years ago. Greaves Hall, the mansion of Lord and Lady Scarisbrick and now long demolished, was once surrounded by the farms of the estate.

The village has a number of Victorian estate cottages amongst older ones. The area was thought to have been a monastic settlement in the past. It was formerly called North Meols, meaning 'the northern sand banks'. Much land has been reclaimed from the sea over the past two centuries. Farmland is divided from the marshes by a long, high, earth sea wall. One of the village lanes is called **Ralph's Wife's Lane**. Ralph was a local fisherman. He was out fishing one night when a great storm sprang up. When he did not come back, his wife went out looking for him. Her voice could be heard across the marshes calling her husband. He did not return and her ghost is said to haunt the mudflats.

The pulpit, pew and choir stalls of the **church of St Stephen** came from St Peter's pro-cathedral, which was in Church Street, Liverpool until its demolition. St Stephen's, built in 1868 on the main road through the village, has in the churchyard, to the right of the south wall of the building, a memorial to some local fishermen who drowned at sea in 1901, when their boat capsized.

Managed by English Nature, **Ribble Marshes Nature Reserve** is an area of 5391 acres (2182 hectares) of sand and mud, hosting thousands of redshanks and terns. This stretches west along the coast towards Southport and east along the Ribble estuary to Hesketh Bank.

To the east of the village is the hamlet of **Hundred End**. The name clearly indicates that it was the division between two hundreds, that of Leyland and West Derby. The station that used to be here was the dispatch point for the tons of celery that were grown in the area.

BARLEY [Pendle]

SD8240: 4½ miles (7km) E of Clitheroe

Witches and Quakers are an unlikely combination, but both are associated with Pendle Hill which looms over the village of Barley. In the early 1600s, the families of two old women, Demdike and Chat-

tox, lived on the slopes of the hill. They were known locally as witches. In 1612 Alizon Device, a granddaughter of Demdike met a pedlar on the road. When he refused to give her some of his wares, she spirited a dog out of the air. The dog attacked the pedlar and badly injured him. Alizon was arrested and brought before a magistrate. He ordered evidence to be taken from the whole of the family and some of them confessed to witchcraft. Alizon, along with Demdike and her daughter, Ann Redfearn, were taken to Lancaster Castle. Meanwhile, more people were arrested on flimsy testimony. The trial at the castle ended in guilty verdicts. Nine so-called witches were publicly hanged on 20th August.

One day in 1640, the young **George Fox** climbed Pendle Hill. At the top, he had a vision of 'a people to be gathered to the Lord'. He saw Christ gathering people into victory over Satan. Out of this came the founding of the Society of Friends, better known by its derisive nickname, the Quakers. Opposed to state religion, many Quakers were imprisoned for offences such as refusing to speak deferentially to judges, meeting in forbidden religious assembly, or refusing to pay the compulsory church tithe. In court, they refused to take the oath on the basis of the words of Jesus, 'Swear not at all.'

The village is an access point for walkers to **Pendle Hill**, Black Moss and Ogden reservoirs and Stacks Wood. It is dominated by the 1831ft (558m) of the hill. There was a Bronze Age burial mound here, and later a beacon to warn of enemy invasions. There is a tradition that to avoid a curse, a stone has to be carried to the top and placed with the hundreds of others already there. Pendle Water flows through the village of white, stone cottages. The Barley Mow and Pendle Inns are at its centre.

Cattle and sheep farming once provided the main source of employment in the village, but that gave way to looms and mills with the arrival of the Industrial Revolution.

At the hamlet of Narrowgates, next to the car park, are weavers' cottages and a mill which has been converted into a house, although the original chimney still stands.

BARNOLDSWICK
[Ribble Valley]
SD8747: 4½ miles (7km) N of Colne

The feet of Roman soldiers used to tramp along the old Roman road which passed near the town of Barnoldswick. Sections of this road remain at Brogden and Greenberfield Lanes to the north. In the Domesday Book, mention is made of the settlement of Bernulfsuuic. Then, in 1147, a monastery was founded by Cistercian monks from Fountains Abbey. A hostile local reception resulted in the monks moving on to Kirkstall, where they built the abbey.

After centuries of sheep grazing and handloom weaving, the Industrial Revolution reached the town. Mills were built and cotton produced. The decline of this industry was followed eventually by the arrival of firms such as Rolls-Royce, who researched and perfected the jet engine here.

In a lovely, secluded setting, a mile from the town centre, along Gill Lane, is the **church of St Mary-le-Gill**. It was established by the monks ten years after they had left for Kirkstall. The reason they rebuilt the church in a remote spot was said to be because they did not want it anywhere near the local inhabitants. The roof is 13th century, and the tower dates from 1524. The builders of the tower could not have been very good mathematicians because the Roman numerals for 1524 on the side omit the M for 1000. Inside is a 17th-century three-decker pulpit, and box pews of the same vintage. The font is 14th century, with a Jacobean cover. Alongside it is a 12th-century holy water stoup.

In Gillians Lane, the **Bancroft Mill Engine** belongs to the last of thirteen mills to be built in the town in 1920. Although it closed in 1978, the engine remained, with its two boilers. It is a 600-horsepower, cross-compound machine with a rope drive. The mill, with its 120ft (36.5m) chimney, and the engine were restored. The engine has been back under steam since 1982, using one of the boilers. There are also demonstrations of weaving on two looms.

The old Baptist chapel in Walmsgate dates from the late 17th century, the present one having been opened in 1797.

The highest point on the Leeds and Liverpool Canal is at Greenberfield Locks, off the Skipton Road.

BARROW [Ribble Valley]
SD7338: 2 miles (3km) S of Clitheroe

Barrow is a long, straggling village now bypassed by the A59. Its 19th-century textile manufacture was concentrated on the mill.

A well-known old boy is **Cyril Washbrook** (1914-), the Lancashire and England opening batsman, and first professional captain of his county team (1954-9). His cricketing career spanned thirty-one years, from 1933-64.

A Church of England clergyman who was expelled from the church in 1662 because of his refusal to adhere to the Book of Common Prayer is commemorated by the **Jollie Memorial Congregational**

Church, situated next to the primary school at the north end of the village. After holding services in secret on Wiswell Moss, Thomas Jollie founded this chapel.

BARROWFORD [Pendle]

SD8539: 2 miles (3km) W of Colne

Pendle Water runs through the centre of the small town of Barrowford, adjacent to Nelson. Originally dependent on farming, Barrowford expanded rapidly as a textile town during the 19th century. There were few mills built, however, because at the end of the domestic weaving era mechanised production moved to Nelson, which had better rail and canal facilities.

The best local legend is that of the **Lamb Club**, a group of local young men who were partial to nettle pudding. Before they were allowed a drink, they had to go out onto the moors to eat the pudding and then recite the rhyme, 'Thimblethwrig and Thistlethwaite, who thinking to thrive through thick and thin, through throwing three thimbles hither and thither was thwarted and thwacked by thirty three thousand thick thorns.'

The Bannister family, a dynasty of local farmers, lived at **Park Hill** from the 15th century. Roger Bannister, who ran the first four-minute mile, is a descendant. The present building, adjacent to the road bridge, was erected in the 17th century. It is now the home of the **Pendle Heritage Centre**. At the rear of the house is a walled garden containing organic fruit, vegetables, flowers and herbs. A 17th-century cruck barn from the Cliviger area, with an oak frame and oak-pegged doors, has been reassembled.

On the corner, across the bridge, stands the **Toll House**. The small building is so designed that the road can be seen in both directions. This ensured that no one on the old Marsden to Long Preston turnpike road could slip by unnoticed, so avoiding the fee. On the front of the 1803 house is the renovated board indicating the various toll prices.

In 1774 John Wesley, the Methodist leader, had to hide in what is now the **White Bear Inn,** on Gisburn Road, when he was chased by a local mob. Built in 1607, its name is thought to be connected with bear baiting that took place. It was, at the time of Wesley's visit, the residence of the cotton magnate, John Hargreave. Opposite the lake and just off the Gisburn Road, it was in use as an inn by 1775. Wesley preached from **Th'Owd Brig'**, at Higherford in the northern part of the village, on his visit to the village. Leading into the pinfold, this 16th-century packhorse bridge is open to foot traffic only.

One of the few remaining towel weaving factories, the **East Lancashire Towel Company**, founded in 1932, operates from Park Mill in Halstead Lane.

In 1964, a disastrous fire devastated the **church of St Thomas** in Church Street. The remains of the original 1841 building are found in the Remembrance Garden. What looks like a tower pinnacle in the graveyard is actually that. Four local men had agreed to finance pinnacles for the tower. The verse on the solitary pinnacle indicates disappointment that three of them reneged on their agreement.

Bank Hall, otherwise the Lamb Club, stands further east from the church along Church Street. A Jacobean house dating from 1696, there are mullioned windows on the second floor and the porch on the second floor is wider than the lower one. At the bottom of the carved finials are faces, which were thought to act as a protection against witchcraft.

A regiment of trees called the **Waterloo Trees** is at **Carr Hill**, west of the village. After Colonel Clayton's regiment had been involved in the Battle of Waterloo in 1815, he planted here an avenue of lime trees in the shape of the deployment of his troops at the conflict. Those trees standing in front of the others represent the officers of the regiment. The 17th-century hall was demolished in 1954.

At the western end of Summit Pool, east of the town at **Barrowford Locks**, seven locks take the Leeds and Liverpool Canal in a descent of 65.5ft (20m) to Burnley Pool. The reservoir nearby was built in 1885 to take overflow water from Foulridge Reservoirs.

BARTON [Preston]

SD5237: 4 miles (6km) N of Preston

The name 'Barton' derives from the word for a corn field, but the village is strung out along the busy A6.

At the end of an avenue of trees, next to the Boars Head on the main road, the **church of St Lawrence** is built with a warm-looking stone. It underwent major restoration in 1895, having been first erected in 1577.

Barton Hall, which was used by the Ministry of Aviation during the Second World War, is now an Animal Health Centre. A long drive leads off the main road to the south of the village. The collection of buildings looks out over the extensive estate from a hilltop site.

Cardwell Bridge spans the brook that runs through the estate. The steep drop to the bridge made it the scene of many accidents in the last century. Apparently, to avoid further mayhem, two local sisters paid to have the road down to the bridge lowered, to make it safer.

In 1863 a large Roman Catholic church, found by turning off the main road to the north of the bridge, replaced **Newsham Chapel**, which was built in 1741.

BASHALL EAVES [Ribble Valley]

SD7043: 2½ miles (3km) E of Clitheroe

The tiny hamlet of Bashall Eaves, in the midst of fields and narrow lanes, is not far from the banks of the River Hodder. Its sandstone houses and cottages surround the village green.

The **Red Pump Inn** has a pump on the wall and others around the building. Built in 1756, it was once a farm. On one occasion a boy hid in the hay here to escape the press-gang. It was later a coaching inn.

The **Fairy Bridge** is said to have been built by fairies who were helping a woodcutter to escape from witches who were chasing him. It is found by turning right, north of the Red Pump Inn. Pass through the little cluster of houses and at the second sharp bend in the road, a footpath goes right down a lane and through a farm to the bridge. At a sharp bend north of the post office, a footpath leads off the road to the restored **Roman Bridge**. In spite of its name, it is of a much later date. The new stonework has holes as a habitat for bats.

Two miles (3km) north of the village, **Browsholme Hall** has been the family home of the Parker family since the 16th century. They were bow-bearers of Bowland. Set in extensive grounds containing a lake, the hall of pink sandstone is Tudor in origin with an Elizabethan façade. It also has a Queen Anne Wing, and a West Wing which was reconstructed in 1604. Inside there is a collection of family portraits including one of Thomas Parker, one-time Lord Chancellor. Furniture, arms, armour, textiles, stained glass and memorabilia such as stone age axes and a piece of a Zeppelin are also displayed. In a cupboard in the house is a skull. The tale is that this must never be seen by anyone other than members of the family or some disaster will occur. Another legend relates that when a death in the family is imminent, it will be preceded by the sight of a ghostly white horse in the grounds.

On the banks of Bashall Brook, 2 miles (3km) south-west of the village and east of Bashall Town, stands **Bashall Hall**. The Talbot family owned the house in the 15th century. Thomas Talbot had his own private army. The half-timbered building behind the hall, by the stream, is believed to have been the quarters of his troops. Because he betrayed Henry VI during the War of the Roses, Thomas received a pension from Edward IV. At the end of the approach lane is an old packhorse bridge.

BELMONT [Blackburn]

SD6715: 5½ miles (9km) E of Chorley

Lying at the southern end of Belmont Reservoir between Smithhills and Longworth Moor, the village of cottages, built from local stone, lies on the A675, the former Bolton to Preston turnpike. Standing high on the West Pennine Moors, 900ft (275m) above sea level, it was, in the last century, a busy centre of the bleaching, dyeing and quarrying industry. Until the name was changed to Belmont, meaning 'beautiful hill', in 1804, it was known as Hordern, a name still used at Hordern Pasture and Hordern Stoops to the west of the village. The population trebled during the last half of the 19th century with the coming of the textile industry, but has fallen again as the village has reverted to a moorland community.

Good examples of millworkers' cottages are found on Maria Square and along the High Street. Although the **Belmont Bleach Works** is still active in Egerton Lane, it is tourists and walkers who swell the population. Ward's Reservoir and the Spring and Ornamental Reservoirs are recreation areas close by. To the north of Ward's Reservoir, up the Rivington Road beyond the church, the **Potato Pie Path** is up on the moors. In the 19th century, villagers used this short path to transport peat down from the moor. The landowners tried to prevent them doing so by blocking the path. For a week, the villagers held a sit-in on the path. They were supplied with potato pie to sustain their vigil. Eventually, the landowners admitted defeat.

Built on conventional lines, the **church of St Peter** is a large parish church with a broach spire. It is situated in an elevated and spacious position opposite the Black Dog pub, at the start of the Rivington Road. In 1850, the local Squire Wright gave the land on which it is built.

BELTHORN [Hyndburn]

SD7225: 3½ miles (5km) SE of Blackburn

At 900ft (275m), Belthorn is one of the highest villages in Lancashire. Seen from a distance, it looks like a biblical city set on a hill. From the steep hill on Belthorn Road, the houses and cottages seem to the onlooker to stare down into the valley below. Most of the buildings on this main street are weavers' cottages from the early 19th century. One of the houses was built in 1791 and was once the Bell in the Thorn Inn, a name derived from a bell that was placed in a thorn bush. Whenever a horse bringing a load up the hill got tired, the bell was rung to summon a substitute.

BICKERSTAFFE [West Lancashire]

SD4504: 3 miles (5km) SE of Ormskirk

Bickerstaffe is a widely scattered farming community sliced in half by the M56. Its name means 'where the beech trees grow'. Excavations in Glass Hey Field revealed evidence of a 17th-century glass-making kiln. From the field, the road towards the hamlet of Barrow Nook is part of the Coach Road, which led to the Derby family home at Knowsley Hall. Part of a previous mining history is indicated by the old pit mound by the M56 junction.

Most of the land in the parish is part of the Lord Derby estate. It was the Derby family that built the **church of Holy Trinity** in 1832.

Opposite the church is **Bickerstaffe Hall**. There have been a number of buildings on the site since the first was erected by Ralf de Bickestath. The present one is Georgian, but retains some items from previous halls, such as the bell which used to summon estate workers to their tasks.

The road north from the church passes over the motorway. On the right is the **windmill**, now a private residence. This was built in 1757, but became steam powered in 1885 after the sails had blown down.

The Barracks, a cottage to the right of Church Lane, got its name when a German prince who was a guest of Lord Derby in the 19th century commented that it looked like an army barracks. At the crossroads to the east is **Stanley Gate Inn**. It was transferred from the half-timbered house across the road in the early 19th century.

The village has long associations with the Quakers. The **Burial Ground** in Graveyard Lane, off the A506 at the west end of the village, is the resting place of over 200 Quakers. Dating from 1665, there are no headstones since Quakers did not believe that their graves should be marked.

BILLINGTON [Ribble Valley]

SD7235: Half a mile (1km) SE of Whalley

Placed just across the River Calder from Whalley, the battle of Bilangahon took place here in AD798. This was the basis of the names of Billington, now a dairy farming community, and the village of Langho across the A.59.

The **church of New St Leonard** was built in 1880 to replace the Old St Leonard at Old Langho, a mile away. The latter was built c1557 with a one-roofed nave and chancel and low walls containing stone from the demolished Whalley Abbey. It is possible that the piscina and stoup came from the abbey also.

Hacking Hall faces the River Calder near its confluence with the Lune. It has five gables and a regularly-proportioned front. A cruck-framed tithe barn, built by the Abbey monks, stands in the grounds.

BILSBORROW [Wyre]

SD5140: 6 miles (9km) N of Preston

The village of Bilsborrow takes its name from the Danish king 'Billingr', and in the Domesday Book is referred to as 'Bilevurd'. The A6 cuts the parish in two. The Leeds and Liverpool Canal is parallel to it on the west side and the railway and M6 are nearby to the east.

Centuries ago the area was on the coastline, and a local tale recounts that a large pipe that was being laid into the road completely disappeared overnight into the quicksand.

Jane Salisbury, the owner of the now-demolished Myerscough Hall, who met her death crossing the railway at Brock in 1922, left money to build the stone **church of St Hilda**, with its sturdy tower. It was completed in 1927. The tower is 90ft (275m) high, and the bells were installed as a war memorial. Erected near the site of the manor house of 1654, **Bilsborrow Hall** is an early 20th-century structure in Bilsborrow Lane, immediately over the motorway.

The **Green Man Inn**, on the A6 in Brock, north of the village, formerly acted as a toll-house on the London to the North turnpike road.

The **Lancashire College of Agriculture** now occupies the grounds of **Myerscough Lodge**, 1½ miles (2km) west of the village. The only remains of the lodge are a wall by the reception centre.

BISPHAM [Blackpool]

SD3040: 2 miles (3km) N of Blackpool

The cottages of the old village of Bispham have now been swallowed up in the residential and holiday complexes that have spread from Blackpool. The name comes from 'Biscopham', which means 'the house of a bishop'. One of the older buildings remaining is the **church of All Hallows** in All Hallows Road, which used to be the main street. First dedicated, in the 13th century, to All Saints, the church was rebuilt in the 17th century and again in 1881. As well as the holy water stoup, there are fragments left from the Norman church. In particular, there is a doorway with the signs of the zodiac on the arch. A cross in the churchyard may have been a wayside cross. It is now a sundial.

BISPHAM [West Lancashire]

SD4914: 5½ miles (9km) SW of Chorley

The quiet, small hamlet of Bispham, comprising the Eagle and Child pub and a few houses, is centred on the village green and set amongst small, hedged fields. Placed at the edge of the West Lancashire plain, Harrock and Parbold Hill form the background to the west.

The name of the pub is a reference to the arms of the earls of Derby, the Stanleys. Sir Thomas Latham, one of the family's 14th-century ancestors, had an illegitimate son. Secretly, he had the baby placed beneath a tree in which an eagle nested. He then took his wife for a walk around the estate, 'discovered' the infant, and persuaded his wife that they should adopt the child. Henceforth, both the eagle and the child have featured in the arms of the family.

BLACKBURN [Blackburn]

SD6828: 9 miles (14km) E of Preston

Blackburn is the gateway to the Ribble and Hodder valleys. There had been a textile industry in the area since the 17th century, but its industry expanded rapidly when the Leeds and Liverpool Canal provided the means of transporting its products. There are many impressive Victorian buildings and mills remaining from that era. The copper-domed **Imperial Mill** on the east side of the city was built in 1901. Situated by the canal, it was one of the world's largest mills, having almost one hundred thousand spindles at work at one time.

It is known that there was a church here in the fifth century, and in the time of Edward the Confessor it was a royal manor. The modern town is now involved in industries such as heavy engineering, and has a prosperous commercial life based on a reconstructed central shopping area.

The only cathedral in Lancashire is the **cathedral church of St Mary**, in Church Street, opposite the railway station. It is the mother church of the Anglican diocese of Blackburn and is situated in an open green area. It is conspicuous for its newly restored lantern tower. A church was recorded on this site in AD596, and again in the Domesday Book in 1086. In 1826 a new church was built to replace the old one, which was beyond repair. It is this church that is the nave of the present cathedral, consecrated in 1926. Extension work was carried out in the 1950s and 1960s. The building is in the shape of a cross. At the meeting point of nave and transept is the square high altar. Above it is a corona depicting a crown of thorns. Modern art and sculpture are well represented, particularly by the Josephina de Vasconcellos statue of the Madonna, and a large sculpture by John Hayward, entitled 'Christ the Worker'. In addition to fine, modern stained glass, there are also some medieval glass fragments. A replica of a medieval pax is on show, the original of which is held in the treasury. St Martin's Chapel is a memorial to the East Lancashire Regiment. Outside, the site of the old church, whose surrounding gates and walls still stand, is outlined on the lawn.

A wide-ranging display of painting and local and natural history is found at the **Museum and Art Gallery** in Museum Street. It is housed in a Grade II listed Victorian building. Inside the main entrance are carvings depicting scenes from the 19th-century history of the city, including millworkers and merchants. The art collection comprises a number of British paintings, including eight by J.M.W. Turner, and a number of Japanese prints. The Hart collections of medieval, illustrated manuscripts is priceless, as are a number of rare books. The museum lays claim to the largest display of Eastern European icons, many of them Russian. The Asian population of the town is recognised by an exhibition of Pakistani and Gujerati culture. In addition, there are displays of ceramics and coins and a display of the East Lancashire Regiment memorabilia.

The **Lewis Museum of Textile Machinery** in Exchange Street traces the development of the spinning and weaving industry. Both the house and the collection were bequeathed to the town by Thomas Lewis in 1937. Models of the flying shuttle, the spinning jenny, the spinning mule and a 19th-century Lancashire loom are on display.

The warehouses and wharf master's house at **Eanam Wharf**, by the canal off Higher Eanam Road, on the east side of the city, date from 1816 and have been restored. They have been converted into a business complex and restaurant, but include a small exhibition of the effect of the canal on the growth and prosperity of the town.

The **King George's Hall** in Northgate was built in 1913 to seat 2000 people. It is used for concerts, meetings and exhibitions. At the back of the stage is a corridor known as 'The Ghost Walk' because of the apparitions that have been seen over the years. A story attaches to the building of the Italianate-style **Town Hall**, opposite Town Hall Street, in 1856. The builder was asked by a workman how high a wall would be. He was informed that he would be told when to stop. Unfortunately, the builder forgot and the wall finished 20ft (7m) high rather than the intended 6ft (2m). The buildings bear a resemblance to the Mansion House in London. The **Market Hall** is traditionally famous for its black pudding and sarsaparilla stalls.

The **Grundy Art Gallery** includes a collection of Japanese netsuke, modern British paintings, prints and jewellery.

Part of the 1807 **Thwaites Brewery**, in Penny Street, still remains at the site of the new one. The drays were drawn by shire horses, some of which are still kept and appear on special occasions.

A weathervane in the shape of a shuttle stands atop of the **church of St John the Evangelist**, built in 1789 as a proud reminder of the town's industrial history. It is in a conservation area, which includes the Georgian-style Richmond Terrace and Victoria Street. In the churchyard is the tomb of Daniel Thwaites, the brewer.

The **church of Holy Trinity**, built in 1846, is a large edifice standing alone at Mount Pleasant. Inside, on the flat timber roof, are embossed the emblems of the people who donated towards its erection. The Roman Catholic **church of St Joseph**, built in 1869 in Audley, is notable for having the church on the second floor of the building. The ground floor was designed as a school.

The **Ewood Aqueduct**, south of the city centre, takes the canal over a road and the River Darwen. It was erected in 1815 with one large span. **Corporation Park**, one of six parks in the town, is in a valley to the north-west and laid out on traditional Victorian lines, complete with lake and conservatory.

Blackburn Fig Pie, a tart containing figs, currants, spices and treacle, used to be a traditional Mothering Sunday treat.

BLACKO [Pendle]

SD8642: 3 miles (4km) N of Nelson

On the old turnpike road to Gisburn, the village of Blacko looks out to Pendle Hill to the west.

North of the village, high on the hill-side, is **Blacko Tower**, a small, battlemented folly. It is thought to be on the site of Malkin Tower, where Mother Demdike and some of the Pendle Witches hid before their arrest. The present tower was built by Jonathan Stanfield in 1891. Local folklore tells that it was erected so that he could see his girlfriend in Gisburn from it. When he found that he could not, he left if unfinished, to be completed by others.

BLACKPOOL [Blackpool]

SD3036: 15 miles (24km) W of Preston

The arrival of the railway in 1885 helped to turn what was once the small fishing village of Blackpool into a flourishing holiday resort. People were able to reach it, particularly from the north of England, with comparative ease. So the 7 miles (11km) of beaches and 5 miles (9km) of promenade became the Mecca of the working classes, giving them a well-earned break from the toil of mill and factory. 'Blackpool offers more fun for less money than anywhere else,' was the claim of a newspaper at the end of the 19th century.

The name of the original village came from 'Black Poole', the stream which connected Marton Mere to the sea. The remnants of the mere still offer a home to over 100 species of birds. The village had become a resort for the gentry by the end of the 18th century and was further developed by Henry Banks, who was known as the 'Father of Blackpool'.

One of the most visible attractions of the town is the **Electric Tramway**, running 11 miles (20km) from Starr Gate to Fleetwood. It was established in 1885, and by 1959 the length of track had increased from 2 to 35 miles. There were

124 trams carrying 34 million passengers.

Opened as a tourist attraction in 1894, **Blackpool Tower** took three years to build on a foundation of Accrington bricks, using 2493 tonnes of steel and 93 tonnes of cast iron. Designed as an imitation of the Eiffel Tower in Paris, it is 518ft (158 m) high. At the time, it was the tallest building in the country. Inside the Tower is an aquarium, circus and the ballroom, with its Wurlitzer organ made famous by Reginald Dixon.

One of the oldest fairgrounds in the country is the **Pleasure Beach**, erected in 1903. The River Caves ride was first constructed in 1904 and refurbished in 1974. The Flying Machine was designed by Sir Hiram Maxim, of machine-gun fame, for the Crystal Palace. It was moved from there to Blackpool in 1904. The 1933 Roller Coaster and the 1935 Grand National are other historic rides. Modern high technology is represented by the 1994 Pepsi Max 'Big One'. At a cost of £11 million, it is one of the world's highest rollercoasters.

The **Winter Gardens and Opera House** of 1878 are a large group of white-faced buildings, including the Pavilion and Empress Ballroom. The Opera House has undergone renovation twice, but the original glass dome has remained.

Of the three piers, the **North Pier** was constructed in 1863 with a total length of 1405ft (428m). The **Central Pier** dates from 1868 and is 1518ft (463m) in length, but has been constantly refurbished because of frequent fires. The **South Pier**, with its grand pavilion, was finished in 1993.

The original interior of the **Grand Theatre**, in Church Street, remains unchanged from its original condition in 1894.

BLEASDALE [Wyre]

SD5745: 3 miles (5km) NW of Chipping

The small farming community of Bleasdale is on the southern edge of the Forest of Bowland. The post office and restaurant have taken over the former Higher Brock Mill on Bleasdale Lane. Opposite the post office, a metalled lane leads up to the lonely **church of St Eadmor**. This was built in 1835, with a chancel added in 1897. One mile (2km) north-west of the village, **Bleasdale Tower** dates from the middle of the 19th century, while 1 mile (2km) south-east is the small house **Blindhurst**, built in 1731. Surrounded by its large farm, its long approach lane links paths onto the fells. By the school, just below the church, is an information point about **Bleasdale Circle**. This is reached on a short concessionary path from Vicarage Farm, higher up the lane beyond the church. Dating from around 2000-1700BC, the circle, discovered in 1898, was unique because of its use of wooden posts. In 1937, the 12 posts of the circle, plus one in the centre, were removed from the circle. They were sent to the Harris Museum in Preston and replaced by concrete pillars. Other points that make this circle interesting are the distance between the stones and the outer wall, plus the width of the entrance opening. The circle, which was a burial place from which the remains of two caskets of ashes were exhumed, is 150ft (46m) in diameter. The caskets are also in the Harris Museum.

BOLTON-BY-BOWLAND [Ribble Valley]

SD7849: 6 miles (9km) NE of Clitheroe

Placed just above the V-neck of the confluence of the River Ribble and Tosside Beck and on the edge of Bolton Park is the small village of Bolton-by-Bowland, with its stone cottages, church and inn huddled around a green. Bowland, called 'Bodeton' in the Domesday Book, means 'bow in the river'. The main green is split by a road. On one half are the remnants of a market cross and village stocks, and on the other half is the war memorial.

Standing on the perimeter are the Coach and Horses Inn and the church. Just beyond the church is the second, tree-lined, smaller green, separating cottages from the highway. Halfway along this green is the **Old Courthouse**, at which the Law of the Forest was made known. As tends to happen in villages which have been part of an estate, there are few modern structures.

A road starting opposite the church runs through the grounds of what was Bolton Hall, demolished in the 1950s. After passing the remains of an ancient cross on the left, the road ends at the outbuildings of the hall, now restored as residential accommodation. The hall was the historic home of the Pudsay family. It was Sir Ralph Pudsay who gave refuge to Henry VI there, after the king's defeat at the Battle of Hexham in 1464, during the Wars of the Roses.

Another member of the family, William, was responsible for '**Pudsay's Leap**'. The story goes that he was caught counterfeiting money. He escaped from the pursuing government officials only by making his horse jump from a high cliff over the River Ribble. He rode on to London to seek a pardon from Queen Elizabeth I, which she granted. In a hollow, alongside the restored buildings, is a dome-shaped, small, stone building known as **King Henry's Well**. This was a bathhouse built over a spring of water.

The lid of Sir Ralph Pudsay's tomb in the Pudsay Chapel of the **church of St Peter and St Paul** gives a complete account of his family. Besides his twenty-five children, his three wives are engraved on the cover of the tomb. In the manner of a scoreboard, Roman numerals indicate the number of children produced by each wife. The chapel also has a number of monuments to the Pudsay family. At the entrance to the chapel there is a holy water stoup in the wall. The stone altar in the sanctuary is probably the original medieval one. The church pews have three names of previous owners inscribed on them. One even has an address. The 19th-century pulpit incorporates two older Flemish panels. At the back of the church is a 16th-century font with heraldic shields of the Pudsay family on the eight sides. On the font cover look for the mouse, the sign that Robert Thompson left in the many churches he worked in. Over the inside of the main entrance door is a 13th-century stone. Examine the dog-tooth carvings and find that there are four and a bit.

BOLTON-LE-SANDS
[Lancaster and Morecambe]
SD4867: 2½ miles (4km) S of Carnforth

The sands in question are now half a mile (0.5km) away because the shoreline has receded from this former fishing village. Known as 'Bodeltone' in the Domesday Book, 'Le-Sands' was added to Bolton in the 19th century to distinguish it from Bolton-by-Bowland. On the route of the West Coast railway line, it is claimed to be the only spot from which the coast can actually be seen.

The old village, up Main Street off the A6, has a street lined with whitewashed 17th- and 18th-century cottages. Although there has been much post-war building on both sides of the A6, there are still many ancient buildings to be seen in the older part, including the **Old Grammar School** of 1637. Past traditions of the parish were a Shrove Tuesday paper chase and pace-egging on Easter Monday.

The **church of Holy Trinity**, next to the Blue Anchor Inn at the top of Main Road, was erected in 1794. It was much restored in the 19th century, as the plaque on the outside of the wall nearest the road indicates. It was originally dedicated to St Michael. The tower is 15th century. Inside, a stone in the sanctuary has a pre-Christian inscription on it, and there are also an early 18th-century chest and candelabra. In the churchyard, a small millstone rests on the top of a grave, perhaps to make sure that no one escapes. The **Packet Boat Inn** stands at the lower part of the old village, at the junction of Main Road and Packet Lane. Adjacent to the Lancaster Canal, it is a reminder of the halcyon days of the canal, when the inn met the needs of canal workers and travellers.

BORWICK [Lancaster and Morecambe]

SD5272: 2½ miles (4km) NE of Carnforth

Although close to the M6, Borwick, along with the nearby hamlet of Priest Hutton, is a quiet refuge, with its old cottages and village green set amongst fields and narrow lanes. It is situated on a rise above the surrounding countryside. The green is enclosed by a triangle of roads and the Lancaster Canal skirts the edge of the village.

Two main buildings on the main road by the green constitute **Borwick Hall**, namely a 15th-century pele tower and a house. The four-storey tower has a turret on one corner. The Elizabethan house of three wings was built around the tower, at different times in the 16th century, by the Blindloss family of Kendal. They were Royalists who gave hospitality to Charles II in 1651, as he was travelling south after being crowned King of Scotland at Scone. He was defeated at the Battle of Worcester by Cromwell's forces. Inside the house, which is surrounded by terraced gardens, is a spinning gallery. The gatehouse and stables, although built in Elizabethan style, actually date from 1650. There is a priest's room with access to a hiding place. Restoration took place at the start of the 20th century. Much of the building has been turned into residential accommodation.

BRACEWELL [Pendle]

SD8648: 1½ miles (2km) NW of Barnoldswick

Henry VI managed to stay in many places after his escape from the Battle of Hexham in 1464. The village was one of them. Today it remains much as it was when the king was there.

King Henry's Parlour is the stone barn in which he hid. Turn left up a lane after Hopwood Hall and Farm and the church. The barn is on the right, in front of the farm, alongside a small group of houses and cottages.

A unique, two-stage tower makes the small **church of St Michael** stand out. The original church was built by the Tempest family in the 11th century. They were the lords of the manor and lived at the hall next door. The chancel is dominated by a large sanctuary window and the 14th-century tower arch opens onto the nave. Above the arch is a small 'leper's squint' window. Some of the windows contain fragments of 14th-century glass.

BRETHERTON [Chorley]

SD4821: 5 miles (8km) W of Leyland

In the middle of flat farmland reclaimed from the marshes, the village of Bretherton has no natural centre, the houses having been built in a linear fashion along the road.

Set back amongst the trees from the busy A59, **Bank Hall** is now in a ruinous state. Efforts are being made to restore it to a good condition. Built in brick in 1608, it has passed through the hands of three local families. The clock tower incorporates a balustraded oak staircase from the 17th century. In 1832, the Legh-Klek family undertook a major restoration which was sympathetic to the Jacobean style. The west wing and front porch was added at this time. The building has been empty since 1945, but is being restored.

North of the hall, at a roundabout on the A59, is **Carr House**. This was home to the Barry Elder collection of dolls. After his death it was moved to the Judges' Lodging Museum in Lancaster. Over the porch is an inscription, which states that the house was built in 1613 by 'Thomas Stones of London, haberdasher and Andrew Stones of Amsterdam, merchant'. The porch of the brick house reaches to the upper floor. Inside is a rare 'cage--Newell' staircase. This was also the home of **Reverend Jeremiah Horrocks**, an early astronomer. From a room above the porch, he observed the transit of Venus across the sun on 29 November 1639 at 3.30pm. At the time he was curate at Hoole parish church.

Halfway between the hall and Carr House, off the A59, is a residence that was a working **windmill** from 1741 to 1904.

In the village itself, the **church of St John the Baptist** was built in 1840, with a gallery at the back. The small spire is, unusually, built over an archway. An ancient holy water stoup stands in the entrance vestibule. The chancel was added in 1909. East of the church is the present school. Immediately before it, the original schoolhouse of 1653 is one of two attached cottages. A stone over the doorway gives details. Opposite is an imposing house dating from 1698.

BRIERFIELD [Pendle]

SD8436: 2½ miles (4km) N of Burnley

Brierfield is a large village which looks towards the Thursden Valley. In the 19th century there were coal pits, but the textile industry soon became predominant. The mill buildings still loom over the town.

The village has strong associations with the Quaker Movement. There is a Meeting House at Marsden Cross, on Walverden Road near the junction with Halifax Road. Built in 1760, it is a single-storey, stone building. Off Railway Street, below the station, **Quaker Bridge** is a two-arched, 17th-century structure.

Extwistle Hall, 2 miles (3km) to the south-west, is a late 17th-century building, which looks a little lopsided with one half being low and the other high.

BRINDLE [Chorley]

SD6024: 3½ miles (6km) NE of Leyland

Brindle, surrounded by rolling hills and fields, centres on the parish church and the ancient Cavendish Arms Inn. Although the M65 is nearby, and the road through the village a busy shortcut to

Blackburn, it is possible to escape into quiet countryside in a couple of minutes.

The name comes from 'bryn' meaning 'spring', and the history of the parish goes back over 800 years. It is thought that the Battle of Brunaberg may have taken place near the village.

Down the centuries, farming was the main source of income. After weaving arrived and departed as a local industry, farming continued to be predominant.

A local legend tells of the 'Brindle cuckoo'. The villagers were led to believe that if they could find a way of persuading a cuckoo not to leave after the summer, then summer would continue for as long as the cuckoo stayed. So, having found a fairly docile one, they hit on the brilliant idea of building a wall around it. For some reason, the scheme did not seem to work! For many years babies born in the village were called 'Brindle cuckoos'. Until early in the 20th century, Brindle races drew large crowds, with an estimated attendance of 20,000 in 1905. The race was run from the Rectory to the canal at Wheelton.

The nave and the chancel of the **church of St James**, on the B5256 in the centre of the village, are both 19th century. There are some fine stained-glass windows and two old fonts. One is Georgian and the other late 17th century. It has a 15th-century tower and a chapel dedicated to the Cavendish family. On the outside of the east wall are some ancient grave covers. Nearby are an empty stone coffin and the remains of a preaching cross.

The name of the lords of the manor is also remembered in the form of the **Cavendish Arms Inn**, opposite the church. This was once the home of the previous lords of the manor, the Gerard family. Sir Thomas Gerard had to sell his estate to the Cavendishes of Holker Hall in Cart-

mel. This was to raise money to buy his release from the Tower of London, where he was held for supporting the claims of Mary, Queen of Scots, to the throne during the reign of Elizabeth I. A plaque at the inn indicates that it was called 'Mrs Holland's Cavendish Arms Inn'. Presumably, she was the landlady at the time.

Before the Roman Catholic **church of St Joseph** was built in 1780, masses had to be said in secret through fear of arrest or persecution. To indicate where the mass was to take place, washing was hung out at the appropriate spot. A leading recusant was Edmund Arrowsmith. He was eventually arrested and executed at Lancaster Castle. Arrowsmith House still keeps the room in which he said his secret masses. The church is signposted off Hillhouse Road, between the village and Gregson Lane.

Brindle Lodge, south of the A675, half a mile (1km) west of Hoghton, has excellent plasterwork inside. This stone building, built on rising ground, dates from the early 19th century and has a tower folly in the grounds.

BRINSCALL [Chorley]

SD6322: 5 miles (8km) E of Leyland

Previously devoted to farming, the linear village of Brinscall grew in the 19th century with the arrival of handloom weavers and calico printing. A local industrialist built **Brinscall Hall**, 1 mile (1.5km) south of the village, in 1876. In **Wheelton Plantation** on the other side of the Goit, a wide track takes walkers past the ruins of the calico works.

Kathleen Ferrier, the renowned contralto, was married at Hillside Methodist church in School Lane.

BROOKHOUSE [Lancaster and Morecambe]

SD5465: 4 miles (6km) NE of Lancaster

This small community, adjacent to Caton, is set in the midst of farmland. There are rows of white stone cottages, as well as a pub and a church. Except for the 16th-century tower, most of the **church of St Paul** was rebuilt in 1865. It is thought that there was a church on this site in 1230. Situated along New Street from the Black Bull Inn, it also serves as the parish church of Caton and Littledale. Built into the west wall of the church is part of a 12th-century doorway bearing the figures of Adam, Eve and the serpent from the temptation in the Garden of Eden. Inside are a number of monuments, including a number of 14th-century coffin lids. The doorway is reinforced with stones from the previous building, including one with the cross and sword Crusader emblem. It may have come from the grave of a Knight of St John of Jerusalem, whose order owned the surrounding land. In 1953 two ships' bells replaced the three bells of 1605, 1617 and 1724. They were refurbished again for use in 1964. The pulpit and prayer desk were made from portions of the oak roof of the former building. A finely carved 18th-century chair from the now demolished Littledale church is placed at the west end of the north wall.

A plague stone is set into **Bull Beck Bridge** at the Black Bull Inn end. Money was dipped in vinegar and left in the hollowed-out stone in exchange for provisions. This was to avoid the tradesmen catching the plague.

Eulogised by Turner in his painting and by Wordsworth and Gray in their poetry, the **Crook o'Lune** attracts many visitors. This loop in the River Lune, north of the village, is a beauty spot that has escaped unscathed from modern development.

BROUGHTON [Preston]

SD5235: 3½ miles (6km) N of Preston

Because of its proximity to Preston, the village of Broughton is sought out by commuters, but there are still cottages and houses from the time when it was a rural village community.

Woodplumpton Brook flows by the **church of St John the Baptist**. Despite the nearby M55, here, just off the A59 south of the main part of the village, is a small oasis of unexpected tranquility. Apart from the tower of 1533, there is little left of any of the older buildings on the site. The bells are 17th century, but the rest of the church was completely rebuilt in 1826 and the chancel added in 1906. Fortunately, some relics of the old church remain inside. Outstanding is the Saxon font, to the right of the entrance door. It was thrown out as surplus to requirements in 1887 and demoted to use as a vase in a garden in Barton, north of the village. Sixty years later it was recovered and reinstated. It is placed on a more modern base. Also worthy of notice is a holy water stoup found near the church at the end of the 19th century. Old stocks, refurbished in 1902, and a mounting stone are near the tower entrance to the churchyard. **Church Cottage**, in the grounds of the school behind the church, was once the church inn. Although the date of construction is not known, it was in existance in 1806. It is recorded that on Guy Fawkes Day 1923, the bell ringers drank 20 pints of beer here. It is now fully renovated, with the interior restored to the original condition and used as a small museum. Across the road from the church is the 16th-century grammar school building.

The delightful higgledy-piggledy **Toll Bar Cottage**, between the post office and the traffic lights, juts out into the road. It is reminder of the turnpike road which is now the A6.

Broughton House, almost opposite the lane to the church, is the headquarters of the Lancashire Ambulance Service. Built in brick in 1833, it has large windows and an attractive, flat-roofed design.

BURNLEY [Burnley]

SD8432: 5 miles (8km) E of Accrington

A market charter was granted to Burnley in 1293, but its history can be traced back to settlements in the Stone and Bronze Ages. A charter granting St Peter's Church to Pontefract Priory in 1122 calls the settlement 'Brunley', the name meaning 'field by the River Brun'. In 1801, the population was 5000, but the Liverpool and Leeds Canal led to a dramatic growth. Although the wool industry had made Burnley a thriving market town from the 13th century and there was later coal mining, textiles made the town into the world's largest producer of cloth. It was always a weaving rather than a spinning town. Twelve mills were erected between 1900 and 1914.

The **church of St Peter** stands in what was once the centre of the town, enclosed on three sides by the River Brun. It is known that there was a church on this site in the early 13th century. The present one is of various architectural periods, including a 1790 south aisle and a 1803 north aisle. The local influence of the Towneley family is demonstrated by a family chapel, a communion rail from Towneley Hall and a 16th-century font emblazoned with the family arms.

Approached down a long, tree-lined drive, **Towneley Hall Art Gallery and Museum**, 1 mile (2km) south, is fronted by a large pool. It was the home of the Towneley family until the end of the 19th century. Over the preceeding centuries,

the building had been constantly altered. The oldest part is probably the south-east wing, dating from the middle of the 14th-century, which contains two spiral staircases. The central block and the north-east wing were completed in the middle of the 15th century. In 1729, the great hall was replaced by an entrance hall, sumptuously plastered by Vassali, the Italian artist. The walls of the hall are 6ft (2m) thick. The house also contains a 17th-century Minstrels' Gallery, kitchens from the late 19th century and a chapel with a 16th-century reredos of oak made in Antwerp. The font cover is 15th century. A prized exhibit is a collection of vestments from Whalley Abbey, rescued at the time of the dissolution of the monasteries. In other rooms of the house are the Long Gallery, a hiding place for priests, and a fireplace in the style of Adams.

The head of the early 18th-century Francis Towneley was kept at the hall until 1947. He was executed because of his support for the Jacobite cause. It was later placed in the family vault at St Peter's Church.

The Art Gallery holds 250 paintings from the 18th and 19th centuries. Watercolours include four by Turner and there are oils by Constable. The hall was purchased by the Corporation in 1901 and became the base for the town's museum and art gallery service. The museum has archaeological and natural history exhibits. The hall is surrounded by a 24-acre (9.5 hectares) park, which has a 19th-century underground ice house and a natural history centre. An aquarium demonstrates the variety of fish to be found as a river flows from its source to the sea.

The hall is reputedly haunted. Sometimes soft voices are heard in the Long Gallery and at other times lights, which cannot be accounted for, are seen in the house. People also say that they have heard the ghostly steps of a pony (near the park) belonging to the last owner of the Hall.

Amongst a number of Victorian buildings is the **Town Hall** in Manchester Road. Built of Yorkshire stone in classical Renaissance style in 1888, the clock tower has a copper dome and cupola. The interior is notable for the mosaic floors and ornately painted ceilings in the council chamber. A reminder of the Victorian endeavour to meet the social and training needs of the workers is the **Mechanics' Institute**, next door to the Town Hall. Built in 1855, it is now an arts and information centre.

At one time the **Manchester Road Wharf**, accessed from Manchester Road, was the terminus of the canal. It was built in 1796 with a large warehouse and tollhouse. This has been turned into the visitor centre. Within, there is an exhibition about the life and development of the area. From here a walk to the west takes the visitor through the **Weavers' Triangle**. This is an area of mills and warehouses situated by the side of the canal, close to the Town Hall at Burnley Wharf. Here it is possible to get the feel of the life of a mill town in the 19th century. It is now an industrial heritage site. Also to be seen are a Victorian classroom recreation, a weaver's house and a display about the workers' holiday weeks with a working model of a fairground. A five-minute walk will bring you to **Oak Mount Mill** where a restored steam-engine can be seen.

From the Manchester Road wharf the towpath leads in an easterly direction towards the Burnley Embankment, a long, northern stretch of the canal. This is the 'Straight Mile' (although it is less than that) which carries the canal over the River Calder. It is regarded as one of the outstanding examples of Victorian engineering. Some of the material used to make it came from the Gannow Tunnel, reached along Gannow Lane, off Padiham Road, near the M65. The tunnel had to be 'legged'. Because it was not wide enough to include the tow path, the bargemen had to lie on their backs with their legs on the tunnel roof to propel the boats through.

An exhibition of photographs about historic Burnley is found at the **Heritage Centre**, a three-storey building built in 1879. Amongst the other exhibits are a Lancashire loom and a recreation of a kitchen and living room in the 1930s.

The cost of the **church of St Mary** in Yorkshire Street was originally met by a steward from the Towneley estates from the prize money he received when his horse won the Oaks. Built in 1849, it has a 19th-century altar designed by E.W. Pugin.

It is claimed that **Heasandford House**, off Netherwood Road, east of the centre, is the oldest occupied house in the town. It was originally Worsthorne manor house, parts of it remaining from the 15th century.

The only surviving steam-powered cotton mill in Europe is **Queen Street Mill**, at Harle Syke in the northern part of the town. The mill was named after the brook which fed the boilers. The name itself means 'the shallow muddy ditch with wild flax growing beside it'. It was opened as a workers' cooperative in 1894. Except for a fire in 1918, it remains as it was at the height of its productive power. It eventually closed in 1982 because the ancient machinery had become uneconomical to run. Reopened by the County Museum Service, visitors can gain an insight into the turning of yarn into cloth. The central attraction of the mill is the 500-horsepower steam engine called 'Peace'. It drives over 300 looms in the weaving shed.

BURSCOUGH
[West Lancashire]

SD4311: 3 miles (4km) NE of Ormskirk

The village is built on a small ridge and surrounded by rich, arable land. Most of this was reclaimed over the years from the large shallow lake of Martin Mere. The cutting of the Leeds and Liverpool Canal in 1774 caused the population to begin to rise. Coal, wool and timber were the main cargoes and boat-building became an important local industry. Near the road bridge over the canal are some renovated quay buildings. In more recent years the village has grown into the size of a small town as more residential areas have been built.

At **Top Locks**, along the canal to the east of the village, the Leeds and Liverpool Canal makes a junction with the Rufford Branch. The purpose was to provide easier passage than that which existed on the River Douglas. Here is a little group of canal workers' cottages, dry dock, toll-house and locks. The pool is known as 'Wannin' Pool'. The word means to 'turn around'. The barges that brought wheat up to Ainscough's Mill (on the canal by the railway bridge), turned round at this point to make their way back to Liverpool.

There are only two piers left of the 1190 Augustinian foundation of **Burscough Priory**. It is reached along a footpath down Abbey Lane, off the A59 on the south side of the village. It was quite small and had a staff of seven monks. For many years the priory provided the vicar of Ormskirk. Three of its canons were suspended in 1454 for practising black magic. Amongst the members of the Stanley family, who were buried at the abbey was Thomas Stanley. It was he who placed the crown which had been found under a bush at the Battle of Bosworth in 1485 on the head of his stepson, Henry, Duke of Richmond. After the dissolution of the monasteries, some of the stone was used to build a tower at Ormskirk parish church to house the bells of the priory. The large font was used as a trough on a farm until it was moved to Lathom Park Chapel. **Burscough Hall**, at the end of Chapel Lane, was the home of the Burscough family of Lathom until 1585. It is thought that Roman Catholics held their services here after the destruction of the priory. After the Battle of Waterloo in 1815, the Government decided to spend a million pounds on providing churches for the expanding population. The **church of St John**, opposite Burscough Bridge station, is one of these Waterloo churches. The three original galleries have been retained. Closely associated with the naturalist Peter Scott, **Martin Mere Wildfowl and Wetlands Trust**, signposted from the railway bridge, was established in 1976. It covers 363 acres (147 hectares) of land and plays host to over 130 different species of wildfowl, particularly geese and swans migrating from the northern polar regions. There are habitats such as a Flamingo Pool and Swan Lake, plus a number of hides. In the visitor centre, which is constructed of logs and has a turf roof, there is an exhibition hall, a shop and provision for refreshments.

CABUS [Wyre]

SD4948: 10 miles (16km) S of Lancaster

In an area of sheep and cattle farming, the village of Cabus spreads out widely around the A6. The old toll-house, at the junction between the A6 and the old Garstang road (B6430), still has one of the toll posts outside. This was discovered during excavations for the widening of the road and replaced in its original position. The house was on the route of the Preston to Lancaster road, which became a turnpike in 1751.

CALDER VALE [Wyre]

SD5346: 10½ miles (17km) SE of Lancaster

Richard and Jonathan Jackson were Quakers who decided to build Calder Vale in 1835 as a model of how the mill industry should be run. Set in the wooded valley of the River Calder, the village is built on the slope of the valley, with a number of open greens. Over the bridge, at the bottom of the valley, the four-storey **Lappet Mill**, next to the Methodist chapel, is still in use. By turning left by the green and walking along Long Row, one of the terraces built by the Jacksons to house millworkers, the mill race and pond are reached. These remain from the days when the mill was water-powered. The other mill was **Low Mill**, which is now little more than a heap of stones and the remains of the basement. It can be seen by turning sharp right at the top of Victoria Terrace and following the sign to Primrose Cottages. As the bumpy track goes beyond the cottages, the remains are on the left.

The **church of St John the Evangelist**, erected in 1863, is a remarkably large building for what was a small population. With the little school next to it, it is an imposing, stone, towered building in rural surroundings. It is seen by following the footpath from the end of Long Row or by taking the lane opposite the Moorcock Inn in Oakenclough. North-west of the pub, by the large mill buildings, is **Calder**

Bank. Now a restaurant, it was the home of the Jackson family.

CAPERNWRAY [Lancaster and Morecambe]

SD5372: 2½ miles (4km) NE of Carnforth

Capernwray is a widespread area of scattered houses and farms, with no village centre.

The Member of Parliament for Lancaster, George Marton, had **Capernwray Hall** built in 1844. His family remained there until 1946. Set in spacious landscaped grounds, 1½ miles (2.5km) south-east of Borwick, it has a symmetrical, crenellated façade and a tower at the rear. Inside, there is a hammerbeam roof and a staircase rising to the top of the building. A prized possession is the screen of a minstrels' gallery, which was obtained from Lancaster Priory church. A Victorian chapel stands in the grounds, opposite the road to Over Kellet. The hall now belongs to the Capernwray International Missionary Fellowship.

Take the road opposite the hall's chapel, and **Capernwray Old Hall** will be found as the canal comes close to the road. It is next to the farm and is now residential accommodation. It dates originally from the 12th century. A sign to 'New England' is not a short cut to the USA, but leads towards New England Cottages. By following the canal to the right of the bridge, the span of the canal over the River Keer is reached. By turning left over the canal bridge and then right down the lane by Mill House, an ancient packhorse bridge crosses the river under the towering arches of the railway viaduct.

CARNFORTH [Lancaster and Morecambe]

SD4970: 6 miles (9km) N of Lancaster

Its location, at a crossing point of the River Keer, gave Carnforth its name. There was a Danish settlement here, as ancient objects found in the marshes over the years have proved. Mention is made of the community in the Domesday Book.

By the 18th century, the cutting of the Lancaster Canal had helped the development of sand quarrying. At **Tewitfield**, 2 ½ miles (4km) north-east along the A6, eight locks raise the canal 75ft (23m) within a distance of half a mile (1.5km). Major expansion came with the arrival of the South Durham and Lancashire Railway, which led to the building of the Haematite Iron Company's factory in 1870 to smelt iron ore. The latter closed 60 years later. The town continued to be an important rail centre.

The film *Brief Encounter*, starring Trevor Howard and Celia Johnson, had some memorable scenes which were filmed at the station.

On the site of the last depot of the London, Midland and Scottish Railway to be built, the **Steamtown Railway Centre**, in Warton Road adjacent to the station, contains over 30 steam engines, including the *Flying Scotsman*, the *Sir Nigel Gresley*, *Lord Nelson* and *Le France*. On occasions, some of the engines can be out on other lines. The humble tank engine is also well represented, as well as a range of coaches. One of these, a Directors' Saloon from the early 19th century, is the last word in luxury. The line terminates at the hamlet of **Cragbank**, 1 mile (1.5km) to the north. In addition, there is a workshop, one of the last operative coaling plants, a vacuum-operated turntable, a 1876 signal box and a 15-inch (38cm) narrow gauge railway.

CASTERCLIFF [Pendle]

SD8938: 1 ½ miles (2km) NE of Nelson

Outside the village of Castercliff is an Iron Age **hill fort**. In a commanding position on high ground, villagers would shelter behind the ramparts for protection against marauding tribes. Two ramparts and a ditch remain of what was evidently a much larger fortification. Over the years, locals removed material for their own building purposes. There are also signs of opencast mining from the eighth century.

CATFORTH [Preston]

SD4836: 5 ½ miles (9km) NW of Preston

Tales of priestly skulls add an air of mystery to the widespread village of Catforth, which is surrounded by farmland and narrow lanes. Although there are three chapels and a Roman Catholic church, unusually there is no Anglican place of worship. The buildings of the smithy and tithebarn still remain.

At the north end of the village, **The Running Pump Inn**, built in 1843, is a reminder of the draining of the surrounding marshland. Before being drained, it was an area of pools and springs of pure water.

The skull of a martyred priest is kept at the Roman Catholic **church of St Robert**, which was built in the 19th century. The church is well hidden down the long and narrow Benson Lane, just south of the main village. In the years before the Second World War, up to 2000 visitors a year made pilgrimages to the church. The resident priest at the time, Father Waring, had received from the Holden family of Chaigley the relics of one of the English Martyrs, which the family had in their possession for many years. The relics included a skull, a Mass Missal and a number of vestments. They are believed to be of either Father Philip Holden or, more probably, the Blessed Miles Gerard, a relative of the Holdens. They are still kept in the church.

The **Methodist church** in Chapel Lane was built in 1863, replacing an earlier one. The story is told of a preacher who was not invited to stay for dinner after his long walk to take the service. Next time he preached, he brought a packed lunch with him and hung it by the pulpit. To reinforce each point in his sermon, he pointed to the lunch and stated, 'This is as true as the fact that my lunch is in that bag.'

Now a nursing home, **Swillbrook House** is reputedly haunted by the ghost of a boy who was accidentally killed by his father. The solid, stone building is by the canal bridge to the south of the village.

CATON [Lancaster and Morecambe]

SD5365: 3½ miles (6km) NE of Lancaster

In Domesday Book, the village is recorded as 'Catun'. Now a growing residential area, this was, in the 19th century, a village with eight mills. Most of the mill buildings have been converted to more modern uses. When the turnpike road was built in the 18th century, the population grew. There is no church in the village because it grew from Brookhouse, the adjoining village to the west.

At the entrance to 'The Croft', by the Ship Inn, west of the roundabout, is an old, gnarled oak tree. At the foot were the fish stones where the monks used to sell their fish. West of the tree, past the Quernmore road, a lane on the right leads to **Low Mill**. A splendid construction of

three storeys and a tower, it was built by John Hodgson in 1783. It continued as a mill until the 1970s and was converted to residential use in 1994.

Records state that **Gresgarth Hall**, standing in landscaped grounds laid out in 1810, half a mile (1km) south of the village, was a retreat house for the Abbot of Furness in the 11th century. A number of renovations have taken place over the years, including the addition of an extra wing in 1805. The crenellated building was erected on the site of a pele tower. It is the home of the Lennox-Boyd family.

A visit to the beautiful 'Crook o' Lune' area of the River Lune is best started from the car park on the northern side of the bridge, on the Halton road, west of the village. The railway closed in 1960 and is a path for walkers.

CHAPELTOWN [Blackburn]

SD7315: 5 miles (8km) SE of Darwen

Chapeltown is a moorland village of 17th- and 18th-century stone cottages. High up on Chetham Close, to the west of Green Arms Road, the northerly continuation of the High Street, is an ancient stone circle with a diameter of 51ft (15.5m). The stones are no taller than 3½ft (1.5m).

Halfway along the High Street are the **Old Grammar School, Chetham Farm Cottage** and the 18th-century **Chetham Arms**. At the northern end of the street, the village cross and stocks are to be found in the small rest garden of the conservation area. The wooden top part of the cross was erected in 1990.

It is thought that there has been a place of worship on the site of the **church of St Anne**, Turton since the 12th century. Situated at the south end of Chapeltown, it was completely rebuilt in 1841, with a tall spire at the east end.

CHARNOCK RICHARD [Chorley]

SD5516: 2½ miles (4km) SW of Chorley

To most travellers on the M6, the name Charnock Richard is synonymous with the service station. But the village really does exist. As there were two Charnocks, the owner's name, Richard, was added in the 13th century, so that the village would not be confused with Heath Charnock.

The brightly-coloured, stained-glass windows are a feature of the **church of Christ Church**, which stands in a rural setting in Church Lane. Many of the windows are memorials to the Darlington family. James Darlington, of Bourton Hall, Warwickshire built the church in 1869. He married Frances, a member of the Lancashire Radcliffe family. Her marble memorial is in the chancel.

Divided from the village by the motorway, **Park Hall** was the manor house. The grounds have been transformed into the Camelot leisure centre, based on the stories of King Arthur. Camelot includes a rare breeds farm and jousting area.

CHATBURN [Ribble Valley]

SD7744: 2 miles (3km) NE of Clitheroe

A Roman road ran close to the village of Chatburn. A hoard of Roman coins were unearthed near it in 1838. Four hundred feet (122m) above sea level, the community nestles in a hollow between two ridges. There is still industry in the form of quarrying and textiles. The spire of the 19th-century **church of Christ Church**, at the north end of the village, dominates the surrounding land.

CHIPPING [Ribble Valley]

SD6243: 7½ miles (12km) W of Clitheroe

Close to the Bowland Hills, this village of stone cottages has an industrial history. It boasted five mills in medieval times. In the Domesday Book, the village is called 'Chippenden'. Until the 17th century it was a market, and the village name derives from 'Chepyn' meaning 'market place'. The increasing number of sheep in the area led to a thriving weaving and flax-making industry. It is now a tourist centre, but remains a working village.

Pulling faces in church may not be the done thing, but this is a permanent feature at the **church of St Bartholomew**, at the centre of the village, which has some amusing heads carved on a pillar in the north aisle. Thought to have been done in the 14th century, they appear to be pulling faces. More heads and a medieval carving of a serpent appear on other north aisle pillars. The building is 15th century with 16th- and 19th-century additions. Its interior also contains a 12th-century piscina in the chancel. South of the chancel, near the Memorial Chapel, formerly the Sherbourne Chantry, is a Saxon stone, possibly a plague stone. This was discovered during the renovations of 1813. Next to it is a Belgian chest which came from St Bartholomew's Hospital in London. It was originally a present from the Belgian people to the daughter of their British ambassador, on the occasion of her wedding in 1879. Two 1450 holy water stoups and the 1520 font are at the back of the building. Around the font are letters, written upside down, which are the initials for 'Ave Maria Gratis Plens Dominus Tecum'. A window is dedicated to John Berry, who died in 1966. He was a member of the Berry village firm of chair-makers.

There are Berry chairs in the sanctuary. Six of the bells date from 1793.

In the churchyard, to the east of the porch, is a 1708 sundial on the base of the old church cross. A custom connected with weddings is that the gates of the churchyard are tied by children. The wedding couple has to throw money to get them opened.

A legend connects the church with the 18th-century **Sun Inn**, opposite. A young serving girl, Lizzy Dean, worked at the inn. One afternoon, she heard the church bells ringing. Looking through a window, she saw her fiancé arrive at the church to be married to another woman. In despair, Lizzie hanged herself. Her last wishes were to be buried beneath the church path, so that every time her former fiancé went to church he would have to walk over her grave. She is supposed to haunt the inn. In fact, her grave is now found by the 500-year-old yew tree at the south-east corner of the church.

The village still retains its 17th-century layout. **Windy Street** contains many of the most picturesque cottages in the village. By St Mary's Catholic Church is the **Grammar School**, now in private hands. It was founded in 1684 by John Brabin, a wealthy local benefactor. The date can be seen over the main door and inset in the wall. The word 'Girls' is over another door. Brabin also erected the almshouses. His 17th-century home, in Talbot Street, is now the post office, next to the Tillotson's Arms. Brabin was a wool merchant who left London at the time of the Great Plague. In those days such wealthy people were allowed to mint their own coins. One marked 'Brabin' and 'Chipping' was discovered as far away as St Albans. At the end of this street, by the bridge, is the **Waterwheel Restaurant**. This was formerly a mill and takes its name from the preserved waterwheel on the right of the building.

On the north-west fringe of the village is the chair-making firm of Berry and Sons, based in the old mill. Until 1941, Kirk Mill Dam provided the power for the works.

On the front of **Hesketh End**, a 1582 farmhouse, dates from British history are inscribed. Although there is no mention of the Norman Conquest, the battle of Flodden in 1513 is recorded. The house is reached by turning right at the end of a lane opposite the Dog and Partridge pub in Hesketh Lane.

CHORLEY [Chorley]

SD5817: 3½ miles (6km) SE of Leyland

The name of the town means a settlement by the River Chor. It became a borough in 1250 and its market of 1498, the **Flat Iron Market**, still flourishes. It is so-called because the goods for sale were originally placed on the ground.

A burial urn from c1000BC was unearthed at Astley Hall Farm, but there is no evidence of Roman occupation. Chorley was important during the Civil War, when, at the Battle of Preston Moor in 1648, Cromwell defeated the Royalist troops of Lord Hamilton. For an unknown reason, borough status was lost during the 14th century and not restored again until 1881. The wealth of the town developed in the 19th century, mainly from coal and lead. For many years it was thought that **Miles Standish**, who sailed from Plymouth to the New World in the Mayflower in 1620, was a member of the Standish family of the now-demolished Duxbury Hall. Scholars now question this. What is certain is that **Henry Tate** (1819-99), of Tate and Lyle sugar fame, was a son of Chorley. In fact, the son of a local minister. He went from owning a grocery shop in Liverpool in 1839 to becoming a wealthy sugar refiner. In 1893 he gave his collection of paintings to start the Tate Art Gallery in London, for which he paid all the costs. Another noteworthy local is Roger Wrennal who, in 1987, was beatified by the Pope. He was a weaver in the town and exececuted because he hid a priest in his house.

In 1442, Rowland Standish brought back the skull of St Laurence, who suffered torture on a gridiron. Great mystery surounds this relic for it was eventually discovered that animal bones had been substituted. The niche for the relic still remains in the **church of St Laurence**, on the corner of Market Street and Hollinshead Street. Although there is 14th-century masonry in the walls, much of the building dates from renewal in 1861. At that time, two new aisles were added. However, the tower is 15th century, and was erected by the Standish family, who lived at Duxbury Hall. There is a 14th- and 15th-century font and a litany bell from 1250 in the chancel. In the early 19th century, marriages had to be performed before midday. The story is told that when a couple wishing to be married arrived at five minutes before the hour, the sexton stopped the church clock while he went to look for the vicar.

The **church of St George** is a Waterloo church, built with Government money in the 1820s after the Napoleonic wars. Its architect, Thomas Rickman, was one of the leaders of the neo-Gothic architectural movement.

So close to the town centre that it is easily accessible, **Astley Hall**, north-west of the church, stands in a park of 104 acres (42 hectares) near the River Chor. The park contains an ornamental lake and woodland walks. The arch of the entrance gates was brought from a neighbouring estate in 1914. Parts of the original Elizabethan building of 1580 survive in the west front and courtyard. The south front was added during the refurbishment of the 17th century. The east wing was completed in 1820. In 1922, the hall was donated to the town. One of the conditions of the gift was that the hall should serve as a memorial to the First World War. Consequently, there is a small room which houses a Book of Remembrance and photographs.

The hall is furnished mainly in late Tudor and early Stuart style. Through the entrance is the great hall, where there are a number of portraits on wooden panels. These include Drake and Columbus. The plasterwork of the ceilings is mid-17th century. The drawing room, with its decorated ceilings, has 17th-century Flemish tapestries depicting scenes from the Golden Fleece. The shovelboard in the long gallery is 23½ft (7m) long. The game was played by the players pushing metal weights from one end of the table to the other. This was the precursor of the more modern game of shove-halfpenny. The winner was the player who got his weight nearest to the edge of the table, without it falling off. One of the bedrooms contains the bed used by Cromwell when he stayed at the hall after the Battle of Preston. His boots are also on display. The kitchen has a display of the culinary utensils of former years. The hall also serves as the museum and art gallery of the town. On display are furniture, paintings, pottery and lead soldiers.

High up on the hill, overlooking the M61, is the £100 million **Mormon Temple**. Built in 15 acres (6 hectares) of grounds, with a 155ft (47m) spire, it is the northern headquarters of the movement. This was the closest possible site to the first British Mormon branch, started in Preston in 1837. It was dedicated in June 1998.

CHURCH [Hyndburn]

SD7429: 3½ miles (6km) E of Blackburn

We have heard of the balloon going up, but for one unfortunate man in the 19th century, it came down, in the village of Church. On 18 September 1824, Windham Sadler was flying in his balloon from Bolton to Blackburn. Sadly, one of the mill chimneys at Church got in his way. The balloon folded and Sadler was killed.

The village had a chapel run by the monks of Whalley Abbey, hence its name. The lords of the manor were the lords of Clitheroe. Then, in the 13th century, came the Rishtons, followed by the Walmesleys of Dunkenhalgh. A member of the latter family was Judge Thomas Walmesley, who is commemorated in the name of the pub at **Billington**, west of the river bridge crossing into Whalley. The village is an urban area connecting with Accrington. The Leeds and Liverpool Canal runs through the centre of the community. The coming of the canal in the 18th century and the railway in 1848 rapidly increased the growth of textile manufacture. There was a particular emphasis on calico, the uncle of Sir Robert Peel owning a calico works in the village.

It is known that in 1334 the **church of St James** was in such a parlous state that mass could not be celebrated on a rainy day. The nave and chancel were taken down in 1805. Although the nave was soon rebuilt, the chancel was not replaced until 1870 and again in 1895. Only the 15th-century tower and font remain of the previous building. The church, found off Henry Street, via Edward Street and Church Street, stands near Church Kirk Bridge over the canal, at the northern end of the town. In the churchyard, near the main gate, is the grave of James Simpson, 19th-century president of the Vegetarian Society. The dietary regime appears not to have done him much good, because he died at the age of 48.

CHURCHTOWN [Wyre]

SD4843: 9½ miles (15km) NW of Preston

The historic village of Churchtown centres on its beautiful ancient church. On the turn into Church Street is the **Market Cross**. This is really a dial post – a pillar with a ball on top. This was the 18th-century equivalent of a village clock. Further down the street, the **Punch Bowl Inn** was formerly called The Covered Cup. The cup was part of the coat of arms of the Butlers of Kirkland Hall.

Church Street ends at the church itself. Known as the 'Cathedral of the Fylde', the **church of St Helen**, on the banks of the River Wyre, lives up to its reputation. This was the ancient parish church of Garstang, covering a huge area. Seven other parishes were carved out of it a century ago. The oldest parts of the building are the 12th-century pillars in the north aisle. In fact, the building also has material from every century since then. The nave and a window in the south aisle date from that century. Some of the oak beams in the roof of that aisle were given by Henry IV in 1402. The tower, with a stone turret at the top of the staircase tower, is from the 15th century. Part of an inscription in the bell tower reads, 'Whoever a bell doth ever throwe, shall paye two groate before hee goe, And hee that ringd with spur on heele, likewise that penalty shall feele.'

The chancel arch was erected in 1300. The roof is 16th century, as are two chapels. The south chapel has a ceiling dated 1529. It contains a 17th-century wall painting and a rare 15th-century portrait of a bishop. The rear choir stalls have 15th-century misericords. On the north side of the chancel is a 13th-century pillar.

The Lady Chapel, on the south side, was built in 1529. An inscription in it refers to a demon whose role in life was to write down all the gossip he heard in church and report it on the Day of Judgement. The chandelier in the nave is 18th century. It is said to have been a gift from a builder. When, in 1746, the church was in need of rebuilding, he instead diverted the river round it so that the foundations would no longer be damaged by flood water. The pulpit has a 1646 date. Alongside it are the Norman font, which was unearthed in the sanctuary, and the gravestone of a medieval knight. The charnel house, now used as the boiler room, was erected in 1754. It contained bones which had been dug up when the graveyard was full. In the circular churchyard is an 18th-century sundial and the remains of an old cross.

On the other side of the main road from the village is **Kirkland Hall**. The front dates from 1760 and the two wings from 1668 and 1695. Remodelling took place in 1840. The entrance gates came from the village in 1935.

CLAUGHTON [Lancaster and Morecambe]

SD5566: 6½ miles (10km) NE of Lancaster

The village, pronounced 'Clafton', lays claim to being the smallest parish in Lancashire. Nonetheless, there is much of interest to the visitor, including the house that moved. Quarrying in the hills continues after many centuries. An aerial ropeway, at the west end of the village, brings material down the hill, across the road and into the brickworks.

Found off the main road by the Old Rectory Restaurant, the bellcot of the **church of St Chad** is from the late 18th century and houses two bells, one of which, reputedly the oldest in England, has the date 1296. Apart from an east window from the late 14th century, most of the buildings appears to date from 1904.

Opposite the church, **Claughton Hall**, dating from the 13th century, was moved from its original site in 1935 to a position east of the village. The one wing that was left where it was is now Claughton Hall Farm.

The white **Old Toll House,** by the petrol station on the road to Hornby, is one of the oldest in the country. It was outside the Old Toll House garage that the first white road traffic lines were painted on the road. This was done by the owner because he had witnessed many accidents on the sharp corner. The experiment caused much debate. Eventually, and only after the support of King George V was obtained, white lines started to be used more widely on roads.

CLAUGHTON-ON-BROCK [Wyre]

SD4253: 8 miles (13km) N of Preston

The Roman Catholic **church of St Thomas** and Claughton Hall are two of the oldest buildings in this small village. Pronounced 'clighton', the village is some distance from the River Brock, in spite of the name. The church, on Smithy Lane, the main route through the village, is built of white, rectangular blocks. It was erected in 1792, but the impressive façade is 19th century. The hall is from the late 17th century. It is hidden in the midst of its estate, which is accessed through the lodge on the lane west of the church.

CLAYTON-LE-MOORS
[Hyndburn]

SD7531: 4½ miles (7km) NE of Blackburn

A former farming, mining and quarrying community, the cutting of the Leeds and Liverpool Canal led to the increased growth of the textile industry, as well as coal mining, brick-making and calico printing. Before this, there was nothing that could be called a village. The name derives from 'Clayton-super-moras', which means 'a stretch of barren land'.

The **church of All Saints**, found to the west of the A680 after the canal bridge, was built in 1840. It has galleries from 1852 and a rebuilt chancel of 1882. The pulpit, reredos and font are all of marble. The land was given by **John Mercer**, a Methodist, who invented the process of 'mercerisation'. He lived at Mercer Hall, next door. The grounds, including Oakenshaw Cottage, became a public park in 1913.

The village boasts a number of important houses. **Sparth House** is situated on the corner by the main road traffic lights, north of the canal. Built in 1556, it has mullioned windows, some with their original leaded lights. It is now a restaurant. About 300 metres further north, **Clayton Hall** can be seen from the Clayton Forest Park. The two-storey building, built in classsical style in 1772 to replace an earlier one, is noted for the plasterwork of the ceilings. It was the mesne (tenanted) manor house of Altham, inherited by the Claytons from Hugh the Saxon. **Dunkenhalgh** was the castellated family home of the Petre family, who were the lords of the manor until 1947. There has been a house on the site since the 13th century. The house of 1580 was altered in 1799. It is said to be haunted by the ghost of a French governess. She found she was to have a baby by a soldier and consequently committed suicide by jumping into the river. The house is now a hotel, situated on the A67: between Clayton and Rishton.

CLAYTON-LE-WOODS
[Chorley]

SD5622: 1 mile (1.5km) NE of Leyland

The River Lostock borders this growing residential village, which was once a farming community, centring on Cuerden Hall and its estates.

The graceful spire and bell tower of the **church of St Bede** were erected in 1964. The rest of the building is 19th century.

Cuerden Valley Park, which lies on both sides of Sheep Hill Lane (B5256), was opened in 1981. The River Lostock runs through 600 acres (243 hectares) of fields and woodland between Whittle-le-Woods and Bamber Bridge.

The northern part of the park was formerly the grounds of **Cuerden Hall**. Well-known families such as the Cuerdens, Banastres, Towneleys and Parkers have lived at the hall. The lake was built in 1890 to supply water for the hall. Remains of the building of 1717 survived when, in 1816, Robert Towneley instructed Lewis Wyatt to construct a new house. This was when its belvedere tower, built partly open, was added. The Tatton family bought the house in 1906, since when it has seen use as a military hospital in World War 1 and by the Ministry of Defence from 1958 to 1977. It is owned by the Sue Ryder Foundation.

The **church of St Saviour, Cuerden**, on Church Road, immediately west of Junction 29 of the M6, is built in the style of the 12th century, but dates from 1837.

CLIFTON-WITH-SALWICK [Fylde]

SD4730: 5 miles (8km) W of Preston

The large **British Nuclear Fuels** complex dominates the village of Salwick. At the crossroads is a windmill, now converted into the Windmill Tavern.

A pagan altar turned into a font is the main attraction at the **church of St John the Evangelist, Lund**, situated down Church Lane from the Windmill Tavern. In the early part of the 17th century, the right to appoint the minister, plus the windmill and four acres of land were bought by Sir Cuthbert Halsall. In 1840, Lund became a separate parish, covering Clifton-with-Salwick and Newton-with-Scales. Since the chapel was in a delapidated condition, a new building was erected in 1824 and the chancel added in 1852. The imposing tower of 1873 is 60ft (18m) high, with a turret on top. A 'scandalous trough', referred to in records of 1701, is inside the present church. This is the font, which is in the region of 1600 years old. It was found on the old Roman road. The church bell dates from 1684. In the churchyard are the 19th-century graves of two people who were drowned when trying to cross the marshes to Freckleton.

North of the railway station is **Salwick Hall**. The Lancaster Canal passes between the hall and the road. This was the home of the Clifton family, and until the late 18th century, local Roman Catholics worshipped in the chapel. In the village of Clifton itself, quietly off the A583, **Clifton Hall** is now owned by Milano International. The brick and stone building, in Tudor style, was erected by the Clifton family in 1832, as a farm.

CLITHEROE [Ribble Valley]

SD7441: 9½ miles (17km) NE of Blackburn

The town is the second oldest borough in the county, its charter being granted in 1147. It stands on a hill and is the gateway to the Forest of Bowland. A long-standing tradition is that the meeting at which the council convenes to choose its next Mayor is known as the Cockle and Mussel Feast, because these are part of the menu.

On Castle Hill, only the keep of the **Castle**, with its 9ft (2.5m) thick walls, remains of the original, 11th-century building. It stands on a small outcrop of rock. The smallest keep in the country, this is all that is left from the destruction that the forces of Cromwell wrought in 1649. The castle was handed over to the local authority in 1918, along with the extensive grounds. It had been the property of the crown for over 300 years. In the nearby Rose Garden is a turret which was removed from the House of Commons during building work in the 1930s. The Castle Museum concentrates on the story of the Ribble Valley over the centuries. This is demonstrated through the use of documents and photographs. An Edwardian kitchen, a Victorian printing press and the workshop of a clogger are also on view.

Castle Hill is also the base of the **North West Sound Archive**, containing over 85,000 recordings of people who lived and worked in the Ribble Valley. There is also a restored Hacking ferryboat on display, and an exhibition of Lancashire during the Second World War.

The 15th-century tower and chancel of the **church of St Mary Magdalene**, in Church Street, survived the major rebuilding work of 1823. The twisted spire was built in 1846. Inside, there are some 17th-century panels on the altar in the south aisle. A memorial on the south wall remembers Reverend John Webster who was at various times a vicar, headmaster, metallurgist and astrologer, as well as being author of a book on witchcraft. His memorial also includes a mathematical puzzle. The sobering epitaph on one of the graves reads, 'Passengers, stop as you pass by. As you are now, so once was I. As I am now, so you must be. Therefore prepare to follow me.' The bells are dated 1658.

The **Old Grammar School**, in Well Terrace, was founded in 1554.

Low Moor Mill, at Low Moor, west of the town, was erected in 1782, along with 28 houses for the workers. By 1841 there were 238 houses, planned in the form of an early model village. The **church of St Paul**, on the corner of St Paul's Road and the main road, was built alongside the former one in 1869.

Limestone has been produced at **Salthill Quarry** since the 17th century. Now that this has finished, part of it is a nature reserve and a Site of Special Scientific Interest. Many ancient fossils have been found here over the years. It is reached via Salthill Road.

The **Sculpture Trail**, exhibiting the work of local artists, is on the Ribble Way between Brungerley Bridge, on the B6478, and Croshill Quarry. By the bridge, on the Waddington road, **Waddow Hall** is a large, 19th-century building of nine bays. It is now a Girl Guides centre. Half a mile (1km) south, **Standen Hall** is a 1757 building of seven bays, with a porch of Tuscan columns.

COCKERHAM [Lancaster and Morecambe]

SD4652: 5½ miles (9km) SW of Lancaster

The small village of Cockerham, on Morecambe Bay, looks out towards Pill-

ing Embankment and the vast stretches of Cockerham Sands. The name, spelt 'Cocreham' in the Domesday Book, derives from 'a homestead on the River Cocker'. The village suffered a disastrous fire in the 17th century and had to be almost completely rebuilt. A local legend tells the tale of a schoolteacher. He gave the devil a number of tests, on condition that if failed, the devil would leave the village. The first one was to count the number of drops of dew on a hedge. This task was completed successfully. The next was to add up the number of ears of corn in a field. This was also achieved by the devil. He failed on the third, which was to make a rope of sand and then wash it in the river. The new village surrounds the Manor Inn at the road junction.

Most of the original, late 15th-century, timber-framed structure of **Cockerham Hall** remains. It is a rare example of this type of building, and is situated on the west edge of the village, on the A588. Further west is the **church of St Michael**, although it is best visited along the lane east of the B5272 junction with the A588. Before the fire, the church was at the centre of the village. Now it is in an isolated position. The floor of the porch gives the date of a rebuilding in 1814. Apart from the tower and bells that are said to have come from Cockersand Abbey, there is little remaining from previous structures on the site. In the churchyard is the grave of a vicar who, after burying 11 of his flock during the Great Plague, eventually succumbed himself.

At **Cocker House Bridge**, on a minor road east from the B5272, is an old boundary stone. Only the chapter house remains of **Cockersand Abbey**, 2 miles (3km) north-west of the village. This was because the chapter house was the burial place of the monks and so escaped the destruction of the rest of the buildings when they were razed to the ground on the orders of Henry VIII. Stones from the rest of the building were used to help make a sea wall. The chapter house has a vaulted sandstone ceiling and is one of the few remaining octagonal structures of the type. It later became the burial place of the Dalton family of Thurnham Hall, who took control of the abbey lands after the dissolution. In 1180, Hugh Garth had a hermitage on the site, which he developed as a hospital for lepers and the sick. Ten years later the Premonstratensian monks arrived, and it soon became one of the most prosperous abbeys in the country, owning land throughout Lancashire and the Lake District. It was known in those days as 'St Mary's of the Marsh' because of the boggy nature of the land. So treacherous was it that in 1496 the Abbot of Shap requested a guide to get him to the abbey from Lancaster. The buildings were originally long and narrow, with transepts and no aisles. In the 14th century a Lady Chapel was added. The choir stalls were removed to Lancaster Priory church. Previously it had been home for Hugh the Hermit and then a hospital for lepers. The site was excavated between 1923 and 1927. Fragments of glass and lead found then were removed to Lancaster Museum. The abbey is reached by taking Moss Lane from Thurnham to the seafront at Bank Houses and then walking north along the coastal footpath. The lighthouse beyond the abbey, at the mouth of the River Lune, is **Plover Scar**, erected in 1843.

COLNE [Pendle]

SD8939: 3 miles (4km) NE of Nelson

Sited on an old Roman road, with Brontë

moorland beyond, the town of Colne has one long main street, stretching along the valley. It is a typical Lancashire mill town, finding new life and industry in the modern age. In 1861-2, a weavers' strike brought much distress to the local workers. William Hartley, the jam manufacturer, was born here. So, too, was Wallace Hartley, leader of the band on the *Titanic*. He conducted the music as the ship floundered. There is a memorial bust near the war memorial in Albert Road.

Probably the oldest building in the Pendle area, part of the tower of the **church of St Bartholomew**, in Church Street, dates from the early 12th century. The rest of the building is mainly from the 15th century. Inside are a 16th-century font and screen. In the churchyard are a charnel house, the stocks and, to the east, the grammar school of 1812.

Opened in 1972, the **British in India Museum**, in Newtown Street, houses a collection of uniforms, paintings, postcards, stamps and model soldiers from the era of the British Empire. Among the exhibits are the Indian clothes worn by the novelist E.M. Forster during his time in the country, a Japanese flag captured in 1944 at the Battle of Kohima, the last Union Jack flown in Lucknow, the skin of a tiger and a number of regimental neckties. In addition there is a display of photographs from the royal archives of Queen Victoria and her Indian servants and a working model of the Kalka-Simla railway.

A heritage display, including a history of production methods up to the present time, is found at **Empress Mills** in Empress Street. The library, in Market Street, houses the **Colne Heritage Centre**, where more can be discovered about the history of the town. The **King's Head Inn**, in Church Street, sheltered unpopular magistrates at the time of the 1840 Chartist Riots. It is now a Greek restaurant. **Emmott Hall** at **Laneshaw Bridge**, 2 miles (3km) east of Colne, is a ruined, five-bay, classical-style house of 1717.

The Roman Catholic **church of the Sacred Heart**, in Queen Street, is notable for its Italian mosaics.

CONDER GREEN [Lancaster and Morecambe]

SD4656: 5 miles (8km) SW of Lancaster

Scattered cottages and farms make up this small hamlet on the River Conder, where it empties into the Lune estuary. The whitewashed **Stork Inn**, looking out over the green and the river beyond, dates back to the 17th century. The lane running along the bank of the river from the pub terminates at the old railway station. This is now a car park and the former line has been transformed into a cycleway and walkway. All that remains of the days of steam are the station master's house and that of the crossing keeper. By the latter, at the entrance to the car park, are the crossing posts.

The turreted extravaganza of **Ashton Hall** is half a mile (1km) north of the village.

COPPULL [Chorley]

SD5614: 2½ miles (4km) SW of Chorley

The former mill village is now mainly residential and is divided from Chorley by the River Yarrow.

Built in 1911, the **church of St John the Divine**, off Park Road, has a tower and high arcades. The cost of building was borne by James Darlington of Broughton Hall in Warwickshire, who was also responsible for the erection of the parish church at Charnock Richard.

Coppull Ring Mill and **Mavis Mill** are two large buildings, each with a tower with a copper cupola. The mill

Ashton Hall, Conder Green

lodge is also preserved. Ring Mill is now an enterprise centre.

An area of the old coal tips of Chisnall Hall Colliery, **Blainscough Wood Nature Reserve**, has been transformed into wildflower meadows. Found at the end of Springfield Road, off the B5251, it is used for educational and conservation purposes.

The River Yarrow flows through the 125 acres (50 hectares) of lakes, meadows and woodland of the **Yarrow Valley Country Park**. It contains two old mill lodges. The main car park is off the B5251, south of Chorley.

COPSTER GREEN [Ribble Valley]

SD6834: 3½ miles (6km) N of Blackburn

The name Copster means 'a clearing on a hill'. The community includes, to the south, the villages of Clayton-le-Dale, Salesbury and Wilpshire. The large **church of St Peter** at Salesbury was built in 1887 and gives good views towards the Forest of Bowland. The green was the area of common land, where the locals could put their livestock out to graze. When landowners attempted to enclose the green, they were overwhelmed by the resistance of the villagers. There are two areas of green. The first is divided by the main road at the Park Gate Inn. Opposite the inn, the green is surrounded by houses. Earlier in the 20th century, this was used by visitors for picnics. The locals took the opportunity to earn some money by selling refreshments. The green was also used by geese and acquired the name 'Goose Muck Hillock'. By turning left down Park Gate Row, a set of delightful cottages is reached. **Bolton Hall**, at the end of the lane, was built in 1655.

The second green is in Lovely Hall Lane, off the main road in the southern part of the village. **Lovely Hall** was erected in the middle of the 17th century on an earlier site. It was added to in 1874. Pleasantly situated in wooded grounds, it has been twice renovated since that time. At the front of the house is a sundial dated 1668.

COWAN BRIDGE [Lancaster and Morecambe]

SD6376: 2½ miles (4km) SE of Kirkby Lonsdale

The Brontë sisters went to school in this small hamlet. On the roadside wall of **Brontë Cottage**, adjacent to the old road bridge, is a plaque stating that this was where the sisters attended a school for the daughters of clergy. It was run by the vicar of Tunstall, William Wilson, who founded it in 1823. It was not a time the sisters enjoyed and is referred to by Charlotte in *Jane Eyre*, where it is the Lowood of the opening chapters. She rebelled against the puritanical regime. Wilson, the Evangelical vicar, is the Mr. Brocklehurst of the story. It is recorded that sanitation was so bad at the school that 40 of the students went down with illness. Charlotte and Emily were removed from the school after two years, when Elizabeth and Maria died of typhus. The school was later moved to Casterton.

CRAWSHAWBOOTH [Rossendale]

SD8125: 1½ miles (3km) N of Rawtenstall

The early settlement was one of the areas in the Royal Forest of Rossendale used by the monks of Whalley Abbey as pastureland. The name means 'the booth by the crow wood'. In the 17th century it grew as a centre for weaving and sheep farming.

The **church of St John**, on the main road, is difficult to miss. It is a large structure with a tower 122ft (37m) in height. Built in 1892 by Lord Crawshaw, it is known as 'The Cathedral of the Valley'.

Next to the church, standing high at the end of a long drive, **Sunnyside House** was built by John Marriott, a Quaker, in 1757. In the early 19th century it was bought by the Brooks family. Thomas Brooks was made High Sheriff of Lancashire in 1884 and Baron Crawshaw in 1892. From 1965 to 1997, it was the conference house of the Manchester Anglican diocese. The house has a number of early 19th-century additions. There is notable ceiling plasterwork, which may have come from Whalley Abbey, in two of the rooms. The adjacent **Crawshaw Hall** was built in stone in 1831 as an additional residence for the Crawshaw (Booth) family. North of this complex of buildings, signposted off the main road, the **Friends' Meeting House**, in Cooperative Street, was built in 1716 and enlarged in 1736. It is part of the Crawshawbooth Conservation Area. In the Bury Session Rolls of 1716 it is recorded as, 'a certain edifice or building newly erected in the forest of Rossendale for an assemby of persons called Quakers.'

CROSTON [Chorley]

SD4818: 6½ miles (10km) NW of Chorley

Surrounded by farmland, this historic village derives its name from 'the village of the cross'. The three-storey weavers' cottages found in Drinkhouses Lane are a reminder of the village's industrial history.

It received a royal charter in 1283. 'Coffee Day' is a corruption of 'Feoffing Day', the time when the lord of the manor was paid his rent by the tenants. It traditionally became a day of feasting and merrymaking. A little girl is reputed to haunt the cemetery. She died an orphan and was buried in a pauper's grave. This was never maintained and so her restless spirit still appears.

At the end of Church Street, the **church of St Michael and All Angels** is a sandstone building in Gothic style. Although the present building dates back to the 16th century, it is said that this is where the missionaries of St Aidan built a chapel in 651. Of the older buildings, only a Norman doorway remains. A major restoration took place in 1887. Inside is a memorial to Rector Hyett who was expelled from his living in 1660 because of his Puritan sympathies. Some of the tiles in the south aisle carry the letter 'T', which refers to the De Trafford family.

East of the church is the large, impressive **Old Rectory**, with a Baroque façade and Dutch gables. Erected in 1772, it is now a retirement home.

Church Street itself has been described as one of the best examples of a village street to be found in Lancashire. At the entrance to the street is a cross with a 17th-century base. The remainder was hewn from a millstone in 1953. The cottages flanking the street are from the late 18th and early 19th centuries.

The small packhorse bridge adjacent to the cross is called **Town Bridge**. It was erected in 1682 and built of sandstone in a single arch.

The home of the De Trafford family at **Croston Hall**, built by E.W. Pugin, is no longer to be seen. Only Pugin's little chapel remains, behind the trees off Grape Lane, south of the village centre. It serves as the Roman Catholic **church of the Holy Cross**

The sandstone **Henry Croston Almshouses** in Station Road were erected in 1692. They are said to be the oldest in the county.

The **Lord Nelson Inn**, next to the village green, off Town Road, is 18th century.

DALTON [West Lancashire]

SD5008: 4½ miles (7km) NE of Ormskirk

The highest point in the widely-scattered community of Dalton is Ashurst Hill at 570ft (174m). It is crowned by a beacon. In the Domesday Book, the village is known 'Daltone'. From the 11th century to 1733 it belonged to the Barony of Manchester. Between the 17th and 19th centuries it was known for the quarrying of flagstones. Today it is mainly a farming area, but with an increasing residential population.

Lord Skelmersdale erected **Ashurst's Beacon** in 1798, when it was generally thought that the country was about to be invaded by France. A plaque on the tower states that the beacon and the land around it were bought by the wife of a Wigan journalist as a memorial to his love of the area.

Beacon Country Park covers 304 acres (123 hectares) on the western slopes of Ashurst Hill. With extensive views to North Wales, the Pennines and the Lancashire plain, it comprises rolling meadow and woodland, plus a visitor centre and golf course.

Rising high up on the slopes of Ashurst Hill, the **church of St Michael** was built in 1877. A serious fire in the 1980s resulted in extensive interior renovation.

Next to the church, a short distance up a public footpath, is the 17th-century gate-house and dovecote of **Ashurst's Hall**. The rest of the building was demolished long ago.

Priorswood Hall, at the foot of the northern slope of the hill off Lees Lane, dates from the 16th or early 17th centuries. It is thought that it may have had past links with Burscough Priory.

Well off the beaten track, a mile (1.5km) east of the beacon, **Stone Hall** is early 18th century, with an attractive façade and three bays.

DARWEN [Blackburn]

SD6922: 4 miles (6km) S of Blackburn

Originally a farming and quarrying area in the parish of Blackburn, the town then became a centre for the print and bleach industry and coal mining. By the 19th century, most of this activity had been overtaken by the advent of the cotton and paper manufacturing boom. The community of stone houses lies strung out along the valley of the River Darwen. It is surrounded by hills and Sunnyhurst Hey and Earnsdale reservoirs.

In 1931 the town was visited by **Ghandi**, the Indian leader. He was in England for the Commonwealth Leaders' Conference. India was threatening to reduce its imports of cotton, so Ghandi was persuaded to visit some of the northern textile towns to hear local views.

The **church of St Peter** in the town centre has a flat ceiling and three galleries. Formerly called Holy Trinity, it was renamed St Peter's when the congregation was joined by those of St John's and St George's. The latter two churches were demolished. Erected in 1829, the building stands in a prominent, high position. The walls of the **church of St James**, off Winterton Road, are those of the 16th-century building, but extensive renovation took place in the 19th and 20th centuries. Inside, a plaque on the wall gives details of the difficulties that the Vicar of Blackburn had in regaining the building for the Church of England after the period of Oliver Cromwell's Commonwealth.

Built in 1847, the **Independent Meeting House** in Belgrave Sqare has a high porch and triple bell-gable. According to Nikolaus Pevsner, the architectural historian, it 'creates quite a fantastic skyline'.

At 85ft (26m) in height, **Darwen Tower**, on Darwen Hill, west of the town, was completed in 1898 at 1225ft (373m) above sea level. It was built to commemorate the Diamond Jubilee of Queen Victoria, which had taken place the year before. There is both a viewing platform and a parapet walk at the top. There are extensive views across to the Ribble estuary, the Forest of Bowland and Pendle Hill. From 1878 local people fought for the freedom to roam on these moors. This involved at least one fracas with the gamekeepers. Persistence was rewarded when, in 1898, the legal battle was won. The story of this 'battle' is recounted in Paul Salveson's book *Will Yo' Come o' Sunday Mornin'?*

The 300ft (90m) square chimney of **India Mill**, south of the town centre on the A666, dominates the valley. Built in 1867, it is designed to resemble the bell tower in St Mark's Square in Venice. The ballustrade is so spacious that brass bands have performed from it. All the bricks were made locally and the stone block, on which the mill itself was built, is enormous. To get it on site from the quarry, a special road was constructed. At the mill is a steam engine built in 1907. It is a 45-horsepower, cross-compound machine, with a 16ft (5m) grooved flywheel.

The early 19th-century steam engine outside **Moss Bridge Mill**, north of the town centre near the junction of the A666 and the motorway, is direct acting with a vertical cylinder below the crankshaft and flywheel.

The 85 acres (34 hectares) of **Sunnyhurst Wood**, by Earnsdale Road, were bought by public subscription in 1902 to commemorate the coronation of Edward VII. It lies in a valley, which runs in a north-easterly direction and was planted in the 19th century to provide cover for game birds. Sunnyhurst Brook, whose source is on the Darwen Moors, runs through the centre of the valley. There are many species of plants in the wood. Ninety-six were identified by David Bellamy, the botanist, in 1980. What was the keeper's cottage is now the visitor centre, where there are changing exhibitions about local and natural history. Earnsdale Reservoir lies at the eastern end of the Wood.

Bold Venture Park is a disused quarry coverted into open space, with a lake, waterfall and wooded areas, while **White Hall Park** contains floral displays and a 19th-century fountain.

DOLPHINHOLME [Lancaster and Morecambe]

SD5254: 5½ miles (9km) SE of Lancaster

In the 19th century, the village of Dolphinholme was bustling with activity. The mill on the River Wyre, which closed in 1867, provided work for 2000 workers. Its waterwheel was claimed as the tallest in the country. Now the village is a peaceful place divided into two communities: one around the church, at the top of the valley to the west; and the other, known as Lower Dolphinholme, down in the River Wyre valley. The latter's stone cottages huddle together around the river bridge.

Since the height of industrial activity in the 19th century, the population has declined steadily. There are few reminders of the industry of those days, except for the relics of the mill and rows of workers' terraced houses.

Pevsner observed of the **church of St Mark**, at the centre of the higher part of the village, that 'it hugs the ground happily'. Rebuilt in 1897 to replace the 1642 church, it has a low, sturdy tower, with supporting arches added in 1833. Opposite the old mill terrace of Corless Cottages, the church looks down into the valley. On the tower, the weathervane is in the shape of a large fish, one of the early Christian symbols.

As its name indicates, **Wyreside Hall** stands on the banks of the River Wyre, half a mile (1km) south of the village. The grey stone building, with a porch of Ionic columns, is surrounded by a landscaped park. The 1790 building was extensively altered in 1843, and is now used for residential purposes.

DOWNHAM [Ribble Valley]

SD7844: 2½ miles (4km) NE of Clitheroe

The Industrial Revolution managed to bypass the village of Downham, so that farming has remained the main occupation throughout the centuries. Pendle Hill overlooks the small gathering of stone cottages. A brook runs through the centre of the larger of the village greens.

The route of the **Roman road**, crosses the bottom end of Green Lane, north of the village. It ran from Ilkley to Ribchester and is thought to have been a section of the 'Gold Road', which was a 112-mile (180km) route across the country. Irish merchants travelled along it to do business with the Danes.

The Assheton family were lords of the manor from 1558. In the early 19th century they reordered the church, adding a Regency façade, and built a school and vicarage. The family was involved in the building of the estate cottages and much charitable work. They protected the local environment to such an extent that even the electricity wires were put underground. The creation of a baronetcy in 1955 meant the Assheton name changed to Clitheroe. There are two village greens. The smaller one, at the top of the steep hill, is surrounded by the pub, church and hall. **The Assheton Inn**, opposite the church, commemorates the family who were lords of the manor at the hall for many centuries. An 18th-century inn, it was previously called The George and Dragon. The remains of the village stocks are on the green.

The southern, lower green is lined by stone cottages, with Downham Beck flowing through the middle. East of the village, along Twiston Lane, can be seen a limekiln, the survivor of many which were found on farms. The lime was used both on the fields and for building purposes. Because of the shortage of food after the Napoleonic War, barley was grown and Barley Field is a reminder of those times.

The tower of the **church of St Leonard** is 15th century, but the remainder was rebuilt in 1910, following a previous attempt in 1800. Before the building of the 15th-century church, there had been a chapel in **Twiston**, the neighbouring hamlet. Also in Twiston is a 1670 **Quakers' Burial Ground**, which is a walled enclosure near the entrance to Brownlow.

From the church's elevated position there are fine views across the village. Three of the five bells date from the 15th century, although the belief that they were brought from Whalley Abbey has no foundation. Underneath the Assheton Chapel, in the south-east corner of the church, is the Assheton family vault. The family memorials include one by Westmacott, a leading Victorian sculptor. It is said that the bodies of soldiers dug up when the Roman road was excavated in the 18th century are buried in the churchyard. A 1808 sundial is on the south side of the building.

Further up the hill, **Downham Hall** has an 1835 façade and some Elizabethan walls. It is the home of Lord Clitheroe. From the grounds there are sweeping views towards Pendle Hill. A small stone is at the foot of the wall on the village side of the entrance to the hall, north of the farm. It is reputed to mark the last resting place of Roman soldiers who were killed in skirmishes on the Roman road.

Towneley Memorial, Dunsop Bridge

DUNSOP BRIDGE [Ribble Valley]

SD6650: 8 miles (13km) NW of Clitheroe

A modern public phone box on the green at Dunsop Bridge marks the official site of the **centre of Great Britain**. The little cluster of houses that make up the centre of the community is gathered round the humpback bridge over the River Dunsop. From here, a road commences the ascent over the **Trough of Bowland**. A 1739 milestone at this junction indicates the distance to the market towns in 'old miles', which are 40 per cent longer than modern ones. The milepost, which stands below the modern indicators, has an iron signpost from the early 20th century perched on top of it.

On the same road towards the Trough, north-west of the village, stands the Roman Catholic **church of St Hubert**. St Hubert was the patron saint of hunters, so it is fitting to have him remembered in the former hunting forest of Bowland. The church was built by the Towneley family of Burnley, who lived at Thorneyholme Hall, on the Slaidburn road side of the village. There is a memorial to the family in the churchyard, in the form of a large, white angel. The church was built in 1865 with the winnings from Kettledrum, a horse of Colonel Towneley which won the Derby in 1861. The horse is remembered inside the building by four carvings of a horse's head on the side pillars of the altar and the figure of a horse of each side of the apse ceiling. By the church doorway, on the wall, is a font that came from the medieval church at Burholme.

EARBY [Pendle]

SD9046: 3 miles (5km) N of Colne

Referred to in Domesday Book as Eurebi, the village of Earby expanded in the 19th century as cotton mills were built. Albion Mill, on Victoria Road, and Victoria Shed, by the car park, are examples of the mill architecture.

The early 17th-century grammar school on Old Lane now houses the **Lead Mining Museum**. The school had been opened in 1594 and closed in 1945. The building contained the master's lodgings as well as the school room. After doing service as a clinic and library, it became the museum in 1971. For over twenty years previously a group of enthusiasts had been collecting items connected with the mining of lead, not only in the Earby area, but across the Dales. There are over 700 tools and other equipment on display. In the grounds are a big waterwheel and lead crushing mill.

The parable in the New Testament of the man who started to build and did not finish is vividly portrayed by the **church of All Saints**. The building, on Skipton Road, was started in 1909. It was never completed, leaving the north aisle and tower still to be erected.

ECCLESTON [Chorley]

SD5217: 4 miles (6km) W of Chorley

The name literally means 'churchtown'. The older part of the village is around the church. The industrial area grew higher up the road. There was coal mining in the 19th century. Then, following the weaving revolution, the first mill was built in 1884. After the decline in the textile industry, artificial silk became an important product in the 1920s. Some of the mills have now been converted to other uses.

One family who left the village in the 19th century to start a new life in the United States, the Moon family, later helped to start the Mormon Church in Salt Lake City. A famous son of the village is

Richard Seddon, who became prime minister of New Zealand in 1893.

By Eccleston Bridge, north of the main village, the **church of St Mary** stands on the banks of the River Yarrow. The tower, the nave and the chancel were built in the early 14th century; the south aisle a century later. The restoration in 1881 included a remodelling of the Georgian windows. The interior contains a 15th-century font emblazoned with the coat of arms of the Stanley family. An altar tomb from the same century bears a brass called the **Eccleston Treasure**, depicting the figure of a fully robed priest. From the outside, the battlement design can be seen on the south side of the building.

Two ghosts are reputed to haunt **Heskin New Hall**, in Wood Lane, a mile (2km) south of the village. Dating from the middle of the 16th century, it is a one-storey, brick structure. From 1556 to 1739, the manor belonged to the Molyneux family. In 1744, the estate was sold to Alexander Kershaw, a rich Rochdale merchant. One of his heirs, Mary Kershaw, fled on her wedding day, riding pillion on the horse of her lover. The two ghosts are those of a Roman Catholic girl and a priest. The priest converted to Protestantism and decided to prove this by hanging the girl. Cromwell's troops did not find this compelling evidence of his change of heart and hung him as well. Inside is a great hall, a spiral staircase, long gallery and panelled drawing room. The Old Hall, a similar distance north, was demolished in the 19th century.

EDENFIELD AND STONEFOLD [Rossendale]

SD8019: 2½ miles (4km) S of Rawtenstall

The busy shopping centre stands at the divide of the roads to Rochdale and

Blackburn. **Edenfield parish church,** which has no dedication, has escaped restoration and is very much in the same condition that it was in 1778. The only older part is the 1614 west tower. There are box pews and three galleries. The **church of St John the Evangelist** at Stonefold is comparatively modern, having been completed in 1856.

EDGWORTH [Blackburn]

SD7417: 4½ miles (7km) SE of Darwen

The village of Edgworth lies in the valley of the Brock, including the hamlets of Entwistle, Qualton and Broadhead.

A 19th-century mill village, the ruins of the bleachworks and cottages remain. Nearby are Turton, Entwistle and Wayoh Reservoirs. Entwistle reservoir was constructed in 1838 and enlarged in 1840. It was originally to supply water to the bleachworks, but was taken over by Bolton Corporation in 1864. Two and a half miles (4km) north-west of the village is **Fairy Battery**, near Entwistle Reservoir. It is alternatively known as 'Pulpit Rock'. In the 17th century Unitarians, who had been expelled from the Church of England because of their rejection of the doctrine of the Trinity, worshipped there in secret for fear of persecution and arrest.

Entwistle Hall, situated on the road between Entwistle station and Wayoh Reservoir, 1 mile (2km) north-west of Edgworth, was the home of the de Entwistle family. The hall dates from the early 17th century and is now privately owned. It is on the site of a previous building owned by Sir Birtine Entwistle, who fought at the Battle of Agincourt in 1415.

ELSWICK [Fylde]

SD4238: 5 miles (8km) E of Poulton-le-Fylde

The village, including the small hamlet of Elswick Leys, was a farming community over the centuries. It was known as 'Edelesunie' in the Domesday Book. In 1643 the Earl of Derby's forces passed through the village, marching towards Lancaster. The discovery of cannon balls in the area of **Elswick Grange Farm**, down a lane to the south of the village, makes it likely that a skirmish took place here.

Residing in a glass case in the **United Reformed church** is a Geneva Bible, the bible used by all English-speaking Protestants in the 17th century. This particular one was passed down the generations of a local family. The present building, to the west of the village centre, was erected in 1874. The original one of 1753 was in the area of the present Leys Close, just north of the centre. It is thought that the old farmhouse, near the bungalows, might have been the actual building, which was one of the earliest Nonconformist churches in the county.

EUXTON [Chorley]

SD5519: 2½ miles (4km) S of Leyland

Pronounced 'exton', the village is placed in an agricultural setting close to the M6. It had one of the first paper mills in 1611, which operated until 1766. The coming of the ordnance factory just before the Second World War greatly increased the population. The site now belongs to British Aerospace.

It is curious that the small **Euxton Parish Church,** next to, but high above, the A6, has no dedication to a saint. The nave is 14th century and the west wall has a date of 1513. Reconstruction in the early 19th century included a new chancel, although the sedilia are from the old chancel of the 16th century. One of the windows was installed in 1322. The unusual bellcot partly overhangs the front of the building. In the southern area of the churchyard are an old stone font and a sundial. In 1854, the church gained national newspaper headlines when a whisky still was found under the pulpit.

The 1850 structure of **Euxton Hall**, in spacious grounds at the south end of the village, replaced a previous one of 1739. The stone entrance pillars still remain. Formerly the ancestral home of the Anderton family, it is now used as a private hospital and parts of the grounds have been used for residential housing and a nursing home. Belonging to the Anderton family, it was reduced from two to one storey in 1929. There are two stone lodges and a chapel, built in 1866 by E.W. Pugin.

FARINGTON [South Ribble]

SD5425: 2 miles (3km) SE of Preston

Farington is mainly industrial, particularly known for the **Leyland Daf** factory. Formerly known as Leyland Motors, it developed from a small blacksmith's shop in Leyland. **Farington Moss,** to the south, is, by contrast, in a rural setting amidst farmland.

The **church of St Paul** is in the centre of the village. Built in 1840, the chancel was added in 1910.

FENCE-IN-PENDLE [Pendle]

SD8337: 2 miles (3km) W of Nelson

The name originates from the fenced enclosure, which was constructed to contain

hunting deer. The village is now mainly a residential area. Old Chattox, one of the Pendle witches, lived here. So did Sir Jonas Moore, a founder in the 17th century of the Royal Observatory at Greenwich.

The parish **church of St Anne**, just to the north of the A6068 on the western extremity of the village, was erected in 1837. Further west on the main road, the stone **Ashlar House** was the place to which the Pendle Witches were taken in 1612 after their arrest. Almost opposite is **Fence House**, a 15th-century building with distinctive chimneys. A major restoration of the 1547 **Hoarstones House** took place at the end of the 19th century. After a hoax, in which seventeen people were detained as suspected witches in the 17th century, they were brought here. They were all found guilty, but saved from execution after the hoaxer had been exposed. The house is at the end of a long drive, opposite Hoarstones Avenue. The long road through the village comes to the adjacent community of **Wheatley Lane**. The **Inghamite chapel** was built at Wheatley for the followers of Benjamin Ingham. The chapel was restored at the end of the 19th century.

FERNYHALGH [Preston]

SD5634: 1½ miles (2km) E of Broughton

The **church of St Mary**, at the northern end of Fernyhalgh Lane, is a Roman Catholic chapel built in 1790. The story is told of a merchant who wanted to do something to earn the protection of God during his travels across the world. He was led to a wood found further south along the lane, before the motorway crossing, where he discovered a statue of the Virgin Mary by a well. Here, in 1348, he built a chapel called Ladywell. This was used for worship until the opening of the present one in 1790. The well is found in the beautiful grounds of the white **Lady Well House**, built in 1685.

FENISCOWLES [Blackburn]

SD6525: 2 miles (3km) SW of Blackburn

Situated on a loop in the Leeds and Liverpool Canal, the village was ideally placed for the expansion of the textile industry. The area was owned from the early 19th century by the Feilden family of Witton Hall. A number of paper mills were opened in the middle of that century, some of which are still in operation.

On a rise by the river bridge on Pleasington Lane stands the **church of Emmanuel**, built in 1836. Its squat tower and spire give an attractive appearance to the small building, enhanced by the grassland that slopes down to the water. The cost was financed by the largesse of the Feildens.

The forlorn ruins of **Feniscowles New Hall**, below a wooded hill, can be easily missed by those speeding along the A674. By stopping at the river bridge west of the village, almost opposite Tintagell Close, the remains of the hall can be seen. It was erected in 1812 by William Feilden. The remnant of an entrance to it is by the bridge.

FLEETWOOD [Wyre]

SD3348: 8 miles (11km) N of Blackpool

Until the early 19th century, Fleetwood was no more than a small fishing village at the mouth of the River Wyre. It developed as a port and leisure resort because of the vision and efforts of Peter Hesketh-Fleetwood of Rossall Hall. He owned more land in the area than any

other landowner, and the coastline between Liverpool and Southport belonged to him. He saw the commercial opportunities in harnessing the railway to bring workers from the northern towns for holidays at the seaside. To this end, he hired the architect Decimus Burton. Burton's unusual Christian name came about because he was the tenth son in his family. He drew up the plans of a new town to be built on a grid system, radiating out from **The Mount**, on the Esplanade. Work began in 1836 to turn the empty land into a prosperous new area. The cost was enormous. At one stage, Hesketh-Fleetwood almost ran out of money. The rail link with Euston was completed in 1840 so that, in addition to stopping in Fleetwood, travellers could cross to Ireland and Scotland. The **North Euston Hotel**, built on the Esplanade in 1841, is evidence of this link. Although not all Hesketh-Fleetwood's schemes came to fruition, enough was achieved to be of lasting value. When a more direct rail link to Glasgow, via Shap Fell, was opened in 1846, the number of passengers passing through the town slumped. From then on, effort was put into developing the port for cargo and fishing.

In addition to the central point of The Mount in the highest part of the town, two lighthouses were built as aids to navigation along the Wyre estuary. In the early days, they were lit by gaslights. The taller of the two, the **Pharos**, is a replica of the one at Alexandria, which was once one of the seven wonders of the world. Most of Burton's buildings, such as **Queen's Terrace** by the ferries, were built in the classical style. In 1841, he also erected the **church of St Peter** in Church Street, the tower of which was demolished in 1902. The first tram came to the town in 1898, before the route was later linked to Blackpool. There is an exhibition of old photos in the Clock Room of the **Mount Pavilion**, which was built in 1902.

The **Heritage Museum** is housed in the 1838 Customs House, which was later used as the Town Hall. Exhibits and models help to trace the development of the town. Situated on Queen's Terrace, it demonstrates how steam-powered trawlers made the town an important fishing port. Then how the 'Cod Wars' of the 1970s led to consequent decline. Another section records the development of the town as a seaside resort in the rail era.

Only the Georgian gazebo is left of the home of the Fleetwood-Heskeths, in what is now **Rossall School**, immediately south of the town. William Allen, a Roman Catholic priest, lived here. In 1568, during the time of Catholic persecution, he founded Douai College. Jesuit priests were smuggled across from the college, sometimes hiding at Rossall *en route*. It became a school for clergy and gentry in 1884, before becoming an independent school. The headmaster's house contains some panelling, an 18th-century fireplace and 17th-century staircase balustrading from the original house. At **Rossall Point** on the coast many species of birds can be seen such as plover, eider, knot and turnstone.

FORTON [Wyre]

SD4951: 5½ miles (9km) S of Lancaster

The village lies to the west of the A6 and the M6, where a service station bears its name. Called 'Fortune' in the Domesday Book, Forton was originally described a 'fenced in place'. Up to the dissolution of the monasteries, the land was owned by Cockersand Abbey. Farming is the prime activity today. In School Lane, there is one of the earliest independent chapels. It

was built in 1707. The large, stone building stands in a spacious graveyard. The **church of St James**, Shireshead is on the narrow Whinney Brow Lane, the opposite side of the A6 from the main village. Built in 1889, it has a black and white entrance porch.

Covering 46 acres (187 hectares) to the south-east, **Cleveymere Nature Reserve** was formed from old gravel pits on the River Wyre and consists of marsh land and pools.

Close to the Lancaster Canal, half a mile (1km) west of the village, **Clifton Hill** was the home of Robert Gillow, the brother of Richard, the furniture manufacturer. Built in 1820 in neo-classical style, a chapel was added in 1878.

FOULRIDGE [Pendle]

SD8942: 1½ miles (2km) N of Colne

Prounounced 'foalridge', the village had a hat-making industry in the 17th and 18th centuries. This gave way to the manufacture of textiles. Old weavers' cottages surround the village green at **Town Gate**, at the corner of which is the Hole-in-the-Corner pub. Older buildings can be seen at Stoneygate, near the green. Now it is once again a farming community.

The **church of St Michael and All Angels**, pleasantly situated by Lake Burwain on the Colne Road, was opened in 1905. An imposing war memorial stands at the front of the church.

The **canal wharf and tunnel** is at the end of Warehouse Lane, off Town Gate. In 1796, after five years of excavating, a tunnel 1650yds (1500m) in length was opened to take the Leeds and Liverpool Canal through the hillside. Between 1880 and 1937, a steam boat tugged barges through because there was no towpath. In the years on both sides of these dates, the only means of taking a boat through the tunnel was by 'legging it'. This meant the crew lying on their backs and pushing their feet along the roof of the tunnel. Traffic lights guard the entrance to the tunnel. There is a story told of a cow which fell into the canal and swam the complete length of the tunnel. This event is recorded in a picture which hangs in the Hole-in-the-Corner pub. The wharf, 650ft (200m) away, was completed in 1815. The wharfmaster's offices and the stables for the bargehorses have been renovated and converted into refreshment rooms.

The 16th-century **Hobhouse** is reputed to be haunted by ghosts. The long, grey-stone house, with ruined outbuildings, overlooks the lake from the other side of the village. At the time of the Civil War, Colonel Parker, a Royalist supporter, lived at the house. A bloody skirmish took place when a troop of Cromwell's soldiers appeared. Down the years, a ghostly group of Royalists has been sighted on a number of occasions. Most frightening of all, one night in the 1950s, a farmer was in the toilet. To his alarm, the door was suddenly broken down to reveal a man dressed in monk's robes. As the farmer realised that the man's arm was cut off, with blood pouring from it, the figure disappeared into thin air. Since then, unexplained happenings in the house have included windows shattering and stones being thrown down the stairs. Eventually the local vicar was called in to successfully exorcise the spirits.

FRECKLETON [Fylde]

SD4329: 7 miles (11km) W of Preston

An air disaster during the Second World War has etched the name of Freckleton in many memories. Standing near the point where the Rivers Ribble, Dow and Douglas converge, the village is listed as 'Frecheltun' in the Domesday Book, which translates as 'an enclosed area'. It is the largest village in the Fylde. Access to the rivers meant that in Roman times it was the port for Kirkham. Later it became a thriving port in its own right, with slate and grain being imported. A shipyard was opened in 1814 and was big enough to manufacture an ocean-going vessel 60 years later.

The air disaster has made the **church of Holy Trinity**, built in Norman style in 1837 and situated on the main road through the village, a very special place for many people. One day in 1944, an American Liberator bomber took off from nearby Warton airfield. Caught up in a thunderstorm, it crashed onto the school, next to the church. An impressive memorial to the two teachers, 38 children and seven civilians killed stands at the rear of the churchyard. The cabinet in which the book of remembrance rests inside the church is made from beams of the old school. The finely carved, tall, 1633 pulpit came from the church at Kirkham. Because of its shape, it is lovely to look at, but difficult to preach from.

Tales of smuggling at the **Ship Inn** can well be believed. The long, brick building, erected in 1777, looks out over the marshes towards the estuary of the River Ribble, and has had a licence continuously since 1677. An inn has been on the site since the 14th century. It is situated in Bunker Street, a reminder of the coal ships from Wigan that used to dock here.

The toll-house used to be at **Halfpenny Bridge**, on the Preston side of the village. The bridge is easy to miss on the busy main road, although fortu-

Air disaster memorial, Freckleton

nately it is named. The line of the old turnpike road can still be picked out.

A turn down Lower Lane, off the main road beyond the bridge, gives access to the secluded **Quakers' Graveyard**. In the 17th century there was a strong, local Quaker community. There is record of a Quaker meeting in 1689 and the graveyard at Quakers Wood has burials from 1725.

Freckleton Marsh is an area of saltmarshes which attracts lapwing and plover in the winter. Peregrine falcon and sparrowhawk also frequent the area. In summer it might be possible to catch a glimpse of the rare yellow wagtail.

GALGATE [Lancaster and Morecambe]

SD4855: 3½ miles (6km) S of Lancaster

It used to be a case of drunkards beware in this village. Legend has it that the village mayor was elected on the basis of being the first man to be found drunk and incapable after the annual fair.

The village of Galgate is part of the larger, rural parish of Ellel. Situated by the Lancaster Canal and its marina, it was a silk spinning centre from the end of the 18th century. **Chapel Lane**, on the east side of the A6, contains a terrace of mill cottages. Two water-driven stone mills, off the north end of Chapel Lane, date from 1792 and 1830. A third mill opposite was built with brick in 1852. It was originally water-powered too, but later its steam engine powered all three mills. Further along the same road and next to Ellel House retirement home, is the stone, towered **church of St John the Evangelist**, erected in 1907. Although in sight of Lancaster University and the M6, the church is surrounded by fields. Unusually, there is no graveyard, only a war memorial at the front of the church.

Ellel village is a tiny cluster of houses beyond the church. Now a Christian healing ministry centre, **Ellel Grange**, set in extensive gounds, is a large house, standing on top of a rise in the ground, with two towers. It was built in Italianate style in 1859. The long approach road from the A6, immediately south of the M6 junction, passes through the grounds and over the Lancaster Canal. As the road passes the left turn to Crag Hall and continues into the grange grounds, the **church of St Mary**, which has a rounded aspe and a detached rocket-shaped tower, is on the left. It is now derelict.

GARSTANG [Wyre]

SD4945: 10½ miles (17km) S of Lancaster

The town of Garstang stands at the crossing point of the River Wyre and the Leeds and Liverpool Canal, where a one-arched aqueduct takes the latter across the former. A market charter was granted in 1310, but the market eventually faded away and was not restarted until the late 16th century. The coming of the canal in 1792, and its position on the great road to the north made the town a busy commercial centre. The second half of the 20th century has led to considerable residential growth because of close proximity to Preston and other towns.

In the High Street, by the Kings Arms, is the cobbled **Market Square**. This was the site of the original market. At its centre is a market cross, with a pedestal surmounted by a stone ball. This dates from 1752, replacing the original one. Restoration took place in 1896.

A fire in the middle of the 18th century did enormous damage to the **Town Hall**, which had been built 70 years earlier. Near the market cross, its clock tower and other additions added considerably to the dignity of the building.

There was great surprise at the **parish church of St Thomas** in 1997, when a painting which had hung on a wall for 30 years was valued at £5 million, although later estimations were much lower. The piece, *Ecce Homo* by Annebella Carracci, had been thought to be a copy. The growth of the population of the town in the 18th century increased the need for a parish church to be built. Until then worshippers had to travel to the mother church of St Helen in Churchtown. Consequently, the church was erected on Church Street in 1770, although there had been a chapel since the 16th century. The chancel was added in 1876.

The **Discovery Centre**, by the central car park, explores the countryside, history and heritage of Garstang and the surrounding area. Amongst the displays are exhibitions about the history and environment of the Lancaster Canal and the Forest of Bowland.

Now used for other purposes, the **Grammar School**, on Lancaster Road, was built in 1756 and survived until closure in 1928.

John Rennie engineered the **canal aqueduct** over the river, to the south of Church Street, in 1792. A walk east along the river bank arrives at an 18th-century corn mill, now used residentially.

Greenhalgh Castle, between the hamlets of Bonds and Bowgreave and the M6, has meagre ruins remaining on a mound by the River Wyre. At the battle of Bosworth, the first Earl of Derby had put the crown on the head of Henry VII. The erection of the castle in 1490 was a gift from the king. The castle remained intact until it was one of the last Royalist strongholds to surrender to Cromwell's troops in 1649. It was consequently almost completely demolished. Only part of the tower can still be seen. Castle Lane, to the left from the river bridge on the B6430 out of Garstang, leads to the ruins. It is advisable to walk because of the difficulty of car access. Nearby **Castle Farm** is 17th century. A story tells that during the siege of the castle, a soldier met his wife, who had separated from him some years before, at Gubberford Bridge. Her lover then appeared and stabbed him. Her ghost is reputed to haunt the bridge.

The stone-built **Old Toll House**, at the junction of the A6 and the old Garstang road at the north end of the town, still has the original posts at the roadside. It dates from the 1820s, when the Garstang to Lancaster turnpike was realigned. On the A6, on either side of the town, ancient milestones have survived. The ones to the north are 19th century, with triangular Roman lettering, and the ones to the south, with cursive lettering, are 18th century.

The **church of All Saints, Barnacre** is 1½ miles (2km) east of the town. The small, stone building is in an isolated position on the roadside, by a stream running through the vale. Built in 1912, it has the air of a miniature cathedral, with an impressive tower and narrow aisle. The Rushton Chapel was added in 1937.

GISBURN [Ribble Valley]

SD8248: 6½ miles (10km) NE of Clitheroe

Cobbles can still be found in the main street of white-fronted cottages, in this community divided by the busy A59. The borders of the parish encompass many scattered communities, including Rimington, Paythorne, Newsholme, Nappa, Swinden, Horton, and Middop. The village appears in the Domesday Book, and in 1260 a fair charter was granted to the monks of Sawley Abbey. The name of the village was spelled 'Gisburne' until the railway came in 1885. The railway com-

pany decided that the extra letter only added work every time it was written down.

A musical tombstone is located in the graveyard of the **church of St Mary**. By following the blue signposts, the grave of the hymn tune composer, Frances Duckworth, will be located. On the headstone are inscribed the opening bars of her composition 'Rimington', named after her birthplace in the parish. Another unusual headstone is that of Jenny Preston, near the east gate. A witch stirring her cauldron is carved on it. She was executed for casting a spell on someone who afterwards died. The church tower is partly Norman and partly 14th century. The main doorway is 13th century, and in the nave are two huge Norman pillars. The four panels (hatchments) on the walls of the nave and chancel bear the coats of arms of the Earls of Ribblesdale. Their memorial chapel is on the south side of the chancel. On the wall is a piscina, used for the washing of communion utensils, in addition to a holy water stoup. An unwelcome visitor to the church in 1648 was Oliver Cromwell. He put his troops and horses in the church for a night's rest after the Battle of Preston in 1648.

Over the doorway of the **Ribblesdale Arms Inn** is written the information that the house was purchased by Thomas Lister in 1635 for £855. From the two lodge entrances just off the main road, opposite the Nelson turning, a road runs through spacious parkland to the mansion of **Gisburn Park**. Now a hospital, it was the home of the Ribblesdale family. It was also the supposed residence of Guy de Gisburn, who was thought to be the person from whom the legend of Robin Hood arose.

A collection of steam vehicles is found at the **Gisburn Steam Museum** at Todber Caravan Park. The Old Tithebarn, built in 1710, is now a restaurant and has a display of old farm and kitchen utensils.

On the annual 'Salmon Sunday', **Paythorne Bridge**, on the Paythorne road, is a point from which to view the fish swimming upstream.

GLASSON [Lancaster and Morecambe]

SD4456: 4½ miles (7km) SW of Lancaster

The village of Glasson, on the Lune estuary, came into being when a bigger dock was needed because the increasingly large vessels were unable to get up the River Lune to Lancaster. Until then Sunderland Point had served as the port. In 1787 the new dock was completed, after permission had been given by two Acts of Parliament in 1738 and 1749. A boatyard and a graving dock were built by Jesse Hartley, the engineer also responsible for the building of the Albert Dock in Liverpool. The impetus for all this work came from the local lords of the manor, the Daltons of Thurnham Hall. In 1826 the Lancaster Canal was cut through to the village, with a lock to gain access to the basin. Then, in 1887, a dock railway was built from Lancaster, with a station at Conder Green. Although decline had started to set in 30 years before, the line did not close until 1964. The line of the track is now part of the pathway to Lancaster.

Neither canal nor railway was able to stop decline of the port, although the shipyard did not finally close until 1969. The village is still a busy industrial site, with the marina at the dock basin adding extra life, especially during the summer. 18th- and 19th-century cottages plus three pubs are a reminder of past glories. A tiny lighthouse looks out to sea north of the basin. The cottage in which the keeper lived by the lock was built in 1825. The 19th-century **church of Christ Church** is squeezed between the canal and the B5290, to the east of the village.

GOODSHAW [Rossendale]

SD8025: 2 miles (3km) N of Rawtenstall

The main attraction of this small community, which lies in the Rossendale Valley, is the ancient **Goodshaw Chapel**. Situated near the towerless **church of St Mary and All Saints**, it stands on the edge of moorland, looking out across the valley. Erected in 1760, English Heritage have carried out a restoration on the building, retaining the galleries and box pews and a chair which was used by George Fox. Reaching its present size in 1809, it fell into disuse when a new chapel was built on the main road in the 1860s. It was the headquarters of a group of singers from the valley known as 'The Larks of Dean'. They composed hymns and music to sing in the chapel. The Rossendale Museum has a number of the original scores. North of the village is a house once owned by the Towneley family. Further up the narrow lane from the chapel, **Swinshaw Hall** is reputed to be the place where the last wild boar in the country met its end – one among many!

GOOSNARGH [Preston]

SD5536: 5 miles (8km) NE of Preston

Goosnargh cakes can be found on sale in the village, which derives its name from 'the field of the goose'. At the centre of the village are the church, school and two inns, the Grapes and Bushells Arms.

The circular stone incorporated in the

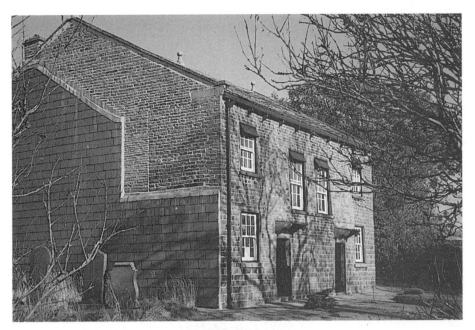

Goodshaw chapel

tower of the parish church, at the north end of the village, was placed as an witch repellent. A chapel of ease since the 11th century, the **church of St Mary the Virgin** became a parish in its own right in 1846. Legend has it that the church was meant to have been built on another site, but fairies kept moving the building material to where it is now. The **Middleton Chapel** was built in 1508 and is now the Lady Chapel. The surrounding oak screen has carved initials of the Rigby family, one being that of the Colonel Rigby who led the Parliamentary forces in the seige of Lathom House. The chancel is 16th century. In the main body of the church is a 15th-century font and an 18th-century chandelier. The building underwent extensive renovation in the mid 19th century. In the churchyard there is a sundial to the left of the porch, and the base of an old cross on the Bushell House side.

Bushell House, next to the church, is mainly 18th century, with a wing added

in 1845. It was built as a hospital for elderly Protestants.

One of the most haunted buildings in the country is **Chingle Hall**, to the west of the village, off the B5269. Adam de Singleton built the first house in 1260. In the 16th century the hall was the home of the Wall family, descendants of the Singleton family. Its most famous member was Father John Wall, who was born at the hall. He met his end when he was hanged for heresy and sedition at Worcester in 1679. He was buried at St Oswald's Church in that city and his head taken to France. Legend has it that his head was brought back to the hall and buried. It is said that if it is ever found, the hauntings will cease. He was canonised in 1970. There are a number of secret rooms, which were used by priests in the 16th century to hold masses in secret, and an oaken 'Praying cross' from before the Reformation. It was only fitting that one step in the reconciliation of the Roman Catholic and Anglican churches

Bushell House, Goosnargh

was the meeting between Cardinal Heenan and the Bishop of Lancaster at the hall in 1962. The moated building dates from 1260 and is in the shape of a cross. It is possibly one of the oldest brick-built domestic buildings in the country. There are numerous stories of hauntings and strange happenings. Noises are heard, objects move without aid and many owners have seen apparitions of people in the dress of centuries ago. It is claimed that there are sixteen ghosts in residence. The most haunted room is the bedroom of Eleanor, the last of the Singletons, who is thought to have been murdered at the hall. Immediately south of the hall is the site of the former Whittingham Hospital, which had at its busiest, 3000 patients and its own railway.

The Rigby family lived at stone **Middleton Hall**, half a mile (1km) north of the village. Its main entrance is on the Inglewhite Road. It was the 17th-century home of Sir Alex Rigby, a right-hand man to Oliver Cromwell.

GREAT ECCLESTON [Wyre]

SD4340: 5 miles (8km) E of Poulton-le-Fylde

Eglestun, as it is called in the Domesday Book, means 'the place of the church'. In the 19th century, rush weaving was important, and farming has always been vital. In the village centre of Great Eccleston, The Black Bull and White Bull Inns face each other across the square.

From the square, the narrow Copp Lane first passes **Leckonby Hall**. In fact, only the stables remain of the original house, which was burned down in 1766. Apparently the owner had got into debt and his creditors were not too pleased. Behind the house is a dovecote from the 17th century Shortly, the **church of St Anne** comes into view. Originating in 1723, and enlarged in the 19th century, it is the parish church of the district. By it is the church school, and opposite is the 18th-century **School Cottage**.

GREAT HARWOOD [Hyndburn]

SD7432: 3 miles (5km) NW of Accrington

'Crying the Fair' was a custom which, every year from 1338 until 1933, announced the annual town fair in Great Harwood. Since then it has been declared open at 9.00am on 21 August, even though it no longer takes place. In the 11th century, the community was called Harwode Magna. Situated by the River Calder and Hyndburn Brook, at the height of its textile prosperity there were twenty-two mills at work in the town. The rows of terraced houses were originally occupied by the workforce at the mills. Much of the cloth produced was exported to India.

The heart of the town is Town Hall Square. In front of the 19th-century town hall stands the **Mercer Memorial Clock.** The clock and **Mercer Hall,** built in 1921, commemorate John Mercer, a local chemist who, in 1850, invented the process of giving a sheen to cotton. The 17th-century school, founded by Roger Nowell of Read Hall, was demolished for road widening, but the lintel has been built into the wall at the bottom of Delph Road.

At the top of the hill, on the corner of Park Lane and Church Lane, the **church of St Bartholomew.** has a 15th-century battlemented tower and 17th-century nave roof. The font is dated 1663, and there is a holy water stoup in the porch. In 1886 the chancel was restored. The Roman Catholic **church of St Hubert,** to the east, is noted for the quality of the 19th-century windows.

The manor house over the centuries has been **Martholme.** The house, near the River Calder, goes back to pre-Reformation days. Thomas Hesketh built the great hall and the gatehouse in 1577. The Fittons and Heskeths were succes-

sively lords of the manor, the gatehouse being used to hold courts and receive tithes from the locals. The wheat sheaf crest of the Fittons can be seen on the gatehouse, with the eagle of the Heskeths on the main house. After passing through a number of hands from the time the Hesketh family moved to Rufford in the 17th century, the house was left empty and deteriorated. Restoration took place in 1969. The house is just under the rail viaduct on Martholme Lane, off the Whalley Road, north of the village.

There is a story behind the building of the ten-arch **viaduct** over the River Calder in 1877. The owners of the land discovered a rich seam of coal. They refused to allow a stone viaduct to be built unless the railway company bought the coal. Just as a wooden one was about to go up, the railway company decided to buy all the coal and the stone structure was erected after all.

GREEN HAWORTH [Hyndburn]

SD7626: 1½ miles (3km) SW of Accrington

The moorland village of Green Haworth was originally called 'Beadlach', the 'lach' meaning 'a bog'. In the 12th century it was owned by Kirkstall Abbey, and by the 17th century its quarries were providing stone for many of the buildings around. A section of the village to the north is called Bedlam. It has good examples of 18th-century cottages.

GRESSINGHAM [Lancaster and Morecambe]

SD5770: 5 miles (8km) W of Carnforth

The stone cottages of the small hill village are dominated by the church and hall. On the road from Hornby is the three-arched, medieval **Loyn Bridge**.

Most of the **church of St John the Evangelist** was altered and restored in 1714 and 1832. However, there is a southern Norman doorway, 16th-century arcade and 1714 pulpit. Two pieces of a Saxon cross are lying at the front of the Marton family tomb. The Martons built Capernwray Hall, living there until after the Second World War. There are a number of box pews and a small, disused organ over the north doorway. The chancel contains an unusual, modern wool-hanging, whilst the pew kneelers were made in the village and dyed with local flowers. One façade of the L-shaped **Gressingham Hall**, next to the church, is 18th century. Inside there is a Jacobean staircase of three flights.

GRIMSARGH [Preston]

SD5934: 4 miles (6.5km) NE of Preston

At the centre of the village is a large green, next to **Grimsargh House**. In the 19th century, the village expanded as the weaving industry grew. The **church of St Michael**, on the main road at the southern end of the village, was built in 1869, re-placing a previous one. On the east side are gargoyles of men's heads; while on the north they are of animals.

GRINDLETON [Ribble Valley]

SD7545: 2½ miles (4km) NE of Clitheroe

Part of the village of Grindleton is clus-tered at the bottom of the hill. The re-mainder lines the road, high above the River Ribble. The population now is only half of what it was in the early 19th cen-tury, when the weaving and spinning industry was thriving.

By the school, on the Sawley road, a little away from the main village, is the small **church of St Ambrose**. Its minia-ture tower gives it a quaint and appealing look.

HALSALL [West Lancashire]

SD3710: 3 miles (4km) NW of Ormskirk

Standing on an outcrop of sandstone in a rich farming area, the village was centu-ries ago surrounded by three meres. The village name of Heleshal in the Domes-day Book indicates a settlement near a bog. During the 19th century, the meres were reclaimed, with the result that the soil is grade one for agriculture. The Leeds and Liverpool Canal cuts through the parish, which includes the hamlets of Shirdley Hill, Primrose Hill, Bangors Green, Barton and Downholland. The first cutting of the canal took place on the Halsall section. An unusual feature of the district is the bituminous turf, which was used instead of candles to provide light.

The tower of the **church of St Cuth-bert**, at the crossroads in the centre of the village, was built in 1762. The spire, with its square base and octagonal sides, was reordered in 1852. The spires of St Mi-chael, Aughton and St Peter and St Paul, Ormskirk are similar. The nave, the chancel and the pedestal of the font are all 14th century. Leading off the chancel, a 14th-century oak door, complete with handle, lock and key, is one of the few examples of its kind. In the choir stalls are misericords from 1533, one of which, the extreme left on the south side, depicts two wrestlers. A brass on the same side tells of a wreath sent by Queen Victoria when one of her maids died. Also in the chancel is an Easter Sepulchre containing the effigy of a 16th-century rector and the tomb of the 16th-century Sir Henry Halsall. The modern St Nicholas window in the south chancel contains fragments from its medieval predecessor. Near it is a memorial to Wilfred Blundell, who was killed during the Boer War. He gave a drink to one of the enemy and was killed by the man in return for his kindness. Attached to the church is the 1593 Grammar School. Outside, on the south-east buttress, is a carving of a man seated at prayer in a boat. In the grounds, reached by a path through the woodland at the rear of the churchyard, are the remains of a priest's 14th-century house. There is a wall 55ft (17m) long, with three doorways and three windows.

The 1750 structure of **Halsall Hall**, opposite the school, replaced the manor house of the Halsall family, who were lords of the manor. The original hall was destroyed by fire in 1700. The present brick house, with mullioned windows, stands on sandstone plinths. During renovations in 1997, a late 17th-century coin was unearthed. It was the home of the rectors of the village until 1906, when a new rectory was built. This latter is now a private residence.

century castle. It may have been erected by Tostig, the lord of the manor, as a defence against Norman invaders. The British Museum has on display a necklace and hoard of coins discovered near the village at the end of the 18th century. The mills of the 19th-century textile industry have now disappeared.

The main body of the **church of St Wilfrid** was completely rebuilt in 1877. Only the 1597 battlemented tower is left from previous buildings. Over the porch is a half-timbered room, while in the southern part of the churchyard, near the road, is an 11th-century cross. It is significant for the fact that one side has Christian motives, whilst the other has pagan themes from the story of Sigurd. At the top are various symbols connected with the Evangelists. A Roman altar was discovered near the church in 1794.

A shadow of its former self, only the battlemented, 18th-century stable block and a 19th-century wing of **Halton Hall** remain, opposite the church. Most of it was demolished in the early 20th century. **Tower House** is a battlemented building from 1760, with two towers and a façade of three bays, while **Halton Hall Park** is an L-shaped, 17th-century building with mid-19th-century extensions.

HALTON [Lancaster and Morecambe]

SD5064: 2½ miles (4km) NE of Lancaster

This widespread village on the River Lune has seen much development over the past fifty years, although it still retains a number of 17th- and 18th-century houses. Many of the inhabitants commute into Lancaster.

Castle Hill, immediately east of the church, with a flagpole on the summit, is the site of both Saxon and Roman fortifications, plus the earthworks of an 11th-

HAMBLETON [Wyre]

SD3743: 2½ miles (4km) NE of Poulton-le-Fylde

On the banks of the River Wyre estuary, north of Shard Bridge, the commuter village is surrounded by farmland. Until the 18th century salt was an additional commodity produced in the area.

A miniature wooden windmill by the road through the village indicates that the wind blows sharply across the flats. **Wardleys Creek** can have changed little over the centuries. Its little creeks and inlets give the necessary atmosphere for its stories of smuggling history. The large **Wardleys Inn**, dating from the 16th century, stands in lonesome grandeur, overlooking the boats moored below. The creek is reached by turning down Kiln Lane, by the Shovels Inn.

A modern, detached, four-sided spire, replacing the original tower, makes the **church of St Mary the Virgin** conspicuous. The rest of the present building dates from the 19th century, but historical references are not lacking. On the south wall is a copy of Henry III's granting of the manor to Geoffrey the Crossbow and also Queen Elizabeth I's confirmation of this to Sir Richard Shirbourne. Both the marble pulpit and font are attractive, along with some colourful, modern windows.

HAPTON [Burnley]

SD7932: 3 miles (5km) W of Burnley

Electricity came to the village of Hapton in 1886, making it the first to use this form of power in the country. The M65 (1983), the railway (1848) and the Leeds and Liverpool Canal (1816) run through this mainly industrialized village. Coal and stone quarrying were the main occupations.

There are ghostly tales at the **Bridge Inn**. A girl who committed suicide in the canal is said to haunt the pub.

One of the few remaining signs of the town's history is at Castle Clough gorge, which was brought into being by glacial action. The rock formation is impressive. There is little left to be seen of **Hapton Castle**, which in 1242 was a fortified manor house. From the 14th century it belonged to the de-la-Legh family, and later, through marriage, to the Towneleys. A footpath from the picnic site on

Mill Hill Lane runs through trees along the edge of the gorge. Just before reaching the railway line, it is possible to discern the remains of the castle walls on the east side of the gorge. As the stream reaches the railway, the remains of an old reservoir which fed the dyeworks is discernible.

Sir John Towneley built **Hapton Tower** on Habeldon Hill, in the middle of his large hunting park, in the 16th century. This was demolished 200 years later, but some water spouts from the tower were used at Dyneley Hall, one of the homes of the Towneley family.

The **church of St Margaret**, on the Manchester Road through the village, is a small, towerless structure with a bellcot for one bell. It was built in 1927. Over the motorway and canal bridge north of the village, **Shuttleworth Hall** is a large, two-winged house, built in the 17th century as a yeoman farmer's house.

HASLINGDEN [Rossendale]

SD7824: 2 miles (3km) W of Rawtenstall

Haslingden is a typical mill town on the edge of Calf Hey and Ogden reservoirs and the open moorland of Haslingden Grane. Charles II granted a market charter to the town in 1676. The old town, called 'Top of the Town', was at the top of the hill, and the centre of the woollen trade. The coming of the Industrial Revolution in the 18th century led to the building of mills, such as **Hargreaves Street Mill**. This was built in 1861 and still stands, near the **King Street Methodist chapel** at which John Wesley once preached. The Grane was a centre of the farming and the weaving industry, as well as an illegal trade in whisky. Quarrying and brick-making were also of importance. After the opening of Ogden

Reservoir in 1912, the population declined rapidly.

The tower of the **church of St James**, at the north end of the town, incorporates a stone at the bottom, believed to be part of a Saxon cross. If this is a correct assumption, then there may have been a church on the site for thousands of years. The present building dates from the late 18th century, except for the tower which was erected in 1827. The interior contains an early 16th-century font, a medieval chest and the stocks.

The **Public Hall**, off Church Street, was erected in 1868. Apparently, when coming to visit the hall, Winston Churchill got lost in the vicinity. Immediately to the south, **Deardengate** was the street in which the market used to be held. To the west are good examples of weavers' cottages, including some loom shops with the workshops on the top floors.

To be drowned by water was the fate of the **church of St Stephen**, Haslingden Grane. The original church of 1868 was demolished to make way for Ogden Reservoir. It was eventually rebuilt further away in 1926.

Anyone interested in motorcycles will make for the **Motorcycle Museum** at Winfields, Hazel Hill, Blackburn Road. The display includes exhibits from the past 70 years.

HEATH CHARNOCK [Chorley]

SD5915: Half a mile (1km) S of Chorley

Heath Charnock is a small hamlet on the outskirts of Chorley. Built in 1724, **Hall o'the Hill** is now the Chorley Golf Club clubhouse. Standing at the top of the hill, it is three storeys high and built with stone from the demolished Duxbury Hall. The

entrance is on the A673, immediately north of Adlington.

HELMSHORE [Rossendale]

SD7821: 1 mile (2km) S of Haslingden

Set in the West Pennine Musbury valley, Helmshore, a small town of stone cottages and mills, grew through textile manufacturing on the banks of the Irwell. The 19th-century **church of St Thomas**, Musbury looks down on the town from a high vantage point.

A collection of early textile machinery is based in two stone buildings, Higher Mill and Whitaker's Mill, at the **Helmshore Textile Museum**, alongside the main street. Both are listed monuments. The machinery is mainly seen in its working day surroundings. Higher Mill was built in 1789 to complete the cloth by the fulling process. It is powered by an 18ft (5m) waterwheel. The top floor of the mill houses a collection of machinery, including an improved Hargreaves Spinning Jenny and an Arkwright Water Frame. Next door is Whitaker's Mill, in which there is a display describing the Industrial Revolution, and the 714-spindle Taylor Lang mules from 1903, which are 82ft (25m) in length. They demonstrate, moving up and down on their tracks, how yarn was spun at the rate of three miles a minute. Guides who once worked in the factory describe this scene, which was once so common in the mill towns of Lancashire. The lower floor contains an exhibition of the history of the textile industry.

South of the village, **Stake Lane** was part of the old Pilgrim's Way. Beyond it, on the moors, is **Ellen Strange Cairn**, a memorial to a woman murdered there in 1735.

HESKETH WITH BECCONSALL [West Lancashire]

SD4423: 6 miles (9km) W of Leyland

The widespread area covered by the parish of Hesketh with Becconsall is bounded on the north by the River Ribble and on the east by the River Douglas. The word 'hesketh' was Scandinavian for a race course. The main industries in the middle ages were agriculture, salt production and, in later centuries, brickmaking. Over the centuries, land has been reclaimed from the marshes by means of the building of earth banks to hold back the tides, which caused much flooding. Until the first was built in 1860, the sea used to come right up to the village. Twenty years later another one was built half a mile (1km) further out. The flat, fertile soil maintains market gardening and farming.

The **church of All Saints**, on the main road to the north end of the village, was built in 1925 to replace the old brick church of 1764, which stands near the boatyard on the River Douglas. This latter is a listed building, but now in a bad state of repair. In its graveyard are some headstones which bear the marks left by a bomb dropped during the Second World War.

In 1967, the conservation society of the West Lancashire Light Railway reopened a short stretch of line which used to run to the docks. The *Irish Mail* steam engine, built in 1903, runs on a two-feet (61cm) gauge. It operates steam engines on occasional weekends, from its depot on the main road through the village, south of the church.

Dating from 1667, **Becconsall Hall** has been the family home of the Becconsalls, Molyneuxs and Heskeths. It is at the end of a lane going east from the village road, just south of the church.

HEYSHAM [Lancaster and Morecambe]

SD4160: 2 miles (3km) NW of Morcambe

A mixture of a modern power station and ancient churches provide the fascination of Heysham. There was a community present in Saxon times and at the time of the Domesday survey, when the settlement was called Hessam. For many centuries it was a fishing village, developing in the 19th century into an important port. Although this usage has declined, ferries still sail to the Isle of Man and Ireland. Heysham is now linked by building to Morecambe. Longlands Lane leads off the main road to an old street leading to the quay and fishermen's cottages.

Tradition has it that St Patrick was shipwrecked near where the **chapel of St Patrick** was built, on a little promontory by the shore. He was escaping from his slavery in Ireland in the fifth century. The little chapel, 22ft (7m) by 7ft (2m), stands on a rocky knoll, looking out to sea. The walls are 2½ft (1m) thick, and built of different sizes of stones. There is doubt about the St Patrick association because the site is not thought to be earlier than the seventh century. Alongside it are graves cut out of the rock, with a hole for a cross cut in each. The skeletons found in these were dated to no earlier than the 10th century. Excavations in 1993 discovered over 1200 artefacts on the land below the stone graves. These proved that people lived here 12,000 years ago. On the site there is also a raised barrow or burial mound from prehistoric times.

Similar in design to St Patrick's, the **church of St Peter**, on the headland below the chapel, was first recorded in 1080. The doorway in the west wall is from Saxon times. Since that time there have been many additions to the original

Ancient graves, Heysham

small church. The chancel was erected in the middle of the 14th century. The south aisle is 15th century and the north aisle was erected in 1864, when an Anglo-Saxon doorway was discovered during excavations. This was rebuilt in the churchyard. The arch in the chancel bears the marks of a rope, a reminder of the fisherman's trade carried out by the saint of the dedication. The oak screen below the chancel may have come from Cockersand Abbey. Although the cover is 19th century, the font is 15th century and bellcot are 17th century. In the south aisle, by the centre door, is a Viking hogback gravestone which has both Christian and pagan carvings on it. One of the best-preserved in the country, it was brought from the churchyard in 1961. By the path to the porch is a cross, part of which is Anglo-Saxon, bearing a carved figure, possibly of Lazarus. Further along the path is a stone coffin, which was found in the chancel. At the front of the church is the 17th-century **Greese Cottage**, which was the old rectory. Greese means 'gradus-steps', referring to the steps down to the road.

The battlemented structure of **Heysham Tower**, built in 1836, formerly stood in the middle of a holiday camp (Middleton Towers). It was originally Heysham Hall, the home of the Fleetwood-Hesketh family. **Heysham Old Hall**, on Heysham Road, was built in 1588 and renewed in 1888. It is now a public house.

Beyond **Heysham Harbour**, to the south, rise the towers of the **power stations**. Heysham 1 and 2 nuclear power produce enough electricity for all of Lancashire. At each station there are two advanced gas-cooled reactors. The visitor centre contains exhibitions and a replica nuclear reactor. A 25-acre (10 hectares) nature reserve is complete with bird hides.

HIGHAM [Pendle]

SD8137: 3 miles (5km) SW of Nelson

At least one 19th-century Higham villager had a smashing time. Thomas Clayton, a local benefactor, decided to pay for a new west window for the **church of St John the Evangelist**, at the east end of the single road that rises through the village. When he saw it, he disliked it so much that he smashed the glass with his cane and ordered another window. This was made by Charles Kemp, a noted local artist, whose signature of a sheaf of wheat is included in the window.

The church was built in 1846. Until then the village was part of Padiham parish. For many years Methodism was very strong. The chapel graveyard has 1400 graves in it, although the chapel no longer exists. Opposite this graveyard is the **Four Alls Inn**, built in 1792, which has the inscription on its sign, 'Parson. I pray for all. King. I govern all. Soldier. I fight for all. Worker. I pay for all.' Close to it is the old mill, now used for furniture manufacturing. Between the pub and the church is **Higham Hall**, next to its old barn. Although the building has been altered on the road side, the rest retains the original 16th-century structure, bearing the emblem of John of Gaunt, Duke of Lancaster. In medieval times it served as the court house. Chattox, one of the Pendle Witches executed at Lancaster, was accused of turning the beer sour at the inn. Jonas Moore, who helped to found the Greenwich Observatory, lived here. From 1920-40 the Higham Balloon Juice Company, which never actually existed, was at the height of its non-existence in the village. It was invented to be a spoof of company life, having board meetings, accounts and annual meetings.

HODDLESDEN [Blackburn]
SD7222: 2 miles (3km) E of Darwen

The Blacksnape Ridge divides this large village from Darwen. The traditional industries were coal mining, pipe-making and textiles. The 19th-century **church of St Paul** was demolished in the 1970s. Only the graveyard remains, on the north side of the village, opposite the reservoir. The church building is now attached to the school. At the **Ranken Arms**, a large millstone from the Lower Darwen paper mill is situated on the cobbled forecourt of the inn. The name of the village is inscribed on it. Opposite the inn, the small green has a war memorial.

HOGHTON [Chorley]
SD6125: 5 miles (8km) W of Blackburn

The name of the village is taken from the family who have dominated the area for over 1000 years. In fact, the de Hoghton baronetcy is the second oldest in the country. Hoghton means 'township at the bottom of the hill'. During the 17th century it was a hotbed of Catholicism. In the 18th century there were weaving communities in the village, and in the hamlets of Hoghton Bottoms and Riley Green. Farming and quarrying were other important local industries. The River Darwen and the Leeds and Liverpool Canal both wind their way through the parish.

Inn sign, Higham

The village has no centre as such, the Boar's Head Inn and village hall making up what focal point there is. The war memorial stands near the approach road to the tower.

Anyone considering the derivation of the word 'sirloin' can find the answer at **Hoghton Tower**, well-signposted from the main road. The approach along the narrow road is dramatic, with the fortified hilltop mansion looking down like some fairy castle. The de Hoghton family (motto *malgré le tort* – 'in spite of wrong') have been lords of the manor since the time of William the Conqueror.

At 560ft (170m), the house dominates the village from the top of the hill. It was built in 1565 by Thomas de Hoghton. In the late 19th century it was extensively restored when the family returned to it after an absence of over a century. It is mainly known for a visit of James I in 1617, when he supposedly knighted a loin of beef. Hence the name 'sirloin'. The event is commemorated by a pub in the village called The Sirloin. After expenditure on three days of royal entertainment, Sir Richard de Hoghton was apparently so much in debt that he was committed to prison.

Entering through the gatehouse, the first of the two courtyards is found. Up the steps is the terrace, with its 18th-century gates. Inside the house are the banqueting hall, where William Shakespeare once performed in a group of travelling players, the King's bedchamber and anteroom, the ballroom and staterooms. Research has shown that as a young man, Shakespeare may have lived at Hoghton Tower for a year. The tower also contains a Tudor well house with a horse-drawn pump and oaken windlass, underground passages with a Lancashire witches display, dungeons where local criminals were imprisoned and the wine cellar. There is also an exhibition of family historical documents. Outside are walled gardens and a rose garden.

Opposite the lych-gate of the **church of Holy Trinity** is a roadside resting place with the inscription 'Travellers Rest 1877'. The building stands on the edge of open fields, by the main road on the Blackburn side of the village. The adjacent farm adds to the rural charm. The church was erected in 1823 and restored in 1887, having been opened to take the place of the worship at the chapel of Hoghton Tower. In the south-west corner of the churchyard are graves of the de Hoghton family. A Mr Gatty, whose claim to fame was the invention of a khaki dye to put in military uniforms, is also buried here.

Information over the doorway of the **Methodist chapel**, immediately over the rail bridge in Chapel Lane, indicates that it was founded in 1794. This makes it one of the oldest in the north-west of England. The view from here up to the tower is impressive. In the same lane, reached by turning off the main road at the Boars Head pub, are some cottages called 'The Barracks', commemorating their use by Cromwellian troops in 1651.

A impressive, three-arched **railway viaduct**, built in 1826, crosses high above the River Darwen at 116ft (35m). This can be seen from the riverside footpath, which starts from the end of a narrow road south from Hoghton Bottoms.

Edmund Arrowsmith, a Roman Catholic priest, said his last mass at **Arrowsmith House** before being arrested. The white-stone house, with a footpath alongside, is opposite the butcher's on the road through **Gregson Lane**, the village to the west of Hoghton. An inscription over the doorway gives the details about Arrowsmith. The sideboard which he used for the mass now forms the altar at St Joseph's Roman Catholic Church in the village.

HOLCOMBE [Rossendale]

SD8729: 3 miles (5km) SE of Burnley

On a hill above Ramsbottom, the village of Holcombe is one of the few that was not changed by the mills of the revolution in the textile industries. All of the industrial growth took place in Ramsbottom by the River Irwell. The village was left as it was when weaving replaced farming as the major local pursuit. Holcombe Brook is now a residential community.

Down the lane from the Shoulder of Mutton pub, the **church of Emmanuel** is a large, 1853 building, and can be seen across the surrounding area. There are two dilapidated mills in the older hamlet of Pot Green. A car park south of the village is the starting point for the climb up to the **Peel Monument** on Holcombe Hill. Eleven hundred feet (335 m) above sea level, it was erected in 1852 as a memorial to Sir Robert Peel, born in Bury in 1788 and the Prime Minister from 1841 to 1846. The tall building has a mill-like architecture, and 'Peel' is in large letters on the front. In the base is an extract from Peel's resignation speech of 1846. A footpath leads $1\frac{1}{2}$ miles (2km) north of the tower to the **Pilgrims' Cross**, which is on the ancient route to Whalley Abbey.

HOLLINS LANE [Wyre]

SD5051: 7 miles (11km) S of Lancaster

In the 18th century, this was a busy village. Now the area is rural, lying between river, railway and motorway.

The **church of St Paul**, Shireshead, east of the village, took the place, in 1805, of a previous church, which, in the 11th century, had been under the jurisdiction of the monks of Cockersand Abbey. It has windows with iron tracery and two bell towers.

HOLME CHAPEL [Burnley]

SD8828: 3 miles (5km) SE of Burnley

The village, with its surrounding hamlets of Walk Mill, Mereclough and Overtown, is situated in the Cliviger Gorge, between Deerplay and Worsthorne Moors. The name derived from an 18th-century chapel. The village sheep fair was one of the oldest in the country. Village stocks are found near the war memorial at the front of the church. Farming, weaving and quarrying were the traditional occupations, while at Walk Mill there were two coal pits. From the road there are superb views towards the heights of Thieveley Scout.

By the main door of the church of St John the Divine is the grave of General Sir James Scarlett, who led the Heavy Brigade into battle at Balaclava in 1854. It fared somewhat more successfully than the infamous Light Brigade. Lady O'Hagan, the last owner of Towneley Hall, also rests in the graveyard. The Whitaker family had the church built in 1794 as a replacement for a 16th-century chapel. It is notable for its attractive cupola.

A field separates the church from **The Holme**, which stands in a little, sheltered hollow. Erected in 1603, the stone, two-storey building is on the site of a previous house. It was the family home of the Whitakers until the 1950s. In the late 18th century, Reverend T.D. Whitaker lived in the house. He was the author of numerous history books, including the story of Whalley Abbey, and also planted many trees in the Cliviger Gorge. He was a friend of the painter, Turner, who paid a number of visits to the house. There is a bust of Whitaker in St John's Church, of which he was a benefactor. The middle portion of the house was rebuilt in 1605 and the west wing added in

1717. On a staircase in the house is a window which is said to have come from Whalley Abbey. The plastered ceilings are 18th century. The house, now a nursing home, is reputedly haunted by the ghosts of a monk and a girl.

East of the village, the **Long Causeway** is an old track used by the Romans and later by the 18th-century wool merchants. The 24-turbine **windfarm** was erected in 1992.

HOOLE [South Ribble]

SD4623: 5 miles (8km) SW of Preston

The villages of Much and Little Hoole are a mixture of commuter and farming communities. Little Hoole is west of the Preston end of the A59. The one-time landlord of the Rose and Crown pub was **Albert Pierpoint**, the last hangman.

The words 'Prepare to meet your God', appear over the porch of the **church of St Michael**. Added to this biblical exhortation are the words 'Believe, Trust, Obey'. The small brick building of 1628, situated on the edge of the village, to the west of the main road, had a stone west tower added in 1772. Inside, there are two galleries and box pews, with a pulpit and sounding board dated 1695. A sundial on the tower dates from 1815 and is inscribed with the words, 'Sine, Sole, Sileo.' This translates as, 'Without the sun, I am silent.' On the clock is written, in Latin, 'As the hours pass, so does life.' It is a memorial to **Jeremiah Horrocks**, curate from 1639 to 1640, who was the first astronomer to detect Venus crossing the sun. This proved that the planets revolved around the sun rather than the earth, which was the common belief at the time. There is also a memorial to Horrocks, who died at the age of 23, in Westminster Abbey.

HORNBY [Lancaster and Morecambe]

SD5868: 5½ miles (9km) E of Carnforth

This historic village, set on the old packhorse route in the middle of farming country, is little more than the long, wide **Main Street**, which is lined with stone buildings, a castle, two churches and a river bridge.

The octagonal Eagle Tower of the **church of St Margaret of Antioch**, at the north end of Main Street, was erected by Sir Edward Stanley in 1514. A tablet has the inscription, 'Edward Stanley, Lord Monteagle, a soldier, caused me to be made.' This was a practical form of thanksgiving to God that Stanley performed on his return from the victory at the Battle of Flodden. Reference to Stanley can be found in Sir Walter Scott's novel *Marmion*. He was also known for dabbling in the occult.

Most of the remainder of the church was reconstructed in the 19th century. The remants of an ancient cross in the tower are carved with loaves and fishes. It is thought to have originally come from a monastery that was once near the site of Priory Farm. A momument commemorates Dr Joseph Lingard, a local Roman Catholic priest and theologian, who turned down the offer to become a cardinal.

'The castle looks, from the bridge, as if seen in a picture book,' is the description of a historian of **Hornby Castle**. Its fame was spread last century by a Turner painting. The original occupants were the Montbegons in the 11th century, who moved into it from Castle Stede. The keep was erected in the 13th century and restored three centuries later. Colonel Charteris bought the castle in 1713 with money gained by cheating at cards. In the 19th century it was restored by Pudsay

Dawson, a rich financier. His family crest can be seen on a fountain near Lamb's Garage at the fork of the roads. A cat has a rat in its mouth. This refers to a time in 1858 when, during the owner's absence, the castle was overrun with vermin. A story is also told of the Harrington family, who lived in the castle in the 13th century. When father and son were killed in battle, an uncle tried to deprive the daughters out of their rightful inheritance. His reward was to be imprisoned by the king. Eventually the daughters married into the Stanley family and that dynasty took over at the castle. It is now in private hands.

On the Gressingham road are the remains of **Castle Stede**, built in the time of King Stephen on a hillock near the River Lune. It is thought to be the best example of a motte and bailey in the county. Near the motte is a pillbox from the Second World War. The **Loyn Bridge**, which spans the river, was built in 1684. **Priory Farm**, by the river to the south, is near the site of a medieval priory.

Dr Lingard was the parish priest from 1811 to 1851. He was responsible for the building, in 1820, of the Roman Catholic **church of St Mary**, opposite the parish church. The adjacent presbytery dates from 1777. The **Castle Hotel**, on Main Street, was one of the village's many coaching inns.

HOWICK CROSS [South Ribble]

SD5128: 2 miles (3km) SW of Preston

Deriving its name from a wayside cross, Howick means a landing place by a creek.

The base of the ancient **Howick Cross** is at the corner of Howick Cross Lane and Liverpool Road. It underwent restoration in 1919 as a memorial to the First World

War. The village took its name from the inlet, which used to run from the Ribble Estuary. Just off the lane is **Howick Hall,** and off Howick Park Avenue, nearby, is 17th-century **Howick House**.

HUNCOAT [Hyndburn]

SD7831. 1½ miles (3km) NE of Accrington

Mentioned in Domesday Book, Huncoat was incorporated into Accrington in 1929. At Town Gate, the heart of the old settlement, are the 1722 village stocks. The carding engine used in the cotton process was invented here by John Hacking. The **church of St Augustine**, on Bolton Avenue, was consecrated in 1909. To the west side of the village, the huge quarries continue to excavate stone.

HURST GREEN [Ribble Valley]

SD6838: 5 miles (8km) SE of Clitheroe

The Longridge Fells provide the background to this picturesque, rural village. A claim to fame is that a road into the village was the first to be tarmacked. J.C. McAdam used it as a trial for his macadamised road surface, which has not been superseded.

Set in a Versailles-like landscape, **Stonyhurst College** is a leading Roman Catholic boarding school. Situated immediately north-east of the village, the long drive leads by the two lakes completed in 1696 up to the imposing buildings. In 1592, the Shireburne family built a new house on the site of a former one, the gatehouse being the first part to be completed. Oliver Cromwell was a guest in 1648. The Shirk (1799), the church (1829 – built in the style of King's College, Cambridge), the west front (1856)

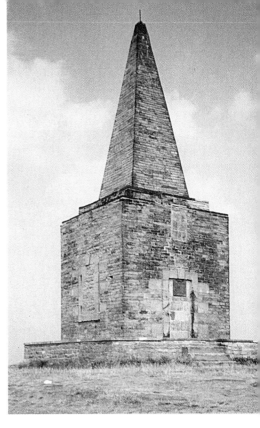

Clockwise from top left: Ormskirk parish church, Brian Wallington; Ashurst's Beacon, Dalton; Greenhalgh Castle, Garstang *(Terry Marsh)*; Hornby Castle and the River Wenning *(Terry Marsh)*.

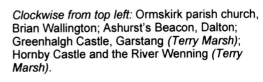

Top to bottom:
Textile museum,
Helmshore;
Clapper bridge;
Wycoller;
Vaccaries at Wycoller.

Clockwise, from top left: Peel Tower, Holcombe; St Patrick's Church, Heysham; Whalley viaduct *(Terry Marsh)*

Sawley Abbey
(Terry Marsh)

Liverpool Castle,
Lever Park and
Lower Rivington
Reservoir,
Rivington.
(Terry Marsh)

Cockersand
Abbey

Cromwell Bridge, Hurst Green

and the south block (1889) complete the assembly of buildings.

In the grounds is a recently restored observatory. In the middle of the 19th century it was one of a small number of government meteorogical stations across the country. This showed that the college was to the fore in new learning, as did the fact that it was the first public building to make use of gas.

In 1702 the male Shireburn heir died at the age of nine, after eating poisonous berries. Eventually, in 1794, after years of neglect, the Jesuits took over and returned the buildings to their former glory. They were from the English College at St Omer and came to Stonyhurst with a small group of pupils.

Inside the college are many priceless items. They include a 7th-century Gospel of St John, said to have been used by St Cuthbert of Lindisfarne, the early northern missionary; the gold cope worn by Henry VII at the Field of the Cloth of Gold; a cope worn by Sir Thomas More and a chasuble belonging to Catherine of Aragon. The main rooms of the college are the great hall, the library, the long gal-

lery (with a priest's hole) and the chapel. Amongst the possessions of Mary Queen of Scots are a jewelled Book of Hours that she had with her when she was executed and some strands of her hair. The war memorial in the college includes the name of Lt Archer-Shee. Whilst at the college, he was accused of stealing a postal order. Terence Rattigan's play *The Winslow Boy*, was based upon this event. The college has produced a number of distinguished old boys. Amongst them were Sir Arthur Conan Doyle, who used the school as the setting for his novel *The Hound of the Baskervilles*, Charles Laughton, the film actor, and the author J.R.R. Tolkien. Gerard Manley Hopkins, the Jesuit poet, was one of the staff members in the 19th century.

Near the entrance to the grounds of the college are the **Shireburn Almshouses**, which were built in 1706 at Kemple End, a small hamlet 1½ miles (2.5km) north. In 1936, they were rebuilt near Stonyhurst College for workers on the estate. The cottages surround on three sides a central courtyard with a ballustrade. At Kemple End there is a Paulinus cross on the south side of the road, half a mile (1km) west of Higher Hodder Bridge. Paulinus was an early 7th-century preacher and missionary.

The ruins of **Cromwell's Bridge** lie downstream from the present Lower Hodder Bridge, on the B6243, 1½ miles (2km) west of the village centre. Cromwell is reputed to have crossed it with his troops on his way to the Battle of Preston in 1562.

HURSTWOOD [Burnley]

SD8831: 2½ miles (4km) SE of Burnley

The River Brun runs through this hamlet in a setting of moorland and woods. At the river bridge, with a red phone box beside it, is the core of the old settlement. The modern housing is higher up the hill. Beyond the village, Cant Clough and Hurstwood reservoirs provide recreational facilities.

Immediately by the bridge is **Hurstwood Hall**, built by Barnard Towneley in 1579 after he had married a 10-year-old girl.

Down the lane by the hall, on the right is **Spencer's Cottage**. It has a roof on three levels and a rectangular entrance porch. Edmund Spencer lived here from 1576 to 1578, after graduating from Cambridge. He was the author of the _Faerie Queen_, which he dedicated to Queen Elizabeth I, and also the _Shepherd's Kalender_, a book about local wildlife.

At the bottom of the lane is **Tattersall House**. This 16th-century structure, with its long roof and narrow windows, was home to the Tattersall racing family.

The remains of an extensive limestone industry are found at **Shedden Limestone Hushings**, 1½ miles (2km) southeast of the village. One of the kilns has been restored. The hushing process was

that of washing away the debris from the limestone rock before it was placed in the kilns to be burnt. The water channels can still be made out.

HUTTON [South Ribble]

SD5027: 3 miles (5km) SW of Preston

The murderer Charles Peace never came near the area, but his violent deeds are remembered at the Headquarters of the Lancashire Police, which has been in the grounds of **Hutton Hall**, at the junction of Saunders Lane and the bypass, since 1931. The hall had been demolished 10 years before. One of Peace's victims was a police constable, Nicholas Cock. A memorial to him was transferred from a church near Manchester and placed at the headquarters. The **Grammar School**, on Liverpool Road, dates from 1764, when it was moved from Longton. Most of the present buildings were erected in 1931. At the end of Tolsey Drive, behind the school, is the **Lodge**, which was moved from the Penwortham Priory site, brick by brick, in 1928.

INGLEWHITE [Preston]

SD5440: 7½ miles (12km) NE of Preston

At the centre of the village is the triangular-shaped green, which is intersected by roads. Around the edge are 17th-century cottages and the **Green Man Inn**, at the beginning of Silk Mill Lane. On the western side of the green is the **market cross**, which was surmounted by the figure of a green man. Only remnants of green remain at the top. It is 10ft (30m) high and on the shaft is the date 1695, plus the inscription 'H.C.I.W.'. This refers to Lord Warren, the local squire at the time. A stone is from the ancient toll bar.

Beyond the pub, the **Congregational Church** was built in 1826. The name of **Button Street**, leading north off the green, indicates that the making of buttons also contributed to the local commerce. A bridge over **Sparling Brook** contains some stones from **St Anne's Well**, which was sited by Well Wood stream. One stone has 'Santae Annae' carved on it. This is found where the stream runs south of Latus House, which is off the Bilsborrow Road, immediately west of the village.

INSKIP WITH SOWERBY [Wyre]

SD4638: 7 miles (11km) NW of Preston

This lowland area has become increasingly residential. Although farming is still important, commuters are in the majority. A 2nd-century millstone was discovered in the village in 1889. **Carr House Green** is a 60-acres (24 hectares) plot of common land, either side of the B5269, south of the village. It gives some idea of the wilder look that much of the surrounding land must have had centuries ago. Tall, slim masts rise to the west of the village, dominating the horizon for miles around. At the centre of the village, the **church of St Peter**, built in 1848, has its tower in the middle of the north wall. The spire was added in 1925. In the past few years its rural aspect has been diminished by the building of houses.

IREBY [Lancaster and Morecambe]

SD6676: 3 miles (5km) SE of Kirkby Lonsdale

Although close to the A65, the hamlet has an isolated feeling. Its stone cottages stand alongside a stream. The lane continues to **Over Hall**, a farm dating from 1690. On the other side of the A65, **Ireby Hall Farm** was built in 1641.

IRWELL VALE [Rossendale]

SD7920: 2½ miles (4km) S of Haslingden

The River Irwell runs through the mill villages of Lumb, Chatterton and Strongstry. The latter two have been conservation areas since the 1970s. At Chatterton recreation ground is the site of Aitken's Mill, which had to be rebuilt in 1826. This was because it had been destroyed during the Plug Riot of that year. Nine people were killed and many injured when the army was brought in to quell the disturbance. Rioters pulled the plugs out of the mill engines to prevent them working. The protestors were workers who found themselves no longer needed with the advent of machinery. West of Strongstry are **Buckden Woods**, 435 acres (176 hectares) which were donated to the National Trust in 1943.

KIRKHAM [Fylde]

SD4232: 7 miles (11km) NE of Preston

Kirkham was granted its borough charter in 1296 and soon became the market centre for the Fylde. It still is the centre for the surrounding farmland and countryside. In addition, agriculture, weaving and flax manufacturing were important past occupations. That the area has been occupied for thousands of years was proved by the discovery of Bronze Age utensils. A fort from the first century, identified at the windmill, demonstrated Roman occupation. The settlement stood on the old Roman road to Ribchester. In the 11th century, the area belonged to

Shrewsbury Abbey and then the Abbot of Vale Royal in Cheshire. After the dissolution of the monasteries, the land came into the ownership of Christ Church, Oxford. The making of sailcloth developed as one of the major industries. The town is now mainly residential.

At the centre of the town is the **Market Square**. On either side of the 1872 lamp are curved fishstone slabs. These were placed there in 1829 and used for the sale of fish on market day. Their predecessors had stood on the same site for the previous two centuries. On the east side of the square is the Georgian **Ash Tree House**, built in 1770. Along Preston Street is a terrace of early 19th-century hand-loom weavers' cottages.

The disabled often find access to churches difficult. The efforts of the **church of St Michael**, down the road from the square, have been recognised with an award. Although there has been a church on the site since the seventh century, the present one was erected in 1822. According to a memorial at the back of the church, the money was raised from a parish rate. The richly-moulded steeple and chancel were added in 1843 and 1853 respectively. Just inside the main door of the nave, the brass on the churchwardens' pew is preserved from 1770. Close by the chancel is a chest with three locks. This meant that the incumbent and both church wardens had to be present for it to be opened. In the centre, hanging from the fine, low ceiling, is a 1725 chandelier. The regimental flag of the North Lancashire regiment was placed in the sanctuary in 1920. The back of the church, underneath the gallery, was tastefully converted into a meeting room in 1986. The stone bearing the Clifton family arms was taken from the old tower and placed on the inside of the west wall of the present one.

The Gillow furniture family donated the money to build the Roman Catholic **church of St John the Evangelist** on the west side of the town in 1845. It is notable for housing the first bells in a Catholic church since the time of the Reformation.

Originally on a site near the church, the **Grammar School**, west of St John's Church, was founded in 1549. It has moved twice since, arriving at its present position in 1911.

A large Roman fort used to occupy the site where the **windmill** now stands on Preston Street. The windmill dates from the early 19th century and is now in private hands.

A supermarket occupies most of **Mill Street**, where millworkers formerly lived. On the corner, by the United Reformed Church, is a lamp erected in 1875 to commemorate the jubilee of Queen Victoria.

KNOTT END [Wyre]

SD3548: half a mile (1km) E of Fleetwood

'Knott' means 'a piece of hard land'. Here, at the estuary of the River Wyre, a small fishing port developed in the 17th and 18th centuries. Today it is a favoured retirement area and has spread rapidly. Bourne End Road leads past the Bourne pub to the ferry for the short passage to Fleetwood. By the main road into the village is the turreted **church of St Oswald**. This is a modern building with a fine, painted ceiling. Hackensall Road leads to the rutted lane to **Hackensall Hall**. The property belongs to the local golf club. The old entrance gates, with fierce animals' heads on top, guard the drive to the 16th-century **Parrox Hall**. It is situated on the B5377, close to its junction with the B5270. The oak panelling in the dining room of the hall is original.

LANCASTER [Lancaster and Morecambe]

SD4761: 5½ miles (9km) S of Carnforth

Lancaster is an essentially Georgian town. Signs of occupation from earlier times have been found on Castle Hill, where flint instruments from prehistoric times were discovered, and the Roman general Agricola built Roman forts in AD79. The settlement grew up at the main crossing point of the River Lune. Later, in 1093, a castle was established by Roger of Poitou on an elevated piece of ground. Having been ceded northern territories by William Rufus, Roger made Lancaster the headquarters of the area instead of Halton. It was a strategic site to choose because the road to the north crossed the fording place of the River Lune. It was possible to spot the approach of an enemy whilst still a long distance away. Although Robert Bruce managed to invade the town in 1332, he was unable to take the castle. In the 18th century the town became increasingly important as a port. Imports included sugar, rum, tobacco, mahogany and cotton, whilst the main export was furniture. Within a century, the challenge of Liverpool and other ports, and the difficulty in getting larger ships up the River Lune, led to a steady decline in trade.

On Castle Hill, in the north-west of the town, **Lancaster Castle** is owned by the Queen in her capacity as Duke of Lancaster. Roger of Poitou built a castle here in Norman times as a defence against the invading Scots, but none of this structure remains. The building has been used as a prison since 1196, although it is expected that this arrangement will end by the year 2000. The old prison buildings and gaoler's house were erected in the period 1790 to 1820. The square keep of 1170, partly remodelled in 1856, has walls 10ft

(3m) thick. The massive gateway, erected in the late 14th century, was strengthened a century later. The gateway is called John o'Gaunt's Tower, with a statue of him above the entrance. Although John did not build the tower, he is thought to have lived in the castle. It was erected by his son, who became Henry IV. Since then the estates have belonged to the Crown. One of the tower turrets was used as a beacon to warn of the coming of the Spanish Armada. The Witches' Tower has dungeons below in which prisoners, including the Pendle Witches of 1612, were held. Its two wells has led to it also being known as the Well Tower. Hadrian's or Adrian's Tower dates from the time of King John, but has been much restored in the intervening years. Inside the 18th-century part of the castle are the Grand Jury Room and the Shire Hall, which is noted for its decoration, shields and pointed windows. The Crown Court retains a branding iron, which fortunately went out of use two centuries ago. Outside the castle, by the round tower, is an area known as Hanging Corner. Here, until 1865, onlookers could witness the execution of prisoners. The victims were tied securely in the Drop Room before being led out to their fate. It was a tradition that before the condemned person was executed, a last drink was allowed at the Golden Lion Inn.

It is known that Roger of Poitou founded a Benedictine monastery on the site of the present **Priory Church of St Mary** in 1094. There is evidence from excavations that there was a church here still earlier, in Roman times. When the monastery was dissolved, the wealth and lands were transferred to another abbey. Part of the bargain was that a new church should be built and so St Mary's came into being. Adjacent to the castle, the main part of the building is from the early 15th century, and the tower was added in 1755. Noteworthy in the interior are a Saxon doorway in the west wall, the oak-canopied stalls, the choir stalls and misericords of 1340 and fragments of an Anglo-Saxon cross. The carved pulpit dates from 1619 and the three chandeliers from 1717. A memorial chapel was built in 1903 for the 20th King's Own Regiment and contains a large collection of regimental flags.

The **Cottage Museum**, at 15 Castle Hill, is a small, furnished cottage restored to its original condition of 1825. It reflects the life of an ordinary working family of that era.

With a date of 1675, the **Judges' Lodgings Museum** in Church Street is reputed to be the oldest house in the town. Thomas Covell, responsible for the imprisonment of the Pendle Witches, lived here in the early 17th-century. For the next two centuries the house served as the lodgings for judges taking trials at the castle. In contrast to the Cottage Museum, it demonstrates the lifestyle of a wealthy family. The ground and first floors are furnished as a town house of the Regency period, with the work of Richard Gillow, the renowned Lancaster manufacturer. The two outstanding pieces are the 'Denton Hall' library table, made in 1778, and a 1821 billiard table, complete with a stand for the cues. The judge's bedroom shows in what sort of way the visiting judges lived. The former Barry Elder Museum of Childhood, once housed in Carr House, Bretherton, is on display, with Victorian and Edwardian toys and furniture. The Gillow Gallery has on show furniture demonstrating the history of the firm. In addition, there is a reconstruction of the workshop of a cabinet maker. A reconstructed Edwardian schoolroom is sometimes brought to life by teachers and

children in period costume. Down below, in the basement, is an old kitchen with open fire.

A Georgian Sessions house is the home of the **City Museum** in Market Square. This was built in 1783 for use as the Town Hall. It covers the life of the area from Neolithic times until the present. Amongst the exhibits are a Roman milestone found at Caton and pieces of a Saxon cross from Cockersand Abbey. On display are clocks and pottery, as well as photographs and maps to explain the development of Lancaster over the centuries. This is also the museum of the King's Own Regiment, whose barracks were in the town from 1880. Memorabilia exhibited includes an early Coptic cross brought back from the Abyssinian campaign of 1868.

The **Maritime Museum** is in the 18th-century Customs House on St George's Quay, at the north end of town. Designed by Richard Gillow, it was renovated in 1985. Inside is the Collector's Office, where duty was handed over, and the Long Room, in which arrangements about the transport of cargo were completed. The museum recalls the growth of Lancaster as a port, especially the trade links with New Zealand and the West Indies. More locally, there is an overview of the Morecambe Bay fishing industry. On display are fishing boats and a reconstruction of a fisherman's cottage. An exhibition deals with the crossing of the Morecambe Sands and the gas field in the bay, including a model gas rig. In the review of the work of the canal is included a replica of a canal packet-boat.

Completed in 1764, **St George's Quay** was at its busiest in the late 18th century. Because of the problems of accommodating the size of large ships, New Quay was built further downstream. A three-storey house built c1735, the **Music Room**, in Sun Street, was originally used as a garden house to a home in Church Street, at present the Conservative Club. It was at this house that Prince Charles stayed during the Jacobite rebellion of 1745. Later the Music Room was divided into two in the middle of the 19th century. It has a fine, baroque, decorated plasterwork interior on the first floor. The theme of the plasterwork is that of Greek gods and goddesses. The one of Ceres decorates the ceiling, and that of Apollo, the wall above the fireplace. This was restored in 1975, after years of neglect. The work took about 6000 man hours to complete. Since the plasterwork has representations of various muses, it is thought that 'Music Room' might be a corruption of 'Muses Room'.

Although the Quakers have worshipped on the site from 1677, the **Friends' Meeting House** in Meeting House Lane dates from 1708, with a later enlargement.

The town has few remains from Roman times, but there is a **Roman bathhouse and the Werry Wall.** The remnants of the bathhouse and a small length of the fourth-century wall near to Vicarage Lane, close to the St Mary's Church, are all that survive of the era. Beneath the floors of the bathhouse, the stone supporting piers remain. It was from underneath the floor that the heat would come to warm the rooms.

Built in 1859 on the east side of the Lancaster Canal, off East Road, the Roman Catholic cathedral **church of St Peter** imitates the style of the 14th century. It has a 240ft (73m) tower, lofty nave and a chancel with a wooden roof. The interior has frescoes, a gilded reredos, a triptych designed by Giles Gilbert Scott and notable stained-glass windows.

The **church of St John the Evangelist**, erected in 1745 in North Road, had a spire added in 1784. The building has five bays and retains the original Georgian box pews and communion rails. It began life as a chapel of ease to the Priory church, before becoming a parish church as the local population grew.

E.W. Mountford built the **Town Hall**, in Dalton Square, in classical style. He was responsible also for the Old Bailey in London. The hall contains some 17th-century corporation plate. The square itself was given by the Dalton family of Thurnham Hall. The money for the hall was donated by Lord Ashton. The council chamber is domed and the concert hall is able to accommodate over 1000 people. The **Victoria Monument**, outside the Town Hall, was donated by Lord Ashton in 1907. The images of prominent Victorians are carved on it in bas-relief. Besides modestly suggesting himself, Ashton ordered 40 carvings, including two women, Florence Nightingale and George Eliot. Ashton himself did not attend the opening ceremony because by then he had fallen out with the town worthies.

The **Covell Cross**, near the junction of Chain and Church Streets, close to the Judges' Lodgings, commemorates Thomas Covell, Keeper of the Castle. Previously there was an ancient cross on the site.

In St Leonardsgate, the **Grand Theatre** has been active for over two centuries. It is said to be haunted by the ghost of Sarah Siddons, the actress, who performed at The Athenaeum, the previous theatre on the site.

Designed by Paley and Austin, leading 19th-century architects, the **Storey Institute** in House Lane is an impressive building, now used for exhibitions and lectures.

The one-storey **Penny's Almshouses**

off King Street, were built in 1720 and named after William Penny, a local benefactor. They stand behind a small courtyard. Next door are the **Assembly Rooms**, which were hired out to raise money for the upkeep of the almshouses.

The **Peter Scott Gallery**, at the University, runs temporary exhibitions as well as having a permanent exhibition of paintings.

Lord Ashton made his fortune through the manufacture and export of oil-cloth and lino. Besides becoming a Liberal Member of Parliament from 1886 to 1895 and later being created Lord Ashton, he was a great philanthropist. After donating the money needed to erect the Town Hall and Victoria Monument, he set about developing the 38-acre (15 hectares) **Ashton Memorial Park**, which had been given to the town and landscaped by his father, James Williamson. Williamson made his fortune from the manufacture of lino, wallpaper and pottery. High above the east end of the town, near the M6, the easiest access to the park is from Wyresdale Road. It was formerly a quarry, and when the effects of the American Civil War caused unemployment amongst cotton workers, the project was seen as a way of keeping them in work. He had it landscaped and provided paths and trees. In 1907, he decided to build a huge, copper-domed folly based on the design of St Paul's Cathedral. This was erected on the summit of the hill in which the park is set. It was to be a memorial to his deceased wife. Two years later, the folly was completed. It included a gallery for viewing the surrounding landscape, with plaques identifying places in the distance. On the second floor of the structure is the Williamson Gallery, used for exhibitions and audio-visual displays of the life of Lord Ashton and the times of Edward VII. In the Edwardian palm house

there is a collection of British and European butterflies. The bird enclosure contains a variety of foreign birds.

A mile upstream, the **Lune Aqueduct** carries the Lancaster Canal over the River Lune. Erected in 1797, it consists of five semi-circular arches designed by John Rennie. The cost was so great that there was not enough money left to build a bridge across the River Ribble. Consequently, the canal could not be linked to the main canal network.

The longest cutting on the Lancaster Canal is half a mile (1km) west of the town. **Deep Cutting** was completed in 1795. At 2 miles (3km) long and 33ft (10m) deep, it avoids the necessity of locks.

Reputed to be the outstanding road bridge in the county, **Skerton Bridge**, erected in 1788, was one of the first flat bridges built. Crossing the Lune in the town, it has five arches.

Aldcliffe Marsh, one mile (2km) west, plays host to thousands of mute swans in addition to mallard, curlew, redshank and shelduck.

LANGHO [Ribble Valley]
SD7034: 3 miles (5km) SW of Whalley

During the 19th-century, new Langho developed as a commercial centre on the railway line. Consequently, old Langho, 1 mile (2km) away, faded into obscurity. A new **church of St Leonard** was built in 1879, because the old one was too far away. The new one itself is now a little isolated from the main village because of the A59 roundabout. It is next to the school on the main road to Billington.

The **old church of St Leonard** is a gem. On a back road north of the A59, it is now used only once a year. It has been suggested that to make sure that the monks did not return to Whalley Abbey after the dissolution of the monasteries, as much of its stone as possible was used for other purposes. This may explain the reason for the building of the church in 1557. The small, low structure has a single roof. The five square-headed windows, the piscina, credence table and the carved stones in the outside wall are all believed to have come from the abbey. The credence table was a holy water stoup during its time at the abbey. The window on the left of the sanctuary has a noticeable tilt. The bench ends have the initials of their owners inscribed on them. At the time when the new church was built, a restoration was undertaken at the old one. A vestry was added, the west wall rebuilt and a font placed at the rear of the building. The bellcot was erected for the 1756 bell. The church is under the care of the Redundant Churches Fund.

The key for the church is obtainable at the **Black Bull Inn**, next door. This black and white, timbered building is both larger and older than the church, having being erected in 1554. On the corner of the road to Langho is **Keeper's Cottage**, which was built in 1775.

By following the road north of the village, a sign to **Brockhall Village** comes into view. Turn left along the lane to be faced with a security guard and a notice warning of video observation. The new village, built on the site of the old hospital, centres on a community of 30 resident artists. They have a vision of linking their work with community and educational groups as well as the general public, in addition to the provision of new housing. One of the most glorious views is found by continuing on the north road. As it turns sharply right, a narrow track goes as sharply left. Down it is **Hacking Hall**. The tall, multi-gabled, stone house looks out over the river. There is a farm attached and an old cruck-framed barn nearby.

LATHOM [West Lancashire]

SD4609: 2 miles (3km) E of Ormskirk

The name is derived from 'latune', meaning 'place of the barns'. The small village lies in flat, agricultural surroundings. Some Roman coins were discovered in a brook in 1949, but little more is known of its early history. When Isabel de Lathom married Sir John Stanley in 1385, the long reign of the Stanley (later the Earl of Derby) family began.

After the Battle of Bosworth in 1485, Henry VII gave the title Earl of Derby to Lord Stanley. As a thank offering, the second Earl built the **Chapel of St John the Divine**, locally known as Lathom Park Chapel. This was restored in the early 19th century, and again in 1964. The earl's retainers and servants worshipped at the chapel, while the earl and his family attended services at Ormskirk parish church. The wagon roof of the chapel is painted in medieval colours, and the chancel screen and lectern came from Burscough Priory. Bullet holes can be seen on the screen, a result of the fighting at the siege of Lathom House. Adjacent to the chapel are eight almshouses which date from the foundation of the chapel as a chantry. In the grounds is the burial vault of the Earls of Lathom and a stone from which the Parliamentary forces are said to have made cannon balls during the siege. In the middle of the 19th century, six skeletons were unearthed, one of which had a musket hole in its head.

The siege of **Lathom House** is one of the great sagas of local history. In the 12th century it was the main house of the de Lathom family, which owned extensive lands for miles around. During the Civil War, the seventh Earl of Derby was a firm supporter of the Royalist cause. In this, he stood almost alone in Lancashire.

During the Earl's absence in the Isle of Man in 1644, the house was besieged by Parliamentary forces led by Alexander Rigby and then by Sir Thomas Fairfax. The house had been built in 1495 and visited by Henry VII. Sited near the remains of its successor, it was said to have nine towers, including the enormous Eagle Tower, with walls six feet (2m) thick and 30ft (9m) high, and a moat 24ft (7m) wide. This helps to explain how the Earl's wife, Countess Charlotte de Tremouille, and 300 defenders were able to hold out. The siege was eventually lifted when Prince Rupert and the Earl arrived to drive the Parliamentary forces away. It was resumed the following year. While both the Earl and the Countess were away, General Egerton and a regiment of 4000 troops forced the garrison to surrender. The house was then completely demolished and its gates were taken away to repair Liverpool Castle. Archaeological discoveries of bricks, bones, glass, pottery and pipes from the 17th century, near to the remaining west wing of the second house, indicate that this was the site of the first house. The second house, designed by the Italian architect Giacomo Leoni, was built in the 400-acre (161 hectares) park by Thomas Bootle in 1734. It was demolished in 1825 except for one wing, which has been renovated. During the First World War the park was used as a training centre for horse regiments.

There has been a building on the site of **Blythe Hall**, in Blythe Lane, since the 12th century. It was purchased in 1826 by Edward Bootle-Wilbraham, who lived at Lathom House. He was later to become the second Lord Skelmersdale, and in 1880 the first Earl of Lathom. In 1922, the third Earl decided to live in the hall since Lathom House was full of dry rot. He extended the building considerably and added a new wing, a swimming pool and a bowling alley. The Earl was a great lover of the theatre and entertained leading artists, such as Ivor Novello, Noel Coward and Gladys Cooper. The hall is now a private residence.

Lady Alice's Drive, opposite Blythe Hall, is so called because the wife of the first Earl of Lathom was killed along the lane. Her pony and trap overturned as she returned from the hunt.

The 1960s buildings of the **Pilkington Research Laboratories** occupy what was once part of Lathom Park.

Part of the original estates of Lathom, the village of **Westhead** lies on the A577, east of Ormskirk. The name of the pub on the corner of Castle Lane is a reminder of **Halton Castle**, whose foundations are in the grounds of Ormskirk Golf Club, to the north. On Vicarage Lane, the 19th-century **church of St James** has traditionally been known as St James, Lathom. The lych-gate is one of the few still to have the central resting place for a coffin.

LEA TOWN [Fylde]

SD4831: 4½ miles (7km) NE of Preston

Although close to the industry of Salwick, the name 'Town' belies a pleasant village with a number of old farmhouses, reached down Darkinson Lane. Part of the village, lying on the path of a Roman road and near the Lancaster Canal, spills over into the Preston district. Bordering the garden of a bungalow opposite the Smiths Arms is a 19th-century cross erected in memory of T.H. Myres, who was responsible for restoring a number of the county's wayside crosses.

Ancient cross at Lea

LECK [Lancaster and Morecambe]

SD6477: 2½ miles (4km) SE of Kirkby Lonsdale

A little huddle of cottages, along with its church and school, make up this small, country village.

The **church of St Peter** stands amid fields near the school. It was destroyed in 1912 when a lamp left alight after choir practice set fire to the organ curtains. The building was resurrected in 1915 to as it had been when originally constructed in 1879.

Further down the road from the church, **Leck Hall**, set in extensive grounds, contains an orangery. It has been altered and added to, particularly since 1717. It is the home of the Shuttleworth family.

It is claimed that Leck Fell House, at the end of the narrow road from Cowan Bridge, has the highest elevation of any farm in the country.

LEYLAND [South Ribble]

SD5422: 5 miles (8km) S of Preston

The earliest record of the town is in Saxon times, when the land was in the possession of Edward the Confessor. The name was then Lailande, denoting cultivated grass land. It was part of the shire called the Leyland Hundred, which is mentioned in the Domesday Book. A hundred was an area that had the capability of supporting 100 familes from the land. Centuries of farming were followed by the weaving and spinning of the Industrial Revolution. During the 20th century, the expansion of the local firm, Leyland Motors, was the keystone in the industrial and commercial prosperity of the town. It commenced in 1890, with the first Leyland bus being manufactured in 1927. Engineering and the production of paint are also important industries.

Although the new town has expanded rapidly, the **Leyland Cross** can still be found at the centre of the old village, at the town end of Church Road. The base and the shaft are original. The top piece was renovated to celebrate Queen Victoria's Jubilee, repairing some damage suffered from Cromwell's Roundheads. Until 1887 it was used to support two gas lamps. There is also a Victorian fountain and water basin. On the western side of the cross are the late 19th-century houses of Towngate, with the exception of number 9, which was built in 1710. To the east is the **Roebuck Hotel**. Erected in the late 18th century, the Court Leet used it as a venue.

The town boasts two 16th-century inns. The **Eagle and Child,** at the west end of Church Road, was said to have been a court house. There are tales of secret tunnels linking to Worden Park. A firemark of the Royal Exchange Company can be seen at 48 Fox Lane. After the great fire of London in 1666, people decided to protect their homes by paying insurance. Those who had a firemark, indicating their insurance, would be attended by the fire brigade.

The chancel and tower of the **church of St Andrew**, in Church Road, date from the early 13th century. Restoration took place in the 15th century and the nave was rebuilt in 1852. Some of the bells are 16th century. The chapel is dedicated to the ffarington family of Worden Hall. A legend involving the church concerns the original intention of building it in Whittle-le-Woods rather than in Leyland. The foundation stone and various materials were placed at the former site. Overnight they mysteriously disappeared and were found in a field in Leyland. The material was returned to the first site and a watch was kept. In the middle of the night, a large black cat was seen to take a stone then soon come back for another. One of the men on watch hit the cat on the head with a piece of wood. The cat retaliated by biting the man in the throat. A second watcher ran to get a priest, but when they returned the man was dead. The cat and the material had disappeared. The result was that the church was built on the field in Leyland to which the cat has been taking the material. A variation on this story gives an angel rather than a cat the credit for moving the material to Leyland. The rhyme spoken by the angel was, 'Here I have placed thee, And here thou shalt stand, And thou shalt be called the church of Leyland.' Part of the 18th-century vicarage is retained in the parish hall on the corner of Worden Lane.

The Roman Catholic **church of St Mary** in Worden Lane seats over 1000 people around the centrally placed altar. The stations of the cross were carved by **Arthur Dooley**, the Liverpool sculptor.

The stone-faced, brick **Leyland House**, next to the church, was erected in 1770. It has had a variety of uses down the years, including being a vicarage and a Roman Catholic chapel. When St Mary's Church was opened in 1845, it became the presbytery.

It is appropriate that in the town that gave its name to Leyland Motors, the **British Commercial Vehicle Museum** should be the largest museum of its kind in Europe. Situated in part of the old Leyland Motors factory, it exhibits over 40 examples of the development of commercial vehicles, from horse-drawn and steam wagons through to petrol and diesel vehicles. Included are the 'Popemobile' used by John Paul II, buses, vans and fire engines. The development of motor transport is traced as it meets the needs of the expanding commercial world. The use of sound and light technology help to make some of the exhibits more realistic.

The old, timbered-faced grammar school, in Church Road, is the venue for the **South Ribble Museum and Exhibition Centre**. Originating in 1524, it was much altered in 1580. It closed in 1976 to be renovated, and reopened in 1977. The museum surveys the archaeological, social and industrial history of the area. This includes items such as Roman remains from Walton-le-Dale, Victorian costumes, an example of packhorse bells and a copy of the scorecard for the first England v Australia cricket match. The Exhibition Centre has changing art exhibitions throughout the year.

Opposite the Exhibition Centre are two items of interest. **St Andrew's Watch-**

house dates from the early 19th century and is thought to have been used for keeping corpses overnight before burial. Since bodies used to be carried for many miles to the church, this seems a likely explanation. **St Andrew's Sundial** is from the early 18th century.

For three centuries the ffarington family lived in **Worden Hall**, set in 157 acres (63 hectares) of parkland at the southern end of the town. It was destroyed by fire in 1941. The buildings that remained were restored in 1976. The Derby Wing, built by William ffarington in the 18th century, houses the Worden Arts and Crafts Centre. The Lancashire branch of the Council for the Protection of Rural England has its headquarters here, whilst various craft workshops are found in the former outhouses. The grounds are thought to have been laid out in the early 19th century by William Nesfield, the designer of Kew Gardens and Alton Towers. Adjacent to the formal gardens is the conservatory, built in 1892. The grounds include a folly in the shape of an archway, a domed ice house, a ha-ha (a concealed ditch), a walled kitchen garden and a maze. Amongst the variety of trees is a 300-year-old Spanish chestnut.

LITTLE ECCLESTON [Wyre]

SD4241: 5 miles (8km) E of
Poulton-le-Fylde

The hamlet is situated by the toll bridge over the River Wyre. Standing by the toll bridge, the **Cartford Hotel** has a reputation for being haunted by ghosts who move objects around and switch lights on and off.

Built in 1718 on the site of a burial ground, the **Quaker Meeting House** is now called Quakers' Rest. It is towards the western end of the old Blackpool road.

Little Eccleston Hall, on Wall Lane, south of the main road, belonged to the ffrance family. It is little altered and now a farm.

Rebuilt in the 1950s, **Larbreck Hall** was home to the Molyneux family. It lies by the A586, half a mile (1km) west of the village.

LIVESEY [Blackburn]

SD6525: 2 miles (3km) SW of Blackburn

Livesey is partly agricultural but linked to the built-up areas of Cherry Tree and Feniscowles. The village has one of the largest playing fields in the vicinity. **Livesey Hall** is a farmhouse with two wings which dates from 1605.

LONGRIDGE [Ribble Valley]

SD6037: 9 miles (14km) SW of Clitheroe

In the shadow of Longridge Fell, the village is the centre of a farming district. Its elevation can be judged by the fact that the step of the White Bull pub is at the same height above sea level as the summit of Blackpool Tower. The two main industries in the 19th century were cotton spinning and quarrying. Much of the stone for the building of Liverpool docks and Lancaster Town Hall, as well as for local houses, came from the local quarries. Some of the mill buildings are still intact, although used for other purposes. **Victoria Mill** is at the end of Mersey Street, **Queen's Mill** off Green Nook Lane and **Stone Bridge Mill** near the junction of Kestor Lane and Preston Road. A number of 18th-century buildings are found in the **Market Square**. The thoroughfare continues into **King Street**, whose cottages were built to accommodate handloom weavers. Some of the first houses to be purchased with a mortgage from a building society are found in **Club Row** on Higher Road. The society was formed by workers in the late 18th century. They put their money together and as the twenty (now listed) houses were built, so the workers drew lots for them.

Higher Road leads out to **Tootle Heights Quarries**, from which came most of the sandstone used for building throughout the county.

Although there had been a chapel of ease at the corner of Chapel Hill and Chapel Brow since the 15th century, the **church of St Laurence** gained the status of a parish church in 1868. The original date of the church is not known, but there were certainly numerous renovations from 1716 onwards. The tower was erected in 1841. The clock came from Alston College, a school which was demolished when the reservoir was built close by.

The coming of the railway in 1840 considerably boosted the industry of the village. Now long closed, some of the station buildings remain on Berry Lane.

A large piece of stone called the **Written Stone** is in the embankment in Written Stone Lane. The stone is found by turning left at the crossroads on the B6243, east of the reservoirs. The inscription on it, along with the date of 1655, is, 'Raiffe Radcliffe laid this stone to be for ever.' It was said to be on the grave of a witch. If it is ever moved, dire consequences will follow.

LONGTON [South Ribble]

SD4826: 5 miles (8km) SW of Preston

The Mormons came to the village in 1840. The Church of Jesus Christ of Latter-Day Saints, to give the movement its official title, had been formed near New York only 10 years previously. It may seem surprising that what would then have been an obscure English village should be visited by Brigham Young, the movement's leader and a group of his adherents, but the first British Mormon church had been opened in Preston three years earlier. The mission was so successful that a number of the villagers decided to emigrate to the USA, where some became Mormon leaders. Longton is literally a 'long village', being 4 miles (6km) from end to end. Although it is now mainly a commuter area, it has a history of brick, carpet and basket-making and brewing. It has been suggested that the reason that the village has such a large number of pubs is because of this local brewing tradition. The **Black Bull Inn**, on Liverpool Road, dates from the 17th century. The bay on the first floor juts out from the rest of the building.

At the crossroads in Longton is the **church of St Andrew**. The chantry chapel of 1517 was demolished in 1773 and a larger building erected. This, in turn, was replaced by the present structure, erected in Gothic style in 1887. The original plans included the building of a tower, but this has never been added. Its font was made in 1725 and was previously in St Mary's, Penwortham. The old village stocks are positioned outside the library.

The former Longton Hall is now **Longton Hall Farm,** in Chapel Lane. The present building was erected in 1662. The initials 'WIW' on the wall refer to the Waltons, who were tenants when the Shireburns were lords of the manor. **Longton Brickcroft Nature Reserve** is on the edge of the village, on Drumacre Lane off Liverpool Road. Covering 27 acres (11 hectares), there is a visitor centre. The southern part is for use of fishermen and walkers; the north is the actual nature reserve for the conservation of wildlife.

A narrow lane to the west of the church leads along Marsh Lane to the **Longton Marshes**. Near the confluence of the Rivers Ribble and Douglas, the area attracts many species of wildfowl. The Ribble Way starts from the tiny, isolated, brick **Dolphin Inn**, at the end of Marsh Lane. This was originally built to serve travellers who had come across the estuary at its narrowest crossing point. Outside the pub is the sign of two dolphins and a ball.

LYTHAM ST ANNES [Wyre]

SD3427: 5½ miles (9km) S of Blackpool

The tourist industry has overtaken both of these previously small hamlets, which are now known under the one name. Until the late 19th century, St Anne's and Lytham were little more than widely scattered farming and fishing communities. The name 'St Anne's' was taken from the chapel of ease in the vicinity. Lytham is called 'Ludum' in the Domesday Book. Most of the land had belonged to the Clifton family since the early 17th century. They controlled the whole area and saw the possibility of developing it as a seaside resort. Consequently, the family and a consortium of Lancashire businessmen financed the planning and building of the new development. With a view to planning an upmarket Blackpool, the St Anne's Land and Building Company was founded in 1874. Until the late 18th century, agriculture and fishing were the main local occupation. The coming of the railway in 1842 helped to give added impetus to the growth of the seaside resort, with its eleven miles (18km) of beach. It soon got the name of the 'Opal of the

West', as visitors flocked to the Pavilion and Floral Hall. In 1922, the two communities were officially joined together as one borough, partly to prevent the area becoming merely a suburb of Blackpool.

Many of the buildings in the resort are 19th century, but some are from the Georgian period.

The original Lytham village green, now the **Market Square**, was replaced by **The Green** on the front. A huge tide, which demolished 40 houses, led to its construction as a barrier. Off West Beach is **Charlie's Mast**. This was put there by a man named Charlie Townsend in the early 19th century, on the spot where the only light to guide boats was positioned in those days.

Lytham Hall is on the site of a monastic farm. It had many different owners after the dissolution of the monasteries. Situated off Ballam Road, beyond the railway station, the hall is an Adams-style brick structure, built by Thomas Clifton in 1764. It replaced the mid-16th-century building, but retained the long gallery and servants' quarters, plus some of the original priory in the kitchens. The house is red brick, with a porch of Ionic columns. Inside there is a decorated ceiling and an 18th-century, mahogany staircase. The last of the family, de Vere Clifton, sold the hall in 1978. He had rooms in London at both the Dorchester and Ritz hotels. When asked why he needed these, he replied, 'If I am passing down Park Lane and feel tired, then I've got somewhere to go.' Between the station and the hall, **Witch Wood** is a small nature reserve run by the Civic Society.

The best-known landmark is the **Lytham Windmill**, on the green opposite the junction of East Beach and Station Road. The windmill, with its cap in the shape of a boat, was erected in 1805 to produce flour and oatmeal. It was damaged by a fire in 1919 that ended its operational life. Rebuilt in 1921, it suffered wind damage in 1929. It still has a set of sails and a fantail, and contains an exhibition of the history of the mill and bread-making. The **Lifeboat House**, next to the windmill, was built in 1851. It is mainly constructed of cobblestones and was financed by the Cliftons. Inside is a museum run by the Royal Lifeboat Society. The part of the green on which the windmill and lifeboat house are situated was a former area of dunes, and donated to the town by the Clifton family in 1923.

The oldest known building in Lytham is a barn, just off Bath Street, which has somehow survived from a mid-18th-century farm.

The body of St Cuthbert is said to have rested at **St Cuthbert's Cross**. The cross stands in Church Road, by the cricket club. St Cuthbert was en route to Durham for burial. The **church of St Cuthbert** was built in 1834 to replace the smaller one of 1770.

The Open Golf Championship is played at the **Royal Lytham Golf Club** every few years. In the clubhouse is the mashie iron used by the American golfer, Bobby Jones, in the first Open championship to be played on the course in 1926.

The sand dunes alongside Clifton Drive North in St Anne's, continuing towards Blackpool South Shore, make up **Lytham St Anne's Nature Reserve**. First established in 1968, it became a Site of Special Scientific Interest in 1991. It is a remnant of a much wider sand dune system and is home to a wide variety of birds and animals, including the dark tussock and portland moths. The whole of the **Ribble estuary** is a National Nature Reserve, and is the third most important for waders. Also to be seen are oyster catchers, plover, godwits and dunlin.

The **Toy and Teddy Bear Museum of Childhood**, on Clifton Drive North, includes model trains and cars, books, dolls and prams. It is a delight for adults as well as children. The centrepiece is a collection of teddy bears called 'Teddies at the Seaside'. A display shows what children used to wear in the past, with clothing, clogs and christening gowns, and there is an exhibition of household appliances, such as cookers and washing machines.

The **Ribble Discovery Centre** at Fairhaven Lake, by Lake Road, is run by the RSPB. The programme includes walks, talks and displays, as well as a schools' project that uses Granny's Bay, a good vantage point for watching the birds.

In the **Alpine Gardens**, near St Anne's pier, there is a memorial to 27 lifeboatmen of the St Anne's and Southport crews drowned in 1886. The lifeboat *Laura Jane* was launched from the old **Lifeboat House** in East Bank Road. It went to the aid of a German boat, *Mexico*, which was sinking. Five of the men are buried at **St Anne's Church**, built in 1873 on the corner of St Anne's Road East and Headroomgate Road. Westward along the former road is the Roman Catholic **church of Our Lady Star of the Sea**. Built in 1890, the weathervane is shaped like a boat.

MAWDESLEY
[West Lancashire]
SD4914: 6 miles (9km) SW of Chorley

Harrock and Hunter's Hill loom over Mawdesley, which is set in farming country on the edge of mossland. A stone axe, a flint arrowhead and workflints (on display at Martin Mere) have confirmed early habitation of the area, but there are no discoveries from the Roman era. In the 19th century, basket-making was an important local activity. The name of the village is thought to be derived from it being part of the dowry when a lady named Maud married William Hesketh in the 19th century.

Until the **church of St Peter** was erected in 1840 in High Street, at the southern edge of the village, the villagers had to go to Croston to worship. Built in grey stone with a thin spire, a chancel was added in 1882. The altar is made of 400-year-old oak taken from the demolished Douglas Chapel in Parbold.

Built by William Mawdesley in 1625 on the site of a previous building, **Mawdesley Hall** is situated on a sandstone outcrop between the war memorial and Black Bull Inn on Hall Lane. At the top of the well-worn steps from the road, erected in 1613, are peepholes, which were used for defensive purposes. Part of the H-shaped structure is half-timbered. The central portion is Tudor, the black and white ground floor is original. One of the 19th-century wings is of sandstone, the other of brick. The Mawdesley family lived here for generations. On the landing inside the house is a coffin rail. This could be removed so that the body of anyone who died in one of the bedrooms could be brought downstairs. The fireplace in the hall dates from 1625. A white lady is said to haunt the house.

The **Black Bull Inn** is a neighbour of the hall. The two-storey sandstone building, with Tudor windows, was erected in the 1580s. It was an inn by the beginning of the 18th century and was later known as 'Hell Hob'. The hob, which Helen the landlady had in her kitchen, is long gone. Only a poker from the early 17th century remains.

Bluestone Farm, east of the Black Bull, was built in 1706. It takes its name from an Ice Age bluestone in the garden.

The home of John Finch, the leading Roman Catholic in the area, was **Lane End House** in Smithy Lane. He was executed at Lancaster Castle in 1584 and beatified in 1929. The brick building has mullioned windows. In the attic is a chapel with no windows. Here worship took place during the time of persecution. It continued in use until the church of St Peter and St Paul was opened. The chapel was restored and reopened in 1966.

The Roman Catholic **church of St Peter and Paul**, at the corner of Ridley Lane and Salt Pit Lane, is a large, barn-like structure, erected in 1831.

The 1772 will of John Ambrose is kept in **Ambrose House,** built in sandstone in 1577, at the bottom of a dip in Bradshaw Lane. The ghost of a lady in black is reputed to haunt it.

MELLING [Lancaster and Morecambe]

SD5970: 6½ miles (10km) E of Carnforth

Situated in the Lune Valley, the village, called Melinge in the Domesday Book, has a narrow main street. A number of the stone houses with mullioned windows that line the street are from the 17th century. The stone **Melling Hall**, at the junction of the main road with the Wennington road, is now a hotel. It was built by the Craven family in the 18th century, but later had a porch with Ionic columns added.

The **church of St Wilfrid** stands high above the main road on the fortified site of Castle Mount. A church was known here in 1094. In the 13th century the rectory was held by the Archbishop of York. Most of the building was destroyed by the Scots in 1322. Most of the present church is mid-14th century, with a 15th-century tower. In the middle of the 17th century, the nave roof was raised and the clerestory added. Heavy restoration took place in the 19th century. The north door is known as 'the devil's door', and is left open at baptismal services to let the devil out. On a window sill in the north aisle are stones dating from Saxon times. The south side of the chancel contains a 'leper's squint'. The west window, behind the font, is 13th century and the pews 17th century. The upper vestry houses an oak cupboard made from box pews. On the wall is part of a Saxon burial slab and, opposite, a section of a 13th-century crucifix. By the window is a 17th-century vicarage pew. Because of the slope, the chancel floor falls away steeply towards the nave.

MELLOR [South Ribble]

SD6531: 2½ miles (4km) NW of Blackburn

As the derivation of the name 'Mellor' indicates, the large village of Mellor is at the top of a small hill, 733ft (223m) in height. There is evidence that a Roman signalling station and church were on the site. From a small agricultural village, it grew as the weaving industry flourished. The main village runs down the hill to Melling Brook. Mellor Brook runs through this straggling hamlet. The mill was demolished long ago.

In Church Lane, the **church of St Mary** was built in 1827 and has some 19th-century, Flemish stained glass and a peal of Guildford chimes.

An old millstone stands outside the Georgian **Millstone Hotel**, on the corner of Church Lane. It was formerly Mellor Hall. **The Old Malthouse** dates from 1684.

MERECLOUGH [Burnley]

SD8831: 2½ miles (4km) SE of Burnley

The **Rockwater Bird Conservation Centre** is near Rough Wood, north of the village. It contains over 80 different species of animals and birds, both domestic and foreign, including Birmingham Roller pigeons. There is also a pets' corner, which children enjoy.

MITTON [Ribble Valley]

SD7239: 3 miles (5km) SW of Clitheroe

'The junction of two rivers' (the Ribble and the Hodder) is the meaning of the name 'mythe', which later became Mitton. Up to the reorganisation of county boundaries, the line between Yorkshire and Lancashire was at the bridge over the Ribble. Great Mitton Hall and Little Mitton Hall date from Tudor times.

The emblem of Whalley Abbey at the **Three Fishes Hotel**, on the main road through the village, is a reminder that until the dissolution of the monasteries in the 16th century, much of the local land was owned by the abbey.

Looking down on the River Ribble below, the **church of All Hallows** is in the middle of the village, with expansive views over the surrounding countryside. Entered from the road opposite the hotel, the nave is from 1270 and the crenellated tower, with its stair turret, 15th century. Inside, the floor slopes between 17th century pews. The chancel screen of 1593 may have come from Sawley Abbey. Its gates portray the story of the Annunciation of the birth of Christ. A triple-seat in the chancel dates from the 13th century. There is a 14th-century leper's squint and a pulpit with carved Jacobean figures. The Sherburne chapel, on the north side of the chancel, has a

16th-century screen. On the chancel side of the screen are some chained books, one of which is a 1710 Prayer Book. The chapel itself, containing family memorials, was added in 1594 by Sir Richard Shireburne of Stoneyhurst. Before this time it was a chantry chapel. In the middle of the chapel is the large tomb of Sir Richard, himself, and his family. One of the other memorials remembers another Richard, who died at the age of nine years after eating berries which were poisonous. In the floor is a trapdoor which gives access to the vault. There is also a holy water stoup. Outside, in the churchyard, amongst ancient graves, are the 1683 sundial, an empty stone coffin and part of a 14th-century cross.

Only the great hall remains of the Little Mitton Hall of the early 16th century. The house was restored in the 19th century, but still contains a wooden screen from the original house.

Across the bridge, **Great Mitton Hall** was erected in 1514. It is now a restaurant.

By the side of the B6243, just north of Mitton Green, is the large base of an ancient cross.

MORECAMBE [Lancaster and Morecambe]

SD4364: 8½ miles (14km) NW of Lancaster

With the mountains and hills of Lakeland in the distance across Morecambe Bay, the town is fighting back from a period of decline as a holiday resort. This has been mainly due to the increase in the popularity of overseas holidays. For centuries the bay was crossed at low tide, as the shortest route to the Furness Peninsular. The monks from Cartmel Priory used to guide travellers across and later stagecoaches took this route. The treacherous sands and fast-filling gullies led to many casualties through drowning as the tide came in.

Until the late 19th century, the fishing villages of Poulton-le-Sands, Bare and Torrisholme were the only populated areas of the coast. One of the few remaining echoes of such places is the gateway of **Poulton Hall,** in the grounds of the present Town Hall. The hall itself was on the site of what is now the open-air market. There are some older houses around Poulton Square and Torrisholme Square. Poulton-le-Sands developed as a port for Ireland and a holiday resort after the arrival of the railway in 1848. The town became popularly known as 'Bradford-on-Sea' as the holidaymakers poured in from the mill towns of Yorkshire to enjoy the sands, which stretch from Fleetwood to Grange, and the funfair. The new transport facility also encouraged the expansion of the shellfish industry. Shrimps were caught from boats known as 'nobbles'.

In 1853, the stone jetty on the promenade was completed as the railway terminus for the ferries. From then on, development proceeded apace and the Winter Gardens, first known as the People's Palace, were completed in 1878. At this stage the name of the area was changed to Morecambe.

Of historical interest at the **Frontierland** fairground in Marine Road West is the Texas Tornado Roller Coaster. It was included in the 1937 Paris Exhibition.

Originally founded in 1745, the **church of Holy Trinity** was rebuilt in 1841 to accommodate the increasing population.

The **Broadway Hotel** in Marine Road East is largely unaltered and a good example of the architecture of the 1930s.

NATEBY [Fylde]

SD4645: 10½ miles (17km) NW of Preston

On a mossland farm at the **Fylde Country Life Museum**, at South Hill Farm, Woods Lane, are displayed various aspects of local country life. There is a range of traditional farm implements and machines, the kitchen of a 19th-century farmhouse, a village store, a blacksmith's, a printer's workshop and a post office.

NELSON [Pendle]

SD8638: 3½ miles (6km) NE of Burnley

Taking its name from the famous admiral of Trafalgar fame, the development of the town dates from the early 19th century. The **Lord Nelson Inn**, by the station, was the immediate inspiration for this christening. Situated in the valley of Pendle Water, the town grew rapidly as a textile community with the coming of rail and canal links. There is easy access to the beauty of the surrounding moorland. The **Pendle Photographic Gallery**, in the Town Hall in Market Street, has changing exhibitions by mainly local artists.

In the north-east suburbs of the town, immediately west of the junction of Townhouse Road and Boulsworth Crescent, is 16th-century **Marsden Hall**. This was the home of the de Walton family until 1912, but partial demolition has taken place. In the park nearby is an 1841 sundial, which gives the time in different parts of the world.

Beyond the hall to the east, **Castercliff Hill Fort** is 550ft (167m) in diameter. The oval fort is surrounded by earthworks. About one mile south-east of the fort is **Walton Spire**. This small monument, of a rocket-like appearance, was erected in 1835.

The **stone circle**, which suffered damage in the 19th century, is on Ring Stone Hill, by Pathole Beck, 1½ miles (2km) east of the town.

NETHER KELLET [Lancaster and Morecambe]

SD5068 and SD5270: 2 miles (3km) SE of Carnforth

The number of old springs and wells in the vicinity demonstrate the aptness of the name 'Kellet', meaning 'spring'. The major occupations have been farming and quarrying. At Nether Kellet, the **Lime Burners Arms**, on the corner of Halton Road and the road to Over Kellet, and the old kilns in the vicinity show that the manufacture of lime was also of importance. The tiny church of St Mark, was built in 1879.

At Nether Kellet, **Dunald Mill Hole** is a large cave, full of boulders, and with an underground stream running from it. see also OVER KELLET

NEWBURGH [West Lancashire]

SD4810: 4½ miles (7km) NE of Ormskirk

At the centre of the village, close to the Leeds and Liverpool Canal, is a triangular green. Opposite is the 17th-century **Red Lion**, an old coaching inn. In the conservation area around the inn there are numerous old houses, including **Spring Cottage** (1762) and **Ash Brow Cottage**. The latter has a plaque indicating that the house and six closes of land belonged to the Peter Lathom's Charity. The surrounding countryside is mainly arable. An annual fair commenced in 1304 and was restarted in 1977.

Woodstock Hall was formerly New-burgh Hall. South of the village, it was built in the 14th century.

NEWCHURCH-IN-PENDLE [Pendle]

SD8239: 2½ miles (4km) NW of Nelson

The eye of God is upon you when you visit this small, residential village, built on the slope of a hill in the Forest of Pendle. Once called Goldshaw Booth, it has a number of 17th-century houses, in-cluding the Boar's Head and Bluebell Inns. With its grey-stone cottages, it has seen little change for over a century. Jonas Moore, the co-founder of the Greenwich Observatory, was born in the village in 1618.

The eye mentioned, somewhat over-shadowed by a modern illuminated cross, is built into the west side of the tower of the **church of St Mary**. Another stone on the tower bears the date 1653. The rest of the church was built in 1740, replacing an earlier one on the same site. The church is easy to miss, standing as it does on a downward slope behind buildings at the north end of the village. The sundial on the western wall dates from 1718. To the east of the porch, up against the south wall, is the reputed grave of Alice Nutter, one of the Pendle Witches. On the head-stone is carved a skull and crossbones. Since the surname is so common in the area, there is no certainty that this is the correct Alice. A shop in the village, with model witches gathered outside, serves as a reminder that the village is in the middle of the witch country.

Every year a rush-bearing ceremony is held. Originally the rushes were used on the soil floor of the church to make it warmer and prevent it becoming muddy when it rained. The rushes, in the form of a bishop's mitre, were brought to the church on a cart. The tradition stopped, but was started again at the beginning of the 20th century. Most of the church building dates from 1740, although there is an older sundial and priest's door.

NEWTON [Ribble Valley]

SD7050: 5 miles (10km) NW of Clitheroe

This tiny hamlet, situated by the River Hodder, is the site of a Friends' Meeting House started in 1767. It is situated on the corner of the road leading out to Dun-sop Bridge and the back road to Slaid-burn. John Bright, a Member of Parliament who played a major role in the passing of the Reform Act, wor-shipped here.

ORMSKIRK [West Lancashire]

SD4108: 16½ miles (26km) SW of Preston

Known for its church with both a spire and a tower, the town stands at the centre of the agricultural and horticultural ac-tivity of the Lancashire Plain. It is possi-ble that the name originates from a Viking leader by the name of Orme, who arrived in AD840. The Viking emblem of a raven is carved inside the church and adds weight to this theory. In 1286 a charter was given by Edward I, allowing the monks of Burscough Priory to hold a market. Following the dissolution of the monasteries, much of the land came into the hands of the Stanley family, later Earls of Derby. In 1849, the Liverpool to Preston railway was opened and Orm-skirk started to become a commuter area for people working in Liverpool. Drain-age of the surrounding moss land meant that agriculture became a thriving concern. The latter part of the 19th century also saw the influx of a large number of Irish folk escaping the famine conditions in their own land. The poor conditions in which they were forced to live brought about a great improvement in local services. In the 20th century, the town has become a market centre for the surrounding farming communities.

Apart from the **church of St Peter and St Paul**, only two other churches in the country have both a tower and a spire. They are both in Wiltshire. Unlike those of Ormskirk, the towers and spires of the Wiltshire churches are not adjacent to each other. Although there is a legend that the situation came about because two sisters could not agree whether there should be a tower or a spire, the reality is more prosaic than that. The spire actually dates from 1435, but has been rebuilt twice. The tower, with its battlements and pinnacles, was erected in 1542, to house the bells from Burscough Priory after the dissolution of the monasteries. At the back of the church is one of the bells, made in 1497. The clock was placed on the tower in 1883. Much of the main body of the church is 12th century, but in the late 19th century there was a major restoration. On the east wall of the chancel are some carvings, which are thought to be from the Saxon period. One has the representation of a raven, hence the suggested link with the Vikings. The sundial over the porch is 17th century.

Just inside the porch are the dog-whippers' seats. They were charged with the duty of keeping unwanted animals from attending worship. The benches have a drawer in which the whips were kept. Inside the church, the Derby chapel is, as the name suggests, the resting place of a number of the Stanley family. Known as The Warrior's Chapel, it is separated from the chancel by a 13th-

century arch. Originally a 14th-century Lady Chapel, members of the Derby family were buried here from 1500 until the middle of the 19th century. Until then the burials took place at Burscough Priory.

There are four effigies here, namely that of the first Earl of Derby and his two wives, the second of whom was the mother of Henry VIII, and the third Earl. The vault contains the seventh Earl and his wife, Countess Charlotte de la Remouille, the heroine of the first seige of Lathom House. The head of the earl, having been executed because of his loyalty to the Royalist cause, is said to be in a separate container. In the adjacent Scarisbrick Chapel, where members of the Scarisbrick family are buried, is a life-sized brass of a 15th-century knight. A rhyme on a copper plate reminds the reader that the Mossock family have been buried there since the 13th century. Reverend Nathaniel Heywood, who was ejected in 1662, is remembered by the east window in the chancel. Heywood lived at Chapel House in Chapel Street and is buried in the vault of the Derby family. Heywood was amongst many ministers who refused to conform when the monarchy was restored after Oliver Cromwell's Commonwealth. Also in the chancel is a statue to Dr Brandreth, a leading 19th-century medical pioneer in the town. To the left of the chancel is a Norman window.

Probably the oldest part of the building is the Royal Chapel, where the Royal Arms can be seen on an arch. It was here that Henry VII came to worship on a visit to Lathom House. The font was given by the Countess of Derby in 1661. A 17th-century bookcase used to be used as the place from which the poor of the parish collected loaves.

The meetings of various courts took

place on the first floor of the **Old Town Hall**, erected in 1779 towards the other end of Church Street. On the ground floor were shops and a market. The eagle and child crest is that of the Derby family.

On the site of the old market cross at the town centre crossroads, the **clock tower** was built in 1876. It contains the old town fire bell from 1684.

The **Buck i'th' Vine Inn** in Burscough Street was a coaching inn on the old Liverpool to Preston turnpike road.

The **Tower Hill Water Tower**, on the road of the same name at the west end of the town, was built in 1850, the first in Lancashire. The water came from underground springs and was pumped into a steel tank. It has been replaced by a modern version at Scarth Hill, which is a landmark for many miles around.

OSWALDTWISTLE [Hyndburn]

SD7327: 2 miles (3km) WE of Accrington

James Hargreaves invented the Spinning Jenny in 1764, when he lived at what is now Stanhill post office, on the west side of the town. His invention revolutionised the spinning process but the resultant loss of jobs meant that Hargreaves was forced to leave the area.

The name of the town means 'the boundary of the kingdom of St Oswald'. He was king of Northumbria from AD605 to AD642. The town expanded from a village when, in the 19th century, calico printing and textiles developed. The father of prime minister Sir Robert Peel, who lived at Peelfold, was a pioneer in calico printing.

Amongst a variety of other attractions is a display at **Oswaldtwistle Mills**, in Colliers Street. It is housed in Moscow Mill, built in 1824. The Textile Time Tunnel traces the three centuries in the history of the cotton industry. The exhibition includes the importance of the invention of the Spinning Jenny, the Wakes Weeks and the hardship resulting from the cotton famine.

The **Aspen Colliery Coke Ovens** are situated on the banks of the canal to the north of the town. These are beehive-shaped ovens and in them coke was produced from coal from the nearby mine. The mine was opened in 1869, but only the ovens and loading dock remain.

OVER AND NETHER BURROW [Lancaster and Morecambe]

SD6276: 2½ miles (4km) S of Kirkby Lonsdale

The small hamlet of Nether Burrow is on the banks of the Leck Beck. Northwards, on the other side of the beck, stands **Over Burrow Hall**, erected in 1740. In the fields opposite is the mound of a Roman fortress built by Agricola in AD79.

OVER KELLET [Lancaster and Morecambe]

SD5169: 1 mile (2km) E of Carnforth

The village green at Over Kellet, with the pedestal of an ancient cross, is the focal point of a small community.

There is a piece of local folklore that tells that St Cuthbert, the 6th-century Bishop of Lindisfarne, once stayed in the village, hence the dedication of the parish **church of St Cuthbert**. Except for the 13th-century west bay of the southern arcade and the 14th-century tower, most of the church dates from the major restoration of 1864. There was a tradition of children singing from the top of the tower on Good Friday.

The 1820 house called **Hall Garth**, amongst the 17th- and 18th-century cottages around the green, is on the site of an earlier one. An ancient font found in its grounds was put in the church, resulting in it being one of the few churches with two fonts.

A monastery was formerly in the grounds of **Birkland Barrow**. In the garden there is a monument with a motif of two black men, indicating, perhaps, that a previous family had servants who came through connections with the slave trade.

OVERTON [Lancaster and Morecambe]

SD4358: 4 miles (6km) SW of Lancaster

Overlooking the Lune estuary, some of the white, terraced cottages on the main street are thought to include stone brought from the demolished Cockersand Abbey. In the 19th century the village was a popular place for holidays.

There is much Saxon and Norman stonework in the **church of St Helen**, to the south-east of the village, along Church Grove from Chapel Lane. Situated on top of the Heysham promontory, looking out over the river, the building is remarkable for having a north transept shorter than the nave.

There are different styles of architecture from the Norman to 19th century. The doorway is 12th century, as is the south nave wall and parts of the north. Except from the first few rows, it is impossible to see the chancel from the transept, which was built in early 19th century, The chancel itself dates from 1771. It is the third the church has possessed. Excavations in 1902 discovered the foundations of the apse of the Norman church.

At the back is a gallery, which was erected in 1830. The pulpit was placed in its present position on the south wall in 1772, but is older than that. The west wall contains stones from either the Saxon or Norman period. If they are Saxon, the church has the oldest foundations in Lancashire.

A 19th-century landlord of the **Ship Inn,** on Main Street, was a fanatical collector of birds' eggs. The remains of his collection are on show inside the building.

PADIHAM [Burnley]

SD8034: 3 miles (5km) NW of Burnley

Although the existence of the community pre-dates the Norman Conquest, it expanded with the coming of the weaving industry. Subsequently, unlike many other places, it did not develop into mechanised textile production. It still has the cobbled streets of the early 19th century. Examples of these are found at the side of the Hand and Shuttle pub and in Mill Street.

The 118ft (36m) tower of the **church of St Leonard** is a landmark. It looks out from its dominant position towards the west end of the long, sloping main street. This large edifice contains a 16th-century font that was given by the Abbot of Whalley Abbey to the previous church, which was demolished in 1868.

One of the major historic houses in the county, **Gawthorpe Hall** is situated in extensive grounds by the River Calder. Sir James Kay-Shuttleworth had the building restored by Sir Charles Barry, who was also the architect for the Palace of Westminster in London, between 1850 and 1852. The Shuttleworth family, who had lived in the area since 1330, had the house built between 1600 and 1605. During the Civil War, Sir Richard Shuttleworth was a strong Parliamentarian. In 1642, he and his troops defeated the far superior army of the Earl of Derby at Read Bridge, thus ensuring the end of Royalist resistance in the north. For a century from 1699, the hall was left empty. Then, in the 19th century, Charlotte Brontë visited the house on a number of occasions.

The Shuttleworth family left the house in 1970. It is now in the hands of the National Trust, who lease it to Lancashire County Council. The hall and the estate buildings have been restored to Barry's original designs. It is claimed that the plasterwork and ceilings in the dining room and long gallery are the best in the county. In the gallery is a fireplace bearing the arms of James I. Beneath the gallery is the date 1605, plus the initials of the three Shuttleworth brothers who erected the hall. There is a collection of 17th-century paintings on loan from the National Portrait Gallery.

The Rachel Kay-Shuttleworth collection of lace and needlework, the second most important in the country after that of the Victoria and Albert Museum, is based here. She was the last member of the family to live in the house. It was her wish that the collection should be used by students of the art. Although there are only 500 exhibits on show, they are merely part of a total of 14,000, which are rotated over the year. It includes some of her own work, in particular the bed hangings and counterpane she embroidered early in the century.

PARBOLD [West Lancashire]

SD4911: 5 miles (8km) NE of Ormskirk

The parish stands close to the valley of the River Douglas and the Leeds and Liverpool Canal. It shelters beneath Parbold Hill, which rises quite suddenly from the

Parbold Bottle

Lancashire Plain. The first historic record of the village is in documents from Burscough Priory and Cockersand Abbey. After belonging to the Lathom family until the 17th century, ownership passed through the hands of a number of landlords before being acquired by the Scarisbrick family two centuries later. The village has been important for coal mining and quarrying, the produce being taken away by canal, but is now a peaceful residential area.

On the east side of the village, on the slopes of Parbold Hill, the **church of Christ Church** was built in 1875 to replace the old Douglas Chapel. A stone cross near the canal marks the site of the chapel. It is reputed to have been erected by the Knights Hospitallers of St John, but can definitely be traced back to at least 1240. Much altered over the years, it was finally demolished in 1875. One of its ministers, John Schofield, started the first Presbyterian chapel in the county, at Tunley in Wrightington, after his ejection in 1662. Built on the slopes of Parbold Hill, the church has a 1648 pulpit which was transported from the old chapel.

Built by Thomas Crisp in the middle of the 18th century, **Parbold Hall**, on the east side of the hill, stands on the site of a previous building. The east side has three storeys, whereas the apparently newer west side has two. At the beginning of the 19th century, the hall was used by Benedictines from France. It is the home of Peter Moores of the Liverpool Littlewoods Pools family.

By turning right along a track off the road just before the top of Parbold Hill, **Parbold Bottle** is reached. Gaining its name from its bottle-shaped structure, it was erected to commemorate the passing of the Reform Act in 1832.

The **windmill** by the canal at the Station Road Bridge was built to replace a watermill of 1794 on the River Douglas, known as Nathan's Mill, It was, in its turn, replaced in 1850 by a larger, steam-driven corn mill, now residential apartments. The adjoining dry dock was the start of the planned canal route through Leyland and Whalley to Skipton.

The Roman Catholic **church of Our Lady and All Saints** on Lancaster Lane, with its tall, slender spire, was built in 1884.

PAYTHORNE [Ribble Valley]
SD8251: 2 miles (3km) N of Gisburn

Once a busy village with a corn mill, Paythorne expanded quickly with an influx of weavers in the 19th century. Since then the population has slowly reduced in size. It is now mainly a farming and residential community. The name derived from the meaning 'a thorn tree belonging to Pai'. Legend has it that this thorn tree was near the pub and was a meeting place of the local community.

PENDLETON [Ribble Valley]
SD7539: 2 miles (3km) SE of Clitheroe

The village lies at the foot of Pendle Hill. There is a stream flowing through the middle, alongside the road. It is designated a conservation area. In 1969, an urn from the Bronze Age was discovered, which can now be seen in the museum at Clitheroe Castle. In the Domesday Book, the name 'Penictune' is recorded. On the parish border with Wiswell, south of the village, is the grave of Jeppe Knave, a poor man who was murdered. Because there was no one to pay for his burial in the churchyard, he was laid to rest near where he fell.

The **church of All Saints**, at the east end of the village, was built as a chapel in 1847. An aisle was added in 1893. Opposite it, the now defunct school was one of the first National Schools to be opened in 1837.

On what was once the main road, at the west end of the street, the **Swan with Two Necks Inn**, built in 1776, was a coaching inn. Its name comes from the practice of marking the bills of swans.

Fiddle Bridge, to the rear of **Standen Hall**, is a stone in the shape of a fiddle which serves as a bridge across the stream. The hall is an impressive stone structure at the end of a long avenue of beach trees. **Devil's Bridge** is an old packhorse crossing.

In a wooded glade one and a half miles (2km) north of the village, **Little Mearley Hall** is a 16th-century structure. The bay windows at its eastern end were brought from Sawley Abbey.

PENWORTHAM [South Ribble]
SD5228: 2 miles (3km) SW of Preston

Being at the lowest crossing place of the

River Ribble made the village an important strategic point. In the 12th century a Benedictine priory, formed with monks from Evesham Abbey, was founded. It was never more than small and poor. It became a manor house in the 16th century, was rebuilt in 1832, but eventually demolished early in the 20th century. The Normans built a castle on Castle Hill to defend the ford. The lower part of the village surrounds the bridge; the upper is around the church. Today the area is mainly populated by commuters.

The main building that most people notice is the strange, tall edifice on the corner of Cop Lane. This is a **water tower**, built in 1880 to upgrade the village's inadequate water system.

An old tramway runs through a hollow at the rear of the **church of St Mary**, reached via Priory Lane, off the A59 in Higher Penwortham. This was the ancient route to the river crossing below.

The earliest record of a church on the site was in 1140. The tower is 15th century, and the chancel from a century earlier. There have been a number of restorations down the years and the nave was completely rebuilt in 1855. Behind the church, which is approached through trees and parkland, is the mound of the Norman castle. Some think that there was a Roman fort on the site previous to that. The site of the priory was somewhere on the approach path to the church. Through the large, wooden lych-gate is the church building, with a battlemented tower. The most historic interior artefacts are two helmets dating from 1590, the 1677 font and some cannon balls from the time of the Civil War.

In 1915 a new crossing replaced the **Old Bridge** of 1759, at the lowest point of the river. This itself had replaced one of 1754, after an arch had given way.

Penwortham Hall is actually in Middleforth Green, off New Lane, south of Lower Penwortham. It was the home of John Horrocks, the wealthiest local cotton manufacturer. Having completed the hall in 1801, Horrocks survived only three years to enjoy it, dying at the age of 36.

At **Hurst Grange Country Park**, in Cop Lane, there are a number of rare water plants, including the penny royal and the flowering rush.

PICKUP BANK [Blackburn]
SD7223: 2 miles (3km) E of Darwen

The small hamlet was, until the early years of the 20th century, active in weaving, coal mining and quarrying. **Old Rosin's Inn**, at the centre of the community, received its name because of the resin which used to be used to polish the dance floor.

PILLING [Wyre]
SD4048: 4½ miles (7km) E of Fleetwood

The old church is the focal point of attention in this village, set amidst the flat, drained land looking towards Morecambe Bay. The name derives from the word for 'small creek'. With the surrounding stretches of marshland, it is ideal territory for birdwatchers. **Pilling Embankment**, north-east of the village, was erected in 1983 as a protection against incoming tides. At **Lanes End** is an amenity area from which it is possible to view birds. Over the river bridge to the east of the village is a windmill, now shorn of its sails.

Little has changed at the old, red sandstone **church of St John the Baptist** down the years. Since the building of the new church within its sight in 1877, it has remained substantially unaltered. The

Old and new churches at Pilling

only change that has taken place was the raising of the walls in 1813 to accommodate the installation of galleries. The simple, low-lying structure was built in 1710, or so the date over the doorway says. Above the door is a sundial dated 1766, with the name of the Reverend G. Holden attached. The warning on it is, 'Thus eternity approacheth.' Perhaps a reference to the length of his sermons.

Inside, there is a gallery on the north side. Underneath it are box pews where the wealthier families sat. The others had to make do with the simple wooden benches on the flagged floor. The triple-decker pulpit is unusual in that the second tier is alongside the other two. The altar is surrounded by circular communion rails.

A village tradition, started by the monks at Cockersand Abbey, is the holding of an annual coffee feast to commemorate the beheading of John the Baptist. There were at least two notable incumbents. One was Reverend James Potter, who in the early years of the 19th century was known as a fighter and a looter of wrecked ships. The other, the above-mentioned Reverend George Holden, vicar from 1758-67, was the author of *Holden's Tide Tables*, which can still be relied upon today.

PLEASINGTON [Blackburn]

SD6427: 2½ miles (4km) SW of Blackburn

In the Domesday Book, the village is referred to as Plesigtune, 'the village of Plessa's people'. It is a residential community bordering on the edge of the River Dunsop and Witton Park.

A hilltop position on Pleasington Lane befits the imposing grandeur of **Pleasington Priory**, dedicated to St Mary and John the Baptist. Although built in 1819, the Roman Catholic church has a range of architectural styles from Saxon to Gothic. Its enormous rose window, on the road side, helps to give the impression of a large Oxbridge chapel. The design of the west doorway was taken from that of the chapter house at Whalley Abbey. The towerless structure was paid for by a contemporary owner of **Pleasington Old Hall,** which had been erected by the de Hoghtons in 1587.

Because the landlord wore clogs and a billycock hat, the name of the Bay Horse Inn was altered to the **Clog and Billycock.** Opposite this and the **Railway Hotel** are good examples of weavers' cottages.

Witton Country Park consists of 480 acres (195 hectares) of wood and farmland, including Billinge Hill. It was at one time part of the estate of Witton House. This had been built by the Feilden family in 1800. They had the largest landholdings in the area. Joseph Feilden was Member of Parliament for Blackburn in the early 19th century. The estate came into the hands of Blackburn Corporation in 1946, but the house had to be demolished in 1954 because of dilapidation and neglect. Only outhouses, the coach-houses and the stables are left. These are the venue for the visitor centre. This contains an exhibition of farm implements, horse-drawn carriages and machinery.

Situated in a wooded valley, **Old Hall Nature Reserve** has a walled garden, specialising in wild and garden flowers, as well as thirteen species of butterfly.

POULTON-LE-FYLDE [Fylde]
SD3539: 3 miles (5km) NE of Blackpool

A staggering discovery took place at Poulton-le-Fylde in 1970. The bones of an elk, with hunters' darts in them, were discovered at Carleton. They were dated to c10,000BC. An indication of Roman activity is a causeway called **Danes Pad** that runs towards Pilling. An ancient settlement centring on the market place, the town serves as the commercial centres for the villages around it. 'Poulton' indicates 'town by the pool', the 'le Fylde' was not added until the mid-19th century. The town was a thriving port in the 18th century and farming made it a busy market place.

A number of the houses surrounding the **Market Place** are 18th century. They were built to replace those lost in the serious fire of 1732. This was the centre of the old village. In the middle of this open area leading to the church, a number of items from the past have been assembled. Nearest to the road are the stone stocks and then, in a neat line, the market cross, the fish stone from which fish used to be sold, the 17th-century whipping post, and a lamp, which was erected in 1887 to commemorate Queen Victoria's Jubilee.

The pirate's grave, near the door at the south of the sanctuary of the **church of St Chad**, is that of Edward Sherdley. It is so named, not because he had any known record of piracy, but because a skull and crossbones is carved on the headstone. Also in the churchyard are the remains of two old crosses.

A church is mentioned in records of 1094, but the present building is the result of a restructuring that took place in 1751. The red brick walls of the church were covered by the stone seen today. The tower is 17th century and the apse was added in 1868. There were further renovations in 1883 and 1955. The inside is Georgian, with galleries that contain box pews, candlesockets and a fine staircase leading up to them. Under the gallery are stately chairs, marked for the churchwardens and sidesmen. A carved 17th-century screen, at the front of the choir vestry, formerly surrounded the Fleetwood-Hesketh family pew. A 1710 chandelier and an ancient bishop's chair are in the sanctuary. Behind the choir stalls are brass memorials from the old church. The pulpit comes from the 17th century, its beautiful panels being discovered only when it was replaced by a new one. Near it is a 17th-century bench. Underneath is a vault constructed in 1699. There are a number of memorials to the Fleetwood-Hesketh family.

PREESALL [Wyre]

SD3647: 2 miles (3km) SE of Fleetwood

Small pools and pits are the only evidence left of the thriving 19th-century salt-mining industry on the River Wyre estuary. Mining began in the 19th century, the salt being taken first to the Fleetwood Salt Works and later the **ICI Hillhouse** complex. Constant flooding of the brine wells led to the end of mining in 1930. Seven years earlier, warning had been given when five acres (2 hectares) of land suddenly disappeared under brine water. The hamlet itself is a small group of houses and cottages clustered together. The only remains of earlier history are ancient flints thrown up in the marshland, and a find of Roman coins at Hackensall Hall.

Hackensall Hall, near the estuary of the River Wyre, on the site of the Viking 'Hakon's Hough', is substantially the building that was reconstructed by Richard Fleetwood in 1656. A stone in a wall of the building bears his initials and those of his wife, as well as the building date. He was the last member of the family to live at the hall. In 1729, Edward Fleetwood sold the hall and estate. From that time on, the hall was lived in by tenant farmers.

Parrox Hall, on the road to Knott End, dates from the late 16th century and has been renovated on many occasions since. From the time the owners of the Hackensall estate no longer lived at the hall, the owners of Parrox Hall became regarded as the local squires. From the middle of the 17th century, the Elletson family were resident. In the early 19th century Daniel Elletson had much to do with the expansion of Fleetwood as a sea resort.

Noted for its sea lavender, **Barnaby's Sands Nature Reserve** is 142 acres (57 hectares) of marshland and shingle near the River Wyre. It lies south-west of the village, beyond the old brine wells from which salt was extracted.

PRESTON [Preston]

SD5429: 5 miles (8km) N of Leyland

'Once every Preston Guild,' has become an everyday phrase to describe something that does not happen too often. This is because the Guild celebrations take place in the town only once every 20 years. Since Henry II granted the right in 1328, the Guild Court has been held here. Members of the Guild committed themselves to a high standard of integrity in work and business. If they did not maintain standards of work and honesty, they had their membership cancelled. From 1542, it was convened every twenty years. Except for the war years, it has been held regularly ever since. Its main function used to be to give local notables the freedom of the town and the privileges that went with that. Nowadays, it is mainly a chance to hold a big festival.

The town grew up at the highest navigable point of the River Ribble and its charters granted by monarchs can be traced back to AD1100. Only the present names of Stoneygate, Friargate and Fishergate are a reminder of earlier times. Friargate was the site of a 13th-century friary.

Although there are not many old buildings still standing, the area around **Winckley Square** has a number of Georgian houses. Many kings and nobles passed through the town over the centuries. Perhaps the most unwelcome was Robert the Bruce, who burned the place down in 1323. 'Proud Preston' as it is often called, soon recovered from the setback. The Battle of Preston in 1648 was a turning point in the Civil War. The Royalists were defeated by Cromwell out on

Ribbleton Moor, and then at the Ribble Bridge. In 1715 the town became the venue of another lost cause when a Stuart army supporting the claims of James was defeated.

A tale is told that the vicar of Preston at the time had the nerve to use prayers for the king. When threatened with death by a rebel soldier, he said, 'Do your duty, and I will do mine.' The soldier withdrew. When the king heard of the cleric's bravery he promised to make him a bishop. In due course, the vicar became Bishop of Chester.

Richard Arkwright, the inventor of the spinning frame, was born here in 1732. The cotton industry arrived with the building of the first mill in 1777, but the name that dominated the local industry was that of John Horrocks. Between 1791 and 1802, he erected four mills, from where his family carried on the business after his death in 1804. His success was due to his idea of having the spinning and the weaving process done in the same place. With many ups and downs in the intervening years, cotton remained the main industry until the 1920s. By then, industry had diversified – the Ribble Navigation Company had been formed and the dock complex built. Now both cotton and shipping are defunct.

In the 19th century, the Temperance Movement started in the town and spread quickly throughout the country.

The town has been the administrative centre of the county since 1798. Based on County Hall, Lancashire County Council has its offices and meetings in the town. It is a prosperous and expanding centre of commerce and industry.

Until the Reformation, the dedication of the **church of St John the Divine**, in Church Street, was to St Wilfrid, an Archbishop of York. As the country ceased to be Roman Catholic, links with the past were removed. The reformers felt that a church commemorating a saint from the Bible was preferable to a Catholic one. In the 16th century, the building was pulled down and rebuilt. The process was repeated in 1855, with the erection of a structure with a pinnacled roof. It is the civic church of the town and noted for heraldic stained glass and the Feibush mural.

The **church of St Walburge**, in Weston Street, is a landmark in the town because of its 309ft (94m) spire. The Roman Catholic church has a steep, hammerbeam roof, but no aisle. It also had a famous architect in **Joseph Hansom**, who built it in the Decorated Gothic style. His fame came not so much from the building of churches, as from his invention of the Hansom cab, originally known as the 'Patent Safety Cab', in 1834. The church opened in 1854, but the tapering spire was not completed until 1866. It is made of limestone, the bottom part of the tower being railway sleepers of that stone. The window at the west end, in the form of a rose, has a diameter of 22ft (7m). It is now a Grade 1 listed building.

Originally the mother church of St Walburge's, the **church of St Wilfrid**, in St Wilfrid Street, was erected in 1793, but was extensively restored in 1879.

Hidden away between St George's shopping centre and the Ringway, off Lune Street, the **church of St George the Martyr** was built in 1723 in Florentine Romanesque style. It is designed in the form of a basilica and its walls and ceilings are covered with paintings and designs. The Father Willis organ is one of the best of its type.

Edmund Harris was a local vicar who left money in his will for the building of the **Harris Museum and Art Gallery**, which is the focal point of Market

Square. A local architect, James Hibbert, who was also an Alderman, drew up a design in Greek classical style. It took eleven years to complete, but the final product opened in 1893. With its fluted columns, it resembles a Greek temple. Some have compared it with the British Museum. From the beginning it housed a collection of British paintings, which have been added to ever since. Turner and Hunt feature amongst the artists who are represented, as well as some 18th-century pieces by Arthur Devis, a local painter. There are a large number of prints from the 16th century onwards on show. Displays of porcelain, pottery and glass include a selection from over 2500 scent bottles, watches, 18th-century drinking glasses, Victorian greeting cards and 18th- to 20th-century women's dresses. The work of local 19th-century poet and doctor, Francis Thompson, is included. His best-known poem is *The Hound of Heaven*.

The 'Story of Preston' gallery traces the history of the town from the time of the Domesday Book. There is a model of one of the mill complexes and reconstructions of a corner shop, a room in an 18th-century terraced house and a 17th-century market stall. There is a constantly changing programme of exhibitions and displays.

The **Obelisk** was erected in Market Square in 1782. In the early 19th century, a gas light was added to it. In 1853 it was removed to Hollowforth Hall, north of Woodplumpton, where it remains at present. A 33ft (10m) replacement was erected in the square in 1979.

The single roof span of the 1875 **covered market**, close to Market Square, is on columns of cast iron and covers the three thousand square metres of the market. The architect of the **war memorial**, unveiled in 1926, was Giles Gilbert Scott,

the designer of the Cenotaph in London, the red telephone kiosk, and Liverpool Anglican Cathedral.

Sadly, Scott's **town hall** of 1867 was destroyed by fire in 1947. The present town hall was opened in 1933 and has carved figures on the exterior representing the main industries of the town.

Based in the old court buildings, the **Museum of Lancashire** in Stanley Street covers the history of the county from the middle ages until the present. Relics from the medieval abbey can be seen, such as a processional cross discovered in the Lancaster area. The political role of county families is developed, particularly in 19th-century local elections. The history of the fire service, police and schools is also to be seen. A schoolroom from Edwardian times and a cell from Darwen police station are particularly noteworthy. This is also the regimental museum of three regiments, namely the 14/20 Kings Hussars, The Duke of Lancaster's Own Yeomanry and the Queen's Lancashire Regiment. Swords, uniforms and a Victoria Cross are displayed, plus reconstructions of a 19th-century officers' mess and World War I trench.

More army history is on view at the **Queen's Lancashire Regiment Museum** at Fulwood Barracks, containing memorabilia of the North Lancashire Loyal Regiment, which is now part of the Queen's Lancashire Regiment. Amongst the exhibits are six Russian drums from the Crimean War, a silver tortoise from the 1806 Battle of Maida in Italy and souvenirs brought back from the Siege of Kimberley in the Boer War.

The **British Commercial Vehicle Museum** in King Street has an important collection of vehicles from the past.

Deepdale Road is the home of soccer's oldest league ground in the world. Preston North End FC will be the venue of the **Football Museum** covering the history of the country's most popular game. Also in Deepdale Road, the **Moor Park Observatory** commemorates Jeremiah Horrocks, the 18th-century Lancashire cleric and astronomer. It is a centre for research managed by the School of Physics and Astonomy at the University of Central Lancashire.

The five impressive arches of the **Ribble Viaduct** are best seen from Miller Park. The viaduct was erected in 1838 on the Preston to Wigan railway line.

Formed from a section of the Walton Junction to Preston railway line, which closed in 1972, the **Preston Junction Nature Reserve** was opened in 1990 and is now an oasis for plants, flowers, butterflies and birds. The line was opened in 1850 and known as the Preston Extension line. Near the bridge over the river, only two arches remain of what was once a 52-arch viaduct.

QUERNMORE [Lancaster and Morecambe]

SD5160: 3 miles (5km) SW of Lancaster

Once part of a royal hunting forest, the name of the village, pronounced 'qworma', derives from the quern or grindstone that was used in a quarry. Today it is still a peaceful village, surrounded by dairy farming country.

The **church of St Peter**, located beyond the main village, looks as if it is 14th century, but it is, in fact, the result of an 1860 rebuild of the previous 1834 building. The east window was originally in a ship. It was placed in the church after it was rescued from the wreckage following a sea disaster.

Half a mile (1km) to the east, the moorland sweeps up beyond Rowton Brook to Clougha Pike. In Tombstone Meadow is the grave of a local farmer. For years he had been in dispute with a neighbour about the rights to peat-cutting in the area. The dispute was never resolved during his lifetime. The farmer gave orders that after his death he should be buried in an upright position, facing the track down which his neighbour travelled daily with his cartload of peat. He wished to be a constant reminder of past grievances, even after death. A track to the left, west of the village crossroads, leads to Rooten Brook Farm, beyond which lies Tombstone Meadow. In the 17th century, a lady named Jenny Cragg lived at the farm. Her son-in-law was a Quaker. Persecuted because of his faith, he was sent to the West Indies, but died en route. His wife, Jenny's daughter, died soon after, leaving two young sons. Jenny travelled to London on her pony and carried the two boys back to the farm.

Set in spacious grounds $1\frac{1}{2}$ miles (2km) north of the village, **Quernmore Park Hall**, formerly the site of a priory, was built in 1793.

RAWTENSTALL [Rossendale]

SD8023: $3\frac{1}{2}$ miles (6km) W of Bacup

Rawtenstall is one of a line of communities along the Rossendale Valley which owe their growth and prosperity to the textile industry. The area had previously comprised a number of scattered dairy farming communities in the Forest of Rossendale. Rawtenstall is the terminus for the **East Lancashire Steam Railway**, the route through the Irwell Valley having been restored in 1991. The railway opened in 1846, linking the Manchester to Bolton line with Radcliffe. After closure in 1972, the efforts of the

Weavers' cottages, Rawtenstall

Preservation Society led to the reopening of the 17-mile (27km) stretch through Ramsbottom to Bury. The town boasts, in Bank Street, the last **Temperance Bar** in the country. Amongst the oldest groups of remaining houses are **Newhouses Cottages**, built in 1695 in Grange Avenue. One of the cottages has a witches' post by the hearth. This was supposed to protect the household against evil.

A tower on the south side of the building identifies the 19th-century **church of St Mary**. There is an archway at the bottom of the tower and one pinnacle on its top. At the side of the church, a clock tower indicates the site of a school built in 1939 by the Whitehead family, leading cotton magnates in the town. Afterwards, the Astoria Ballroom was built there.

Restored by the local Civic Society, the **Weavers' Cottage**, at Fall Barn Fold on the Bacup Road, is one of the last of its type from the 1780s. It was a development from individual weavers working in their own cottages and was a stepping stone to the mill system. The word 'cottage' is a euphemism for a large, three-storey building. The workshops were on the top two floors. They lived in now demolished accommodation adjacent to the cottage. The roof is timber-trussed and the windows mullioned. The weavers worked on the upper floor because it afforded more light. On display is a handloom and spinning wheel, plus reconstructions of a clogger's shop and 19th-century kitchen.

In Whitaker Park, the **Rossendale Museum** concentrates on the local and social history of the area, with information about such matters as transport and the making of clogs. It also includes a reconstruction of a 19th-century drawing room. There is also a collection of art and furniture, and a section on the history of taxidermy. The museum is housed in a building that was erected in 1840 for a 19th-century, millionaire mill owner. The Hardman family were the leading cotton magnates in the town. By 1902 the house had opened as a museum. On Cribden Hill, above the park, is the large dry ski slope, called **Ski Rossendale**.

The Groundwork Trust, responsible

for so much good environmental work in the area, is based in what were the outbuildings of **Hardman's Mill**, which is now used for offices. The area is close by the railway station. The Hardman family had it rebuilt in 1862, with vaults which were constructed of fireproof brick. Around the top of the chimney is a balustrade of cast iron. On the back of the buildings, the words 'Hardman Brothers' stand out in relief. The **Irwell Way Sculpture Trail** starts from here. On the river bank is the 'Willow Tree' sculpture. This is possibly the world's largest live sculpture. The 'Talking Heads' is a wood depiction of two heads in conversation. Besides the main roundabout in Bochalt Way is the 'Bocholt Metal Tree'. Bocholt is the German link town. At Cloughfold is the 'Logarythms', a mathematical construction made of logs. The final two sculptures are both in Waterfoot. 'Monument of Nature', at St Michael's Centre, is built into the hillside. 'Weave', at the Glen, reveals fabric under a microscope.

Holly Mount House was built in 1835 by the Whitehead brothers, another leading cotton family in the town. It has been described as three houses in one. Keen churchgoers, the brothers also founded Longholme Wesleyan church, designed in classical style in 1842. A dispute in the church led the brothers to build Haslington Road United Methodist Free church.

READ [Ribble Valley]

SD7735: 3 miles (5km) N of Accrington

Whins Lane is on the route of a track at least 5000 years old that led to Whalley. This gives some idea of the long history of this rural village. By comparison, the **church of St John the Evangelist** was built as recently as 1884, and its steeple added in 1911.

Set in wooded parkland to the west of the village, **Read Hall** was constructed in 1799 and much altered in the early 19th century. It is of Grecian design with a lead dome. The building it replaced was the home of Roger Nowell, the legal officer instrumental in the Pendle Witches going for trial at Lancaster Castle in 1612. Another contemporary member of the Nowell family, Alexander, became a Dean of St Paul's Cathedral in London. He is said to have been responsible for the invention of beer. After accidentally leaving some ale in water for a couple of days, he discovered that it had become frothy. The hall had come into the hands of the Nowell family in 1364. In 1799, it was bought by Richard Fort, a local Member of Parliament. He is reputed to have gained election to Parliament because his mother put gold coins into the missionary boxes of houses she was canvassing for support. His other claim to fame is that of unsuccessfully attempting to make wine from sycamore juice.

Near **Read Old Bridge**, the Royalist troops were defeated by local supporters of the Parliamentary cause in April 1643.

REEDLEY [Pendle]

SD8536: 2 miles (3km) N of Burnley

A residential area linking Burnley with Brierfield, there are historical remnants of its more rural days. **Laund House** was the home of John and Robert Nutter. They were 16th-century Roman Catholic priests who were persecuted for standing by their beliefs. **Greenhead Farm**, off Greenhead Lane, west of the village and motorway, received many visits from Old Chattox, one of the supposed witches of Pendle.

RIBCHESTER [Ribble Valley]

SD6535: 7½ miles (12km) NE of Preston

Roman history pervades this village, the only one actually on the banks of the River Ribble. The three-arched bridge of 1774 crosses the river at what was once the Roman fording point. It was the general Agricola who established the fort of Bremetennacum Veteranorum in AD80. Soon a thriving community developed and roads radiated to many different parts of the country through the Pennines and the Lune Valley. The garrison was able to guard this strategic centre. It comprised 500 cavalry, the first contingent of whom came from northern Spain. It was replaced in AD175 by soldiers from the country we now know as Hungary. Following Saxon and Norman settlers, the village is mentioned in the Domesday Book. In the Civil War this was strong Royalist territory and a number of skirmishes took place in the locality. From the middle of the 18th century, handloom weaving and flax production became im-portant industries in the village. By the end of the 18th-century, cotton and bob-bin turning had replaced them. After their decline, the village reverted to rural tranquility. Some of the cottages from the textile era can be seen in Church Street.

Built on the site of the Roman fort, the **Ribchester Roman Museum** opened on Riverside in 1914. It is the only one in the county to devote itself entirely to Roman history. There are many objects to be seen from the excavations that have taken place in the past century. Amongst them are coins, pottery, leather and woodwork, as well as stonework in the form of altars and inscriptions. Notewor-thy is the tombstone of a cavalry rider en-gaged in combat. A replica of the Ribchester Parade Helmet is on display, along with other models of what the Ro-man and Celtic people may have looked like. The authentic helmet was unearthed in 1796 and is held by the British Mu-seum in London. Exhibitions follow the social, domestic, religious and military

Almshouses, Ribchester

history of the area from Roman times until the end of the fourth century. Erosion of the river banks over the centuries has meant that there are few external Roman remains left to be seen. Among them are the granaries, part of the west rampart and security ditch and a little of the bathhouse. The Roman site covered six acres (2 hectares). It belongs to the National Trust, but a large portion of this cannot be excavated because it lies beneath the old churchyard.

Behind the museum is the 13th-century **church of St Wilfrid**, dedicated to the seventh-century Archbishop of York. At the Synod of Whitby in 664, he was the main advocate of moving towards the Roman parish system rather than retaining the monastic scheme of the Celtic church. The circular churchyard suggests that the church is erected within the Roman earthworks. The building itself is 13th century, with a 15th-century tower and an Early English nave. To admit more light, dormer windows were installed in the south aisle roof in 1712. The chancel, restored after a fire in 1917, is unusual in that its floor is lower than that of the nave. The small window on its north wall was either a leper's squint or used as an Easter Sepulchre. The ornately carved pulpit, now in a fragile condition, dates from 1636. The Dutton Choir, on the north side, is a 14th-century chantry chapel and contains a mural of St Christopher and a 14th-century aumbry, or wall cupboard, in which the sacraments were kept. This was only discovered during restoration work in 1924. Above the altar is a window which contains some pieces of medieval glass. On the south side, by the chancel, is the Houghton Cage Pew, which has a 14th-century screen. At the back of the church is the 1736 oak gallery. The two stone pillars supporting the gallery are thought to be Roman. Beneath the gallery is a churchwardens' box pew and a simple font, which may be Saxon. Carvings regarding the coming of Christ are found on the steps of the preaching cross in the churchyard. On the sundial near the churchyard entrance are the words, 'I am a shadow. So art Thou. I mark time. Dost thou?'

In what was formerly a Co-op shop, the **Museum of Childhood** in Church Street contains a collection of dolls, toys and models. There are 54 doll's houses, a twenty-piece model fairground in working order, a collection of items connected with Tom Thumb and a flea circus. The latter is linked with a video of the circus in action at the old Belle Vue in Manchester.

Pillars in the porch of the **White Bull Inn**, in Water Street, are thought to have come from the Roman temple of Minerva. The inn was erected in 1707. Behind it are the remains of a 2nd-century Roman bathhouse.

Built in 1789, the Roman Catholic **church of St Peter and St Paul** has a round-corner 'ding dong bell' well outside.

The two-storey almshouses erected by the Sherburnes in 1728 can be found along Stydd Lane. At the front is an impressive flight of steps. From the almshouses, a dirt track across a field leads to the simple chapel that comprises the **church of St Saviour** at Stydd. It is reckoned to be the oldest place of worship for miles around. At one stage belonging to the Knights Hospitallers of St John, the north wall dates from the 12th century, the south wall has a Norman window and the doorway is 13th century. The 15th-century font is carved, and the pulpit and screen are 17th century. It was restored in 1925 and is sometimes used by St Wilfrid's for worship.

RIMINGTON [Ribble Valley]

SD8045: 4½ miles (7km) NE of Clitheroe

Called Renitone in the Domesday Book, the scattered rural community includes the hamlets of Stopper Lane, Martin Top, Newby, Middop and Howgill. There is no parish church in the area. Rimington was the home of Frances Duckworth, the 19th-century hymn writer. One of her best known tunes is dedicated to the village. An old lead mine at Stopper Lane indicates the local importance of the industry in the 18th century.

RISHTON [Hyndburn]

SD7330: 2½ miles (4km) NE of Burnley

The name means 'dwelling place among the rushes'. The village is credited with being the first to produce calico, in 1766. The large, pinnacled tower of the 19th-century **church of St Peter and St Paul** stands at the corner of the A678 and Church Street. Today the village is better known for its cricket team. At one time it employed Viv Richards, the West Indies and Lancashire player, as its professional player in the Lancashire League.

RIVINGTON [Chorley]

SD6214: 3½ miles (6km) SE of Chorley

Scattered on the surrounding moors, burial sites from the Bronze Age indicate very old settlements in the Rivington area. **Pikestones Chambered Cairns**, 1 mile (2km) east of High Bullough Reservoir on Anglezarke, are comprised of five large stones, whereas the damaged cairn at **Noon Hill**, 1 mile (2km) east of Rivington Hall, on Rivington Moor, is circular. It is thought that the name of the village derives from a word meaning

'place of the mountain ash'. A Roman road went along the bottom of the valley, where the reservoirs are now. From the 13th to the 16th century, the lords of the manor were the Pilkington family. At the centre of the small village are the church, chapel, old vicarage, post office and stocks.

The names of Rivington and Lord Leverhulme are forever associated. He was born William Hesketh Lever in 1851 in Bolton. He became a partner in his father's wholesale grocery business. In 1884, William brought out his own brand of 'Sunlight Soap'. So successful was the factory that he set up in Warrington to manufacture it, that he had to build a new, bigger one near Birkenhead. Lever at the same time built a model village named Port Sunlight. The business was so successful that it eventually employed over 100,000 workers. In 1930 the firm became part of the Unilever company. Besides being a devoted churchgoer, Lord Leverhulme, as he eventually became, was Mayor of Bolton and Liberal Member of Parliament for Wirral. His greatest personal enterprise was in the Rivington area. In 1899 he bought Rivington Hall and its estate. He kept 45 acres (18 hectares) for his own use, and donated the rest to Bolton Corporation in 1902, to be used as a public space (Lever Park).

After encountering much opposition, the **reservoirs scheme** was allowed to go ahead in the mid-19th century. Chorley Reservoir was built on Anglezarke Moor in 1850, followed by seven others – Upper and Lower Rivington, Anglezarke, Red Bank, Lower and Upper Roddlesworth and Yarrow – in the years between 1850 and 1875.

Lead Mines Clough, flowing into the north-east corner of the Yarrow Reservoir, took its name from the lead mines which were worked from the 13th century until 1837. The remains of a lime and waterwheel pit and the top of a shaft can still be seen. Above the clough is a memorial to the crew of a Wellington Bomber which crashed on the moor in 1943, killing all six.

Situated on the east bank of Lower Rivington Reservoir, near the southern end, **Liverpool Castle** is a replica, completed as a ruin, of the long-forgotten castle. Although commenced in 1912, it took nearly 20 years to complete the task.

Hall Barn and **Great House Barn** stand at either end of Hall Drive, half a mile (1km) south of the village. Although possibly older, they are known to date from the early 18th century. Because of alterations, only the oak cruck trusses and the stone on which they are built are original. Their main purpose was to act as storage for animal feed and for hay. It was Lord Leverhulme's idea to have the barns renovated and used for refreshments for visitors.

The Pilkington family owned red-brick **Rivington Hall** from 1202 to 1616. It was then sold to the Levers. Originally a half-timbered structure, the façade of the west front dates from 1744. The south wing was added in the 19th century. At the back of the house are some remains of the 17th-century building.

At 1200ft (361 m), the **Pike Tower**, 1 mile (2km) south-east of the village, commands extensive views. The Pike was one of a chain of beacons across the country. It was lit in 1588, when the Spanish Armada was sighted off the coast of southern England. The square tower was built in 1733. Inside is a room with a fireplace and a cellar, but it is not open to the public. After years of neglect, disrepair and talk of demolition, the tower was renovated in 1974. Each year there is a Pike Fair on Good Friday and a Pike Race on Easter Saturday.

The tall television mast of **Winter Hill**, 1½ miles (2km) east of the Pike, dominates the area. Near it is a memorial to a young man of 23 years who was murdered crossing the moor. On an iron pillar is the inscription, 'George Henderson, traveller, native of Annan, Dumfriesshire, who was barbarously murdered on Rivington Moor at noonday, 9th November, 1838.' Apparently his last words were, 'I am robbed, I am killed.'

On the slopes below Rivington Pike, Lord Leverhulme built his **terraced gardens**. In 1901, a fine, wooden bungalow, called Roynton Cottage, was erected as his own private residence. This survived until 1913, when it was burned down by a suffragette. It was quickly replaced by a more durable stone house, known as The Bungalow, to which Leverhulme added a ballroom in 1922. Work on the terraced gardens had commenced in 1905. Over the next fifteen years, Leverhulme spent about £250,000 on his plans. Three lodges were constructed. A bridge was placed over the ravine. A Japanese garden was landscaped around the lake and a walled kitchen garden made. Stone House, a gatehouse with an archway over the drive, was built in 1910. A croquet lawn, tennis court, Great Lawn, Long Walk and Lever's walk were added at various stages, as well as Seven Arch Bridge and a swimming pool. One fascinating building that remains standing is Pigeon Tower, built in 1910. Lady Leverhulme used the top floor as her sewing room, so that she could enjoy the lovely views of the surrounding countryside. When Lord Leverhulme died in 1925, work came to a stop and the gardens deteriorated badly. Liverpool Corporation took over ownership in 1947 and demolished most of the buildings. In 1974 the North West Water Authority succeeded Liverpool Corporation and has done much to improve the area.

In the village itself, the small, turreted **church of Holy Trinity**, on a hill overlooking the reservoir, was built in 1541 by Richard Pilkington. There are records of a previous building in the 13th century. In the churchyard, opposite the main door of the church, is a small, 16th-century tower, built to house a bell but never used for that purpose.

A 19th-century vicar gained the nickname 'Steeple Jackson' when he climbed up the steeple to replace the weathercock. In the church is a 19th-century copy of the Pilkington Picture, which is a picture of the genealogy of the family. The pulpit is 15th century and the chandelier 18th century. The lych-gate was erected in 1923. A number of carved, ancient stones are by the church pathway near the lych-gate, and under a tree a little further along the path. Little is known of their origin.

At the centre of the small number of houses that make up the village is the green, on which are placed the stocks. A tablet in the **Unitarian Chapel** by the green has the inscription, 'Revd Samuele Nevtone driven from ye church on Bartholomew Sunday, 1662.' It was discovered by workmen doing road repairs. The bits were put together and placed in the chapel. Newton was ejected as vicar of Holy Trinity in 1662. The box pews and the majority of the fabric of the original chapel have been retained. A date of 1703 on the chapel gives the year of its foundation. A renovation took place in 1960, but the chapel retains its bellcot.

ROUGHLEE [Pendle]

SD8440: 2 miles (3km) NW of Nelson

This is witch country. White House, on the opposite side of the river bridge from the Bay Horse Inn, carries the large figure of a witch on one of its walls. The houses and cottages of the hamlet line the edge of the narrow road which runs by the side of Pendle Water. Halfway along it, a waterfall drops the river to a lower level. In the 19th century the hamlet possessed two mills, but these, along with the chapel at which John Wesley preached, have long gone.

The home of Alice Nutter, one of the supposed Pendle Witches, was Roughlee Hall. Standing in the centre of the village, it is a stone-built house of 1586, with mullioned windows. Alice was hanged, along with others, at Lancaster Castle in 1612. It is thought likely that the real source of conflict was a boundary dispute she had with Roger Nowell, the local magistrate.

To the north, above the hamlet of Blacko, stands **Blacko Tower**. This was built as a folly by a local grocer, although folklore has it that this is where witches gathered.

RUFFORD [West Lancashire]

SD4616: 5 miles (8km) NE of Ormskirk

The Leeds and Liverpool Canal passes through this village of white houses. The parish includes the hamlets of Holmeswood and Mere Side.

One of the great halls of the county is **Rufford Old Hall**. Set in 14½ acres (6 hectares) of ground between the A59 and the canal, north of the Hesketh Arms, this 15th-century National Trust property is a late medieval manor house in black and white timber. Legend has it that William Shakespeare performed at the hall in the late 16th century as part of a travelling group of actors. In the great hall, built in the 15th century, is a 1485 hammerbeam roof, and a very rare, carved, movable screen, supported by posts made from oak trees. It was only in 1949 that a secret priest's hole was discovered, high in the upper end of the room. Originally the house had two wings, but the west wing was taken down and the east wing replaced with one made of brick in 1661. This houses a collection of 16th-century armour. In the dining room are some Chippendale chairs from the 18th century, furniture from the 17th century and a fireplace of the same vintage.

The **Philip Ashcroft Museum of Country Life** includes a reproduction of a village kitchen and a number of old farm implements, costumes and dolls. The Hesketh family lived at the hall for many years, until handing it over to the National Trust in 1936. The family played a large part in helping to drain the mosslands of the surrounding area.

There have been a number of buildings on the site of the present **church of St Mary**, in Church Road. The first chapel was recorded in the 14th century but was soon replaced. This was gradually enlarged over the years, until Puritans destroyed most of the interior furnishings in the 17th century. Another chapel was later erected, which, in turn, was replaced by a Georgian one. The present building, near the canal bridge, was erected in 1869 in the Gothic revival style. The Hesketh chapel contains family monuments surviving from the previous church. One from 1485 records a family of eleven children. The spire is tall and there is excellent modern glass in the windows.. The base of the 1000-year-old parish cross, which used to stand on the village green, is in the churchyard. It serves the function of a base for the sundial.

In 1798 the Heskeths built **Rufford New Hall** in 304 acres (123 hectares). They wanted a more modern and convenient place to live than the old hall. In the event, they did move back into the old hall in the early 19th century and added a new wing to it in 1821. Set in Rufford Park, immediately west of the village, the New Hall was most recently used as a convalescent home, but now awaits new usage while disrepair and decay threaten it.

Rufford Old Hall

Managed by the Lancashire Wildlife Trust, **Mere Sands Wood Nature Reserve** covers 42 hectares (105 acres). The area, on the Holmeswood road out of the village, was declared a Site of Special Scientific Interest in 1985. The old lake of Martin Mere was nearby. In the middle of the 19th century, Lord Hesketh had the land drained and planted the original wood on the site so that he could use it as a shoot. Sand was quarried for glass-making between 1974 and 1982. Winter waterfowl, breeding waders and woodland birds are the main attractions.

SABDEN [Ribble Valley]

SD7837: 3½ miles (6km) SE of Clitheroe

Between the Rivers Calder and Ribble and overlooked by Black Hill, this is an old, industrial village. The community was on a trade route from Bronze Age times. In the 17th and 18th centuries, this became a packhorse trail. The early hand-loom weavers had a unique way of weaving parkin using oatmeal and treacle. This is the inspiration for the present **Treacle Mines** in the centre of the village, a popular family attraction. An alternative explanation of the treacle association is that cannel, a bituminous coal resembling treacle, was mined locally. In 1831 a calico mill owned by Richard Cobden was opened. As a Member of Parliament he, along with John Bright, was a great supporter of the Reform Act of 1832. The **church of St Nicholas**, on the east side of the village, was built in the style of the 11th century in 1846.

A display of historic items is to be found at the **Pendle Antiques Centre**, based on an old mill in Union Street. The **Pendle Toy and Train Museum** in Watt Street also includes cars and boats in its collection.

The steep road leading north-west out of the village reaches the lofty viewpoint of **Nick o' Pendle**.

SALWICK [Fylde]

SD4732: 5 miles (8km) NW of Preston

Salwick is an agricultural area which includes the hamlets of Newton, Scales, Clifton and Lea Town.

The 16th-century **Salwick Hall**, to the north of the village, by the Lancaster Canal, was the home of the Clifton family. Until the late 18th century, there was a Roman Catholic chapel in the building. In 1945, **British Nuclear Fuels** built the large factory which dominates the village.

SAMLESBURY [South Ribble]

SD6230: 3 miles (5km) E of Preston

Pronounced 'sarmzbury', this widespread village, has no centre as such. It is situated in the Ribble Valley, close to the A59, and is now a predominantly agricultural area. It includes the hamlets of Samlesbury Bottoms and Roach Bridge. Weaving and spinning became the main occupations in the 18th century. Some of the white cottages close to the church were built for weavers. After the decline of these industries in the 19th century, farming once again became important.

From the noise of the traffic pounding the A59 dual carriageway, a left turn down the narrow and easily missed Potter Lane attains entry to a quiet, country world within seconds. Although the M6 junction is within throwing distance, the **church of St Leonard the Less**, next to its school, is situated in a little pocket of peace, close to the River Ribble. There are records of a church on the site at the end of the 12th century. Until 1558 it was served by Cistercian monks, but over the years the building became increasingly dilapidated and it was replaced by a stone-built structure. However, the contours of a 14th-century chapel are still discernible on the gable end. The tower, erected in 1900, has a large turret which bears the clock. A major restoration was carried out in the 19th century. Inside is a Norman font, a triple-decker pulpit reduced to two and 18th-century box pews bearing the initials of their occupiers. The altar rails are 19th century and there are some plates inscribed with the names of local farms. There are also memorials to the Southworth family, local lords of the manor. On a wall is the helmet and sword that are thought to have belonged to the 16th-century Thomas Southworth, who is buried below. In the churchyard are two interesting graves. The first is that of a so-called witch, with iron spikes to prevent her escaping. The other is that of William Lazonby, at one time the best plough-maker in the country, complete with scythe and plough. In the 1612 witches' trials at Lancastle Castle, some women from the village were fortunate enough to be declared not guilty.

The outstanding architecture in the village is found at **Samlesbury Hall**, by the side of the A677. This was the home of John Southworth, who in 1654 was martyred for his faith. The hall belonged to the Southworth family from the 14th to the 17th century. Having become a school in 1824, the place had begun to decay by the turn of the century. A proposal was made that it should be demolished and rebuilt in the USA, but fortunately this did not happen. The hall is now run by a trust. Most of the building was erected in the 15th and 16th centuries, including some windows from Whalley Abbey. A previous hall had been destroyed by Robert Bruce in 1325, during a Scottish invasion after the Battle of Bannockburn. A road constructed in 1824 went through what was the moat of the old, quadrangle-shaped building. The south wing of the hall remains. It was built partly of brick in the middle of the 16th century, the first recorded use of this material in a manor house in the county. One of the windows is thought to have come from Whalley Abbey. The other side of the wing is in black and white, half-timbered with quatrefoils. The 17th-century great hall has a roof supported by cruck oak pillars, which are naturally bent. Inside is a medieval, much-altered screen, a 16th-century fireplace and a minstrels' gallery. There are a number of 19th-century alterations. The hall is used for antiques and arts fairs. The hall is supposed to be haunted by a lady in white. She is Dorothy, the daughter of Sir John Southworth, who lived in the early 15th century. One night she had arranged to elope with her lover. Her brothers discovered what was happening and a fight ensued as they tried to prevent her escape. All three men were killed and Dorothy committed suicide by jumping from her bedroom window.

Samlesbury Old Hall subsided into the River Ribble in 1871. Its foundations remain on the river bank. **Roach Bridge** and **Samlesbury Bottoms**, to the south of the A677, owe their existence to their mills on the River Darwen, both of which are still standing. The weir at the paper mill at the former is particularly spectacular in wet weather. Salmesbury Bottoms has associations with Jennet and Ellen Brierley and Jane Southworth, who were tried at Lancaster as witches in 1612. **Samlesbury Aerodrome**, which fronts on to the A59, was a strategic site during the Second World War. The large acreage is now used by British Aerospace.

SAWLEY [Ribble Valley]

SD7847: 3½ miles (6km) NE of Clitheroe

`Sawley Brow looks down on this village by the River Ribble, which is also known as 'Sally'. The road from the north descends into the small community over the river bridge.

Cistercian monks came from Fountains Abbey in 1148 to found **Sawley Abbey**, of which little remains. After the dissolution of the monasteries in 1536, the monks returned to the abbey during the time of the Pilgrimage of Grace, a northern protest. The last abbot, Thomas Bolton, was implicated in the Pilgrimage and executed in 1537. By this time, most of the monks had left, to be replaced by lay orders. The shortened nave of the abbey gives evidence of the poverty of the establishment. The outline of the domestic buildings can be traced through the low walls. Most of the stone was removed to be recycled in local buildings. The ancient-looking arch is a mishmash of stones from the site, fitted together in the 19th century. Along the wall by the entrance are rows of stone gathered from the ruins. This peaceful spot is by the side of the road through the village, to the south of the Spread Eagle Inn.

SCARISBRICK [West Lancashire]

SD3713: 3 miles (5km) NW of Ormskirk

Pronounced 'scazebrick', this is one of the largest parishes in Lancashire and stretches from Southport to Ormskirk. It encompasses the hamlets of Pinfold and Bescar. The village has no centre, but is a ribbon development along the main road. The chief local industry is horticulture.

'One of the finest examples of the Gothic revival,' is the claim often made for **Scarisbrick Hall**. The Scarisbrick family erected a structure on the site in the 12th century. It remained in possession of the hall until 1945, most of its wealth coming from the development of Southport and the draining of Martin Mere, both of which were part of the estates.

During the Elizabethan era a timber-framed building was erected, which was faced with stone in 1814 and a west wing added at the same time. The work was continued by A.W.N. Pugin, who was given this first commission by Charles Scarisbrick. Charles lived at the hall with his mistress and a number of illegitimate children. On his death in 1860, his sister Anne, who had fallen out with him, became owner of the hall. She instructed Pugin's son, E.W. Pugin, to do further work, including adding the slender 100ft (30m) tower in 1867. He later used the design for the clock tower of the House of Commons. The interior of the great hall contains 17th-century oak carvings, and in the King's Room there is a collection of paintings connected with royalty. The ceilings are richly decorated. It is now an independent school. In the extensive grounds are meadows and a lake.

A gap in the wall surrounding the grounds of the hall reveals a medieval cross. It may have been what is known as a 'Vinegar Cross'. In times of plague, travellers would anoint themselves with vinegar, which was thought to protect them. Alternatively, it may have been a wayside cross, where coffins were rested on the way to burial.

The Marquis de Casteja was responsible for the erection of the Roman Catholic **church of St Elizabeth** in Pinfold Lane in 1889. The Marquis, who owned the hall from 1872, was the son-in-law of Anne Scarisbrick, to whose memory the church was dedicated. The new church replaced the previous building dedicated to St Mary, which had been completed in 1812. The Gothic-style church contains an altar of Caen stone and a 16th-century, richly-carved, continental pulpit. The pulpit had previously been part of a large collection of artefacts which the Marquis had acquired. Apparently the pulpit was too big to fit in and had to be cut down to size.

SCORTON [Wyre]

SD5049: 8½ miles (13km) S of Lancaster

All that the motorist speeding along the M6 sees of Scorton is the parish church. Down below it, the village of neat, stone cottages is amazingly untouched by the proximity of the motorway. It is populated mainly by commuters and retired people. The village name means 'enclosure with long incision', which refers to the gorge at the back of the village. The woodland and lake of **Wyresdale Park**, surround its large, stone hall, to the north-east of the village. They were landscaped by Peter Ormrod who, in the 19th century, owned the village and estates. He was also responsible for building, in 1879, the **church of St Peter**, with its shingled broach spire. He also ran a mill and a fish hatchery on the river. The Roman Catholic **church of St Mary and St James** is at the top of Snowhill, but entered under the stone archway from the square. It was built in 1862 by James Hansom.

SILVERDALE [Lancaster and Morecambe]

SD4674: 3½ miles (5km) NE of Carnforth

Woods, crags, fields and sea surround this lovely village. Its name comes from the Viking 'Sigward'. Many parts of this community of grey limestone houses and cottages, on the banks of the River Kent, command fine views across Morecambe Bay. Until a change of course in the river, the village was a thriving small port. The development of the railway in the middle of the 19th century helped in the expansion of the resorts of Blackpool, Morecambe and Fleetwood. At the same time, Silverdale increased in population as the wealthy, who made their money from the mill towns, bought houses in the village. Since, it has proved popular with visitors and those in search of retirement homes. In addition to the main village, there are a number of closely associated hamlets – Elmslack, The Row, Silverdale Green, Gibraltar and Jack Scout. The latter is just a few houses on National Trust land surrounded by marshland. Farming, quarrying and fishing were the tradiional occupations.

Many areas have considerable significance to natural historians, the whole falling within the Arnside and Silverdale Area of Outstanding Natural Beauty. Over the years it has attracted a number of writers, including Mrs Gaskell and W. Riley, writer of the Windyridge novels. A scheme was suggested in 1864 to reclaim some of the land in the bay. So certain were the proposers of success that they started to build a weir out into the bay. Unfortunately for them, Parliament turned the idea down. What is left of the failed project is now almost completely obscured.

There was a chapel in the village before 1100. It is known that there was one, which was enlarged in 1829, on a site at the junction of Cove Road, Park Lane and Emesgate Lane. The present one, to the north of the village centre, was built in 1886 to replace the old chapel. This is the **church of St John**, which was designed very much in the spirit of the 14th century. It is not known whether the dedication is to John the Divine or John the Evangelist, but the fact that the capitals of the pillars each illustrates a different section of the Book of Revelation seems to indicate John the Divine. One of these decorations has angels among clusters of grapes; another has over twenty crowned kings. Fishes, crocodiles and monsters also feature, along with horsemen chasing each other and the ubiquitous winged dragon. The corbels on the exterior of the building trace the descent of Christ. Adam, Abraham, David and Jesus are illustrated in the porch. One of the church's incumbents, Parson Knagg, found the living here so ill-paid that he felt compelled to work as a quarryman at Blackstone Point, while his wife sold toffee in her grocer's shop. The church has no graveyard, even though there is a lych-gate in which to rest coffins. Gravestones from the old churchyard were brought across and laid along the south wall. Two of the three upright ones recall a tragedy off Jack Scout in 1872. Mary Rodier, a governess, attemped to rescue one of her charges, William Atkinson. He had got out of his depth in a pool. Sadly, they both drowned.

The **Methodist church**, built in 1878, is notable for its large rose window.

Mrs Gaskell stayed at Lindeth Tower, at the end of Lindeth Lane, 1 mile (2m) south of the village. She was sometimes visited here by Charlotte Brontë. South of the house is an old limekiln.

On the coast, along the road to the point from Lindeth Tower, **Jack Scout** is 66 acres (27 hectares)) of National Trust property. Beyond this is **Jenny Brown's Point**. The lady in question was a pig-keeper who lived here in the early 18th century. Five hundred metres inland, the chimney of an 18th-century copper smelting plant can be seen.

On Castlebarrow, one mile north of the village, stands the memorial of the golden jubilee of Queen Victoria. It is known locally as the **Pepper Pot**.

Arnside and Silverdale AONB is bordered by the estuary of the River Kent to the north, the River Keer to the south, the A6 to the east and Morecambe Bay to the west. It covers only 30 square miles (75sq km), and yet this intimate green and silver landscape harbours an abundant variety of natural life. In addition to the many attractions of the Leighton Moss Reserve, the limestone hills that surround Silverdale give outstanding views over a picturesque countryside of deciduous woodlands (many containing yews), winding lanes, stone cottages and fields patterned with hedgerows and dry-stone walls.

Leighton Moss Nature Reserve is signposted to the east of the village, near the station. It has been an RSPB reserve since 1964 and covers an area of 321 acres (134 hectares). The nearby **Morecambe Bay Reserve** was bought by the RSPB in 1974 and 1981 and covers 4140 acres (1675 hectares). More than 255 species of birds have been recorded in the reserve, of which 75 breed regularly. In addition, over 532 plant species have been recorded on the site, along with more than 30 types of butterfly. Large numbers of wildfowl use the open water area for much of the year, whilst the elusive and secretive bitterns are the rarest inhabitants of the reedbeds. Water rails, bearded tits and sedge warblers also frequent the reedbeds. The skies above are patrolled by marsh harriers, sparrow-hawks and peregrines. As well as this range of birds, otters can be seen in increasing numbers. The smaller reserve of Hawes Water is $1\frac{1}{2}$ miles (2km) to the north.

At **Wolfe House Gallery**, at the corner of Hollins Lane and Lindeth Lane, are displays of paintings, glass and pottery in a Georgian farmhouse, while Waithman Nurseries exhibits the Lilian Lunn collection of miniature figures.

SINGLETON [Fylde]

SD3838: 2 miles (3km) SW of Poulton-le-Fylde

The name of Miller predominates in the area. Thomas Miller was a rich, 19th-century cotton magnate, who built the village, the pub, the church and a big mansion. The village name derives from 'shingles', which was a type of roofing used in the area. The community still has very much the feel of an estate village. In fact, ownership of the Millers Arms remained with the family until the 1950s, when it was sold to help pay off tax debts. The village even had its own **Fire Station,** which can still be seen. The black and white building, built in 1882, has a brass sign over the door. When the brigade was started, estate workers had to first catch the horse before the fire could be attended. It was said that by the time that was done, the fire was usually out. On the corner of Church Road and the main road, it has been an electricity substation since 1932 and is kept in excellent order.

The brick and stone, Gothic-style **church of St Anne** was erected in 1860. There have been two other known buildings on the site. Thomas Miller, determined to make his own imprint on the church, demolished the previous structure, although it was only 30 years old. Inside are many memorials to the Miller family. One historical remnant is an oak chair on the left side of the sanctuary. This is inscribed, 'John Milton, author of *Paradise Lost* and *Paradise Regained*, 1671.' To the left of the lych-gate, the churchyard contains the Miller family vault, which is surmounted by enormous crosses. The second lych-gate, across the road, was the entrance to a path to **Singleton Hall**. Before this, the lych-gate was on the site of the previous church. This was for the exclusive use of the Miller family to walk to church. The hall is to the north of the village on the road to Little Singleton, hidden away in the trees to the right. The brick building, with a tower, was built in Gothic style for Thomas Miller in 1855.

SIMONSTONE [Burnley]

SD7834: 4 miles (7.5km) NW of Burnley

Here, at Old Read Bridge, the Parliamentary forces beat the Royalists. **Huntroyde Hall**, $1\frac{1}{2}$ miles (2km) to the north-east, is built on the site of an ancient hunting lodge. Dating from 1576, it underwent a 19th-century restoration. **Trapp Forge** gives demonstrations of both traditional and modern methods of forging iron. The small, stone **Simonstone Hall**, by the main road in the village, was built in the 17th century and refurbished in 1818. It was the home of the Whitaker family.

SKELMERSDALE [West Lancashire]

SD4606: 4 miles (6km) SE of Ormskirk

Designated as a New Town in 1961, the old village has increasingly been surrounded by new estates and factories. The name is thought to have been of Norse origin, but little is known of its history up to the 11th century other than that at the time of the Domesday Book, the land was held by Uctred. The name means 'valley of a man named Skjalmar'. Some coins that were discovered in the area are the only signs of any Roman occupation. Until the 19th century, cereal crops and vegetables were the main source of income. Then, in the early years of the century, coal was discovered. At its peak in 1894, the industry employed 3000 miners at twenty-four pits. In addition, others were employed in textiles, rope and brick-making. The Tawd Vale Colliery operated from the middle of the 19th century until 1897 in the present area of **Tawd Valley Park**. The remains of the old bridge, which collapsed in the disaster at the colliery in 1897 in which two men lost their lives, are still visible. Renamed as Glenburn Colliery, work was resumed from 1905 until 1923. A few buildings from the old colliery and a pond which was part of the old course of the river until it was straightened for mining purposes are on the town centre side of the bridge. Depression in the coal industry led to much unemployment in the 1920s. The coming of the new town gave a welcome boost to the area. **The Dome** marks out the Transcendental Meditation Community, who have made the town its northern headquarters.

There was a chapel of ease in the locality from 1781. In 1878 it was declared to be in a dangerous state because of mining subsidence. It was demolished in 1897, at which time the vault of the Bootle-Wilbraham family was removed to Lathom Park Chapel. In 1906 the **church of St Paul**, in Church Road, was opened. Only the font and pulpit were retained from the old building. A proposed tower was never added.

SLAIDBURN [Ribble Valley]

SD7153: 7 miles (11km) NW of Clitheroe

The bridge over the River Hodder leads to a large green overlooking the river. The road then goes uphill, with stone cottages on either side. The way to the left, towards the church, is again lined with fine buildings. On the corner is the youth hostel, which in former years was the Black Bull Inn. The village stands where many of the packhorse routes used to meet. It is thought that the name comes from a stone that commemorated those killed in a fight against Danish invaders. Another suggestion is that it means a sheep enclosure by a river. Terraced fields beyond the church indicate a settlement in Anglo-Saxon times.

Stocks Reservoir lies 2 miles (3km) north-east of the village. The buildings of the former community of Stocks-in-Bowland (or Dalehead), submerged in 1926, lie beneath its waters. The little church was taken down and rebuilt stone-by-stone along the minor road to Clapham. The bodies from the old graveyard were also taken up and reburied.

They must have had a lot of trouble with dogs at the **church of St Andrew** for two of the whips used to remove the animals from church are on display. More importantly, sometimes villagers have found sanctuary here. There is a bar, which fits into grooves on the south door, turning the building into an impregnable fortress. The villagers are said to have taken refuge in the 12th-century tower during a 14th-century Scottish invasion. The tower has undergone many alterations since it was first erected in the 12th century. Inside, the triple-decker pulpit was erected in 1740, and east of it, the oak chancel screen is from the same era, as are some box pews. The font is 12th century, its cover coming from the Elizabethan period. The tiny Hamerton Chapel, containing two piscinae, is in the south aisle. In the churchyard is part of a 14th-century cross, the bottom part of which has a sundial on it. Next to the church, at the southern end of the village, is **Brennand's Endowed School**, built in 1717 and now the church primary school.

Known as The Dog until 1875, the **Hark to Bounty Inn** in the village centre goes back to the 13th century. One day in 1875, the local squire was having a quiet drink in the inn. Hearing one of his hounds, Bounty, making a loud din outside, he shouted to it to be quiet. Hence the new name. Inside the inn is a courtroom, which was in use until 1937. When the village's old court house fell into disrepair, the court moved its business into the inn. It still has the old benches and most of the original furnishings.

SLYNE WITH HEST [Lancaster and Morecambe]

SD4765: 3 miles (5km) N of Lancaster

Bonnie Prince Charlie, in 1745, followed in the steps of Robert Bruce, four hundred years earlier, as he passed through the adjoining villages with his invading army. It was on the main route from Scotland and the North, and they were heading towards Lancaster and the South. Before then, monks from Furness Abbey, on more peaceful business, had enjoyed the feel of dry land after their dangerous journey across the tidal sands. Hest Bank is the starting place for guided walks across the treacherous sands of Morecambe Bay to Grange-over-Sands. For centuries, travellers walked across at their peril on the route to Scotland.

By the Lancaster Canal, the **Hest Bank Hotel**, built in 1554, was a staging post on the way. Those days seem far away in the quiet residential and commuter community of today.

Out on the sand dunes, the **Nature Reserve**, belonging to the RSPB plays host to thousands of dunlin, grey knots, plovers, godwits and curlew.

SOUTHFIELD [Pendle]

SD8837: 1 mile (2km) SE of Nelson

The hamlet is still just about as small as it was when John Wesley preached here in the middle of the 18th century. The main cluster of cottages and farms is towards the bottom of the hill. Overlooking them is a mound surmounted by a World War II pillbox. North of these, at the top of the brow before reaching the Shooters Arms, a rutted private road leads to **Southfield House Farm and chapel.** The Methodist chapel is unique in that it is built over the top of a barn. In fact, Wesley preached four times at the chapel between 1784 and 1790. There is a commemoration plaque of these visits. The chapel's French organ is one of only two of its kind in the country. Wesley was a great friend of William Sagar, a cotton manufacturer, who built the chapel. He stayed with him at Southfield House, at the bottom of a road which leaves the village road at the same point as that to the chapel.

STAINING [Fylde]

SD3536: 2½ miles (4km) NE of Blackpool

A fully operating **windmill**, complete with sails, is found by turning along Mill Lane by the Plough Inn. It is fascinating to watch the dome go round on the high, 18th-century structure. The mill managed to survive fire damage, although not completely unscathed. Now it is residential accommodation.

Known as Staininghe in the Domesday Book, the area also includes the small hamlet of Newton. The population has gradually increased, with a mixture of homes for commuters, the retired and holiday visitors. A folk tale tells of a man who gave some cream with magical properties to a woman whose daughter had eye problems. Against his strict instructions, she tried it out on one of her own eyes. She was found out when she saw the man stealing sometime later. He thought he was invisible, but the woman could see him because of the cream she had used. Rather nastily, he took his revenge by dealing her a blow in the eye.

The small, brick, 19th-century **church of St Luke** is at the top of the hill on the main road.

STALMINE [Wyre]

SD3745: 4½ miles (7km) NE of Poulton-le-Fylde

Smugglers once trod the area served by the village, and the surrounding hamlets of Staynall, Coldrow and Wardley. Built on a rise, the village commands views over the Wyre estuary, from which the smugglers would have made their way up the many creeks and inlets. The village centre clusters round the church, hall and pub.

Stalmine Hall was built in the 19th century and is now a residential home. Next to it is the church of St James. This small building has a bellcot and was built in 1806. There is a 17th-century sundial by the porch and the remains of a preaching cross. In 1873 the vicar was convicted of an assault upon his churchwarden. The vicar had not been pleased with his appointment and grappled with him in the vestry. Adjacent is the **Seven Stars Inn**. Nowadays salt is extracted from below the marshes by pumps which supply ICI. A wooden track called Kate's Pad goes across the marshland. There are some

18th-century cottages at Staynall, while Warleys now has a marina replacing its old port.

ST MICHAEL-ON-WYRE [Wyre]

SD4641: 7½ miles (12km) E of Poulton-le-Fylde

Sometimes called the 'Jewel of the Fylde', the village, with its lovely church by the river, consists of stone cottages surrounded by farmland. There was a small settlement in Upper Rawcliffe with Tarnacre centuries before the establishment of a church by the fording place of the River Wyre. It is known that there was a church here in the middle of the 7th century. There is note of it in the Domesday Book as being one of only three churches in the Hundred of Amounderness. By the 12th century the village had become known by its present name. In the earlier years of the 20th century, many of the cottages were tea-shops. Before the days of package holidays, visitors came from miles around to walk along the river bank and then 'take tea'.

Tradition has it that the missionary Paulinus founded the **church of St Michael** in AD640. It is in a beautiful position by the River Wyre crossing point. There is now an early 19th-century bridge over the river. Since 1789, the right of choosing the vicar has been in the gift of the Hornby family, the lords of the manor. Although parts of the fabric are 13th century, the building underwent major renovation in the 15th century, with two restorations since then. The nave and chancel are 14th century, with St Katherine's chapel dating from 1480. The building has changed very little in appearance since the early 17th century. A small, infilled window in the tower was a leper's squint, through which any with contagious diseases could watch the service. A list of vicars since 1203 hangs on the south wall. The three bells were cast in 1458, 1663 and 1742 respectively. The faint remains of a 15th-century mural, uncovered in 1956, are on the north side of the sanctuary. On either side of the altar are a 13th-century pedestal, which once supported a statue of St Michael, and a piscina used for washing the utensils used at communion.

On the north wall, a plaque records a disaster which occurred in 1984. Some parishioners were visiting Abbeystead to see an installation to help reduce flooding. Methane gas had become trapped and an explosion caused the concrete roof to fall. Sixteen people were killed and others injured. Near it, in a case, is displayed a 1606 bible with concordance. A board hangs on the south wall, giving a list of those who helped the poor. One of the benefactors, Ralph Longworth, haunted the church until the vicar exorcised his spirit. In the churchyard, southeast of the porch, are the three 'soldiers' stones'. These are thought to be the graves of crew members of a Spanish ship wrecked on the river estuary in 1643. Near the east end of the building is a 1796 sundial with the inscription, 'Our days upon earth are as a shadow.' It is thought that its base is part of a Saxon cross.

The Hornby family has lived for centuries at the 18th-century, two-storey, stone **hall**, which is set in spacious grounds on Hall Lane.

Finding part of a fairground big wheel in the middle of the countryside is an unexpected pleasure. At **Wild Boar Cottage**, 1 mile (1.5km) from the village on Rawcliffe Road, a carriage from the wheel at Blackpool Pleasure Beach has been added to the cottage as a conservatory. The wheel was dismantled in 1928.

Two sisters who lived in the cottage at the time had one of its carriages transported here.

SUNDERLAND [Lancaster and Morecambe]

SD4255: 5 miles (8km) SW of Lancaster

Make sure that you do not get trapped here. The road to the small, coastal hamlet is a tidal one, so it is wise to check the times the way is clear. The hamlet, by the estuary of the River Lune, is now quiet and peaceful, but in the early 18th century it was a busy port. Ships arrived from the West Indies. It is claimed that the first cotton to enter this country was landed here. A merchant, Robert Lawson, constructed the complex in 1728. He lived at **Sunderland Old Hall**, at the south end of the hamlet. It was built in the 16th century with very thick walls. Its verandas give it a West Indian air. Lawson eventually lost his fortune by investing in the ill-fated 'South Sea Bubble', one of the 18th century's greatest financial disasters. At one time the area became known for the tradition of catching salmon by the haaf netting process. Converted warehouses and the quay are the main reminder of the port's past history. It did not thrive for very long as the import centre for Lancaster. With the building of St George's Quay in the mid-18th century and Glasson Dock a little later, Sunderland became increasingly redundant, in spite of enjoying a brief period of prosperity as a bathing resort. A gate-pier on the quay at which ships tied up is called the **Powder Stump** and is a doleful reminder of past glories.

The **Cotton Tree** is said to have grown from a seed of cotton that dropped from a bale.

The days of black slaves are recalled by **Sambo's Grave**. An emotive story tells that Sambo was left at Sunderland by his master. They had arrived by boat in 1736 and the master had to go inland on business. Sambo missed him so much that he pined away and died at Upsteps Cottage, which is on The Lane. More prosaically, it is likely that he died after a bout of fever. What is true is that he was buried just west of the point near the shore. A white arrow beneath the sign for The Lane, points to the burial place near the western shore. Some years later, Reverend James Watson, who was headmaster of Lancaster Grammar School at the end of the 18th century, erected a headstone. Its inscription was, 'Here lies poor Sambo, a faithful negro, who (attending his master from the West Indies) died on his arrival at Sunderland.' The 1736 stone is now well worn. A poem was later added, referring to the 60 years that had passed since Sambo was buried.

TARLETON [West Lancashire]

SD4520: 7½ miles (12km) SW of Preston

Situated on the banks of the River Douglas, the village was a port in the 15th and 16th centuries. In the following century an Act of Parliament made it possible for ships to sail as far as Wigan. They also sailed from Tarleton in the other direction, carrying slate and ore to other ports along the coast and sometimes as far as France. The large warehouse still by the river at Bank Bridge was a storing place for cotton. It was brought from Liverpool along the canal system which linked into the Douglas Navigation. The cotton was then sent on to the Lancashire mills. Rope-making, for navigational use, was also an important local industry. During

this century, market gardening has been a major source of commercial prosperity.

The nearby hamlet of Sollom grew as a canal community. Now a conservation area, it linked the canal to the Great North Road, which ran through the village. At the bottom of Lock Lane is the final lock on the Rufford branch of the Leeds and Liverpool Canal. On the other side of the bridge can be seen the old course of the River Douglas. In the centre of the hamlet are the stables from which Geraldine Wilson went to Aintree in 1980 to be the first woman jockey to finish in a Grand National.

Known as Tarleton Old Church, the oblong **church of St Mary**, built in 1717, stands close to the A59. For centuries the village had been part of Croston parish. Frequent flooding of the river often made it impossible for the inhabitants to attend worship. There was a church in Blackgate Lane End during the Commonwealth period, but that had fallen into decay. St Mary's was erected on the site of an old chapel dedicated to St Helen. Additions were made to the brick building in 1824. A bellcot and stone tower, and porch expanded the original Georgian structure. The interior is simple, with box pews, open benches, a gallery and a flagged floor.

The **church of Holy Trinity** was the more central replacement for the old church. Built in the style of the 14th century, it was consecrated in 1888. The broach spire was added in 1913.

The old cottages and houses of Plox Brow lead down to **Tarleton Mill**, by the canal. The chimney was demolished, but the rest of the building remains intact.

The date 1660 can be seen over the old entrance of the **Ram's Head**. The building, now extended as a restaurant, is near the junction of the A59 and the A565.

TARNBROOK [Lancaster and Morecambe]

SD5956: 6 miles (9km) SE of Lancaster

This is the end of the road. The hamlet, on the Tarnbrook Wyre, is as far as vehicles are allowed to go. It lies in a wild valley beneath Ward's Stone. Beyond lie the moors of the Forest of Bowland. In past years the local cottage industry was hat-making.

TATHAM [Lancaster and Morecambe]

SD6169: 1½ miles (2km) N of Wray

The tiny communities of Lowgill, Thrusgill and Botton Head are on the old Roman road below Tatham and on the Tatham Fells. Out on Tatham Fells, 2 miles (3.5km) south of Burton in Lonsdale, the **Great Stone of Fourstones** stands on the boundary of Lancashire with Yorkshire. According to legend, the 12ft (3.6m) stone was being carried by the devil. His apron strings broke and he dropped it. Restoration work took place in 1887 on the perpendicular **church of St James**, whose tower dates from 1722. This is found in an isolated position by following the wooden sign across the river on the Wennington to Wray road.

Two miles (3.5km) to the south-east of the church, **Craig Hall** dates from 1693. **Outhwaite Farm,** 1½ miles (3km) south-east of the hall, was the site of a Quaker prison. The gaol house and stocks still exist.

THISTLETON [Fylde]

SD4138: 3½ miles (6km) E of Poulton-le-Fylde

This is a hamlet of houses and farms, some from the 17th century. The part-black-and-white and part-brick-built **Thistleton Lodge** was erected in 1907 by the Millers, who had the largest landholdings in the district. It is west of the village, on the A585, and is now a nursing home.

THORNTON-CLEVELEYS [Fylde]

SD3442: 4 miles (6km) S of Fleetwood

The dual-village residential area, sometimes known as 'Thornton-le-Fylde', spans the gap between the Irish Sea and the Wyre estuary. The giant **ICI Hillhouse Saltworks** at Thornton are on the banks of the river. Late in the 19th century, brine wells were dug on the other side of the estuary. Fresh water pumped down the wells brought salt to the surface. It was then pumped across the river. A few years later, salt rock mining began. By contrast, south-east of the saltworks, **Stanah Country Park**, on an outcrop of land as the river narrows opposite Hambleton, is an area of open country. It was created a park in 1989. The **Wyreside Ecology Centre** in the park has a visitor centre which explains the ecology and natural history of the area.

South of the park, **Skippool** was a busy port in the 18th century, importing sugar, tobacco and spirits. It declined in importance with the growth of Fleetwood in the following century. East of Skippool, the A588 crosses the river by means of **Shard Bridge**. 'Shard' means 'a narrow crossing place'. There is evidence that it has been used as such for over 2500 years. The first bridge was built in 1864, with the present one being constructed in 1992. The story is told that the fire brigade was held up on its way to a serious night-time fire, when the gatekeeper insisted on getting up to charge a toll on the firemen.

To the west of Thornton, Cleveleys is a family seaside resort, somewhat less hectic than Blackpool.

The **church of Christ Church** was opened in the 1830s by Peter Hesketh-Fleetwood. The more modern **church of St John** has functioned since 1961.

The foundation stone of the original 1717 building of **Baines Endowed School** can be seen in the replacement, erected in 1908.

Remarkable for retaining not only its sails and gallery, but also its machinery, **Marsh Mill** is 70ft (21m) high. Its working life lasted from 1794 to 1922. Now fully restored, in spite of some gale damage in 1935, it is set in the middle of the **Marsh Mill Village** complex of shops and restaurants. Accessed from Fleetwood Road North or Victoria Road East, visitors can view the surrounding countryside from the top or look at the exhibition of local history. The **Northern Clog Museum** is on the ground floor of the mill.

THORNLEY WITH WHEATLEY [Ribble Valley]

SD6140: 2½ miles (4km) NW of Longridge

Both tiny hamlets, 'Thornley' means 'a field with thorns', and 'Wheatley' is 'an area where wheat grows'. The Roman Catholic **church of St William of York** was founded in 1738. It is situated next to Lee House on the Chipping road from Longridge. There are a number of lime pits in the area, part of which is designated an SSSI. Near **Thornley Hall**, found by turning right at the T-junction north of the church, is the base of some old stocks.

THURNHAM [Lancaster and Morecambe]

SD4654: 3½ miles (6km) SE of Lancaster

Here is a small, scattered, rural community near the Lancaster Canal.

The battlements on the parapet and porch of **Thurnham Hall**, at Upper Thurnham, are based on a 13th-century pele tower, giving the building a castle-like appearance. For 400 years it belonged to the Dalton family. It was John Dalton who erected a new façade in 1823. The great hall is 16th century and the decorated plaster and staircase from a century later. After the family gave up the house in 1983, it was put to a number of uses. At the moment it is a country club.

Charles Hansom was the architect of the Roman Catholic church of St Thomas and Elizabeth, which is found by continuing past the hall and over the cattle grid. It has a broach spire and contains the Gillow family vaults, built to Egyptian design. On the bank of the canal, at the end of the lane opposite the Glasson Dock road, **Conder Mill** produced corn entirely by water power, firstly from the river and later from the canal. The 19th-century building was converted into a hotel in 1991 and is now the Thurnham Mill Hotel. The beams and flagstones of the original structure have been retained.

TOCKHOLES [Blackburn]

SD6623: 2 miles (3km) NW of Darwen

The solitude of this village of stone cottages on the edge of the Darwen Moors belies the hub of activity that there was in the community over a century ago. Then it was a busy centre of handloom weaving and later textile production in its two mills. The information centre is now on

Touchstone, Tockholes

the site of the old Hollinshead Mill. At the height of its activity, it had 300 looms and employed 150 workers. It was demolished in 1903, but the mill lodge and the workers' cottages of Hollinshead Terrace remain. Some of the surrounding farmhouses go back to the 17th century. One of them, the 18th-century Fine Peters, at the south end of the village before the main housing begins, has a reputation for being haunted.

The windows in the shape of a lance in the **church of St Stephen** are most unusual. Found by turning off the Tockholes Road just before the Rock Inn, the church was rebuilt in 1832 to replace a previous building and rebuilt again in 1966. The only remaining part of the 19th-century building is the façade of the porch and the perimeter stones of the old building. Outside are three interesting features. The 9th-century Touches Stone, by the porch, is placed on a large block. The inscription explains that it is from this that the village got its name. The inventor of the weft fork for weaving designs on cotton, John Osbaldeston, is buried here. His invention meant that if there were a break in the thread, the loom would come to a halt before further damage was caused. Osbaldeston could have become a wealthy man, but sadly his weakness for drink was his downfall. When drunk, he would often unwittingly share his ideas with others, who then benefited from them. Lastly, on the right coming through the lych-gate, is the 1854 school building. In the wall, a rare outdoor pulpit is a reminder of the days when congregations were, at festivals at least, too large to get into the church. In front of the pulpit are an old font and sundial.

In Chapels Lane, west of the Victoria Inn, the **United Reformed chapel** is on the site of the original of 1662, but has been rebuilt twice.

Out on the moors, by Stepback Clough, are the remains of **Old Aggie's Cottage,** where the owner was murdered in 1880.

Roddlesworth Woods are a popular area of natural beauty, with a wide diversity of native trees and birds. In other words, a naturalists' and walkers' delight. Covering 200 acres (81 hectares), it was planted in 1904, forty years after the completion of the three Roddlesworth Reservoirs. Kingfishers and woodpeckers make their homes here, and in early spring the display of bluebells is extremely attractive. To be able to walk amongst oak, beech and ash trees makes a pleasant change for those who have come across forests of fir trees. At the southern edge of the woods are the ruins of **Hollinshead Hall**. Here was the early manor house. A building must have been on the site for many centuries, but the remains are of the 18th-century house. The remnants of a later farmhouse are also visible. Fortunately, there is a better-preserved **Well House** to see, complete with a trough and the head of a lion. Legend has it that the waters could be used as a remedy for eye diseases.

Outdoor pulpit, Tockholes

TOSSIDE [Ribble Valley]

SD7756: 10 miles (16km) N of Clitheroe

Straddling the border of Lancashire and Yorkshire, the community is widely scattered. The former village smithy is now the post office. The little **church of St Bartholomew** was built in the 17th century and heavily refurbished in 1873. The pews, pulpit and font remain from the first church.

TOTTLEWORTH [Hyndburn]

SD7331: 3 miles (5km) NE of Blackburn

The unexpected delight of the hamlet is that it has survived in such an unaltered state. Surrounded by the built-up areas of Great Harwood, Rishden and Blackburn, it is remarkable that it has not been swamped. There was a settlement here in Anglo-Saxon times, and the 11th-century ground design is still the same today. Many of the buildings date from the 18th century, although some, such as **Manor House Farm,** are a century older.

TRAWDEN [Pendle]

SD9138: 2 miles (3km) SE of Colne

Clogs and gamblers are the clue to this mill village at the centre of the Trawden Forest, which stretches from Boulsworth Hill to Colne. It was never a forest in the sense of thick woods, but was used for hunting purposes and the rearing of cattle until the beginning of the 16th century. After that time some of the land was enclosed, with the tenants having the right to graze the common land. From the 17th century, coal began to be mined, the last pit opening in 1874. Handloom weaving came into prominence in the first part of the 19th century, followed by the building of mills. The village gets its name from the trough-like valley in which it is situated. Farming continues to be an important activity, as it was before the textile revolution.

One of the early 20th-century vicars of the **church of St Mary**, Canon Dempsey, was well known locally for wearing clogs. Built in 1845, the church stands in a commanding position on the hill, at crossroads at the southern extremity of the village.

On the road west from the church,

Trawden Hall is situated on the corner of Goose Green Lane. The original hall of 1540 underwent extensive alteration in the middle of the 20th century. A bell tower remains in the garden. Beyond the hall is a Quaker burial ground dating from 1686. The nearby cemetery is the final resting place of William Hartley, the jam manufacturer.

In **Winewall**, an adjacent village, an **Inghamite Chapel** was started in 1752. Benjamin Ingham was a Church of England clergyman, much influenced by John Wesley. Refused permission to preach in other parishes by the clergy, he started his own society. Of the thirteen Inghamite chapels in 1814, Winewell, with forty-one members, was second only to that at Wheatley. So keen were some of its members that they emigrated, to establish a church at Brantford in Ontario.

The surrounding moorland was used for mining purposes. The small pit mounds are all that remain. Half a mile (1km) south-east of the church, the waterfall of **Lumb Spout** has worn a deep channel in the face of the rock. In the 19th century the course of the river was changed so that it flowed over the cliff. The old course is evident to the left of the present one. On the way to the Spout is **Midge Hole**, which was a favourite gambling hideout for the millworkers.

Lad Law, 1½ miles (2km) further south-west on Boulsworth Hill, has a stone which is thought to have been a Druid altar.

TREALES [Fylde]

SD4433: 1 mile (2km) NE of Kirkham

Treales (pronounced 'trails'), along with the small hamlets of Wharles and Roseacre, covers an oasis of rural solitude around Kirkham. The area covers a maze of small lanes, farms and cottages.

The school and church are both isolated from the centre of the village, being north along Church Road. The peace is somewhat broken by the roar of the traffic on the nearby M55. The **church of Christ Church** is a small, towerless, stone structure at the end of a short lane. It was built in 1853.

On the road east from the village, there is an old **windmill**, now in private use.

At the centre is the **Derby Arms**, which is a thatched, 18th-century inn.

TUNSTALL [Lancaster and Morecambe]

SD6173: 3 miles (5km) S of Kirkby Londsdale

The Brontë sisters walked along the path from Cowan Bridge, where they were at school, to worship at the ancient church of Tunstall on Sundays. In Charlotte's novel *Jane Eyre*, it is Brocklebridge church. The clergy school which the Brontë sisters attended in Cowan Bridge was run by the vicar of Tunstall. On a minor road north-east of the village, the low, castellated **church of St John the Baptist**, formerly dedicated to St Michael, is mainly 15th century. It is the third building on the site. The room over the porch is where the Brontë sisters used to eat their lunch after the morning service. A Roman votive stone on the left side of the north-east window is dedicated to the goddess of medicine and health. It is thought to have come from a Roman settlement at Burrow. The Norman or Saxon stone altar was restored to its original position in 1957. The East window contains 19th-century Flemish glass. In the chapel lies the 1415 stone effigy of Sir Thomas Tunstall. The font is 18th century and the oak chest under the tower 13th century. Although now in an isolated position, the church is thought to be placed where the original village settlement was.

Tunstall Castle, immediately south of the village, survived great damage from Cromwell's forces in the 17th century and a fire in the 18th century. After years of dereliction, it has been restored for residential purposes.

TURTON [Blackburn]

SD7315: 4 miles (6km) NE of Bolton

A tower and a country park are appealing surroundings to the linear villages of Turton and Turton Bottoms. The populations of nearby Bolton, Chapeltown, Edgworth and beyond ensure that this is a popular area for visitors all the year round. It was just as attractive a century ago, when rich cotton magnates such as Henry Ashworth and Samuel Horrocks lived in the vicinity.

Set in 8 acres (3 hectares) of wooded grounds, which include a Victorian tennis court, **Turton Tower** is off Chapeltown Road. It is two buildings in one, being basically a medieval pele Tower with an Elizabethan farmhouse attached. Some think that the tower was built in the 12th century and its three storeys modernised in the 15th century. Others believe it was all erected in the 15th century, with another storey being added a century later. Early in the 16th century, two cruck-framed farmhouses were added to the house. It was completed with the half-timbered entrance hall and some extra rooms in 1596. The expense of all this refurbishment was so great that the owners had to sell it to meet the bills. In 1628

Henry Chetham, the High Sheriff of Lancashire, came to live at the tower. He was a staunch supporter of the Parliamentary cause during the Civil War, so much so that he was the treasurer of the party. He is better known for being a great benefactor, especially to Manchester, where he founded the Chetham Library. From 1644 to 1835 a succession of tenant farmers took over the property. By the end of this time, it was in a state of parlous neglect. James Kay, a local mill owner, then restored the place to its former glory. He made a few additions of his own, such as plaster ceilings and oak floorboards. These did not meet with everyone's approval. When a railway was built close to the tower, Kay made the engineers build their bridges in an architectural style to blend in with his property. Towards the end of the 19th century, W.B. Lethaby designed an extension in the early English craft style. The tower came into the possession of the local authority in 1930. Inside, there are 12th-century panels and 17th-century Swiss glass in the dining room. One of the bedrooms has furnishing designed by William Morris and C.R. Ashbee. Amongst the furniture, weapons and armour on display, there are two items of particular interest. One is a German chandelier carved out of antlers, and the other a four-poster bed, second only in size to the Great Bed of Ware. During the year there are changing exhibitions. Near the ornate, castellated railway bridge along the track from the tower is a 19th-century waterwheel. This was formerly at Black Rock Mill at Turton Bottoms.

By the road towards Chapeltown is a Second World War pillbox. Six stones in a poor condition remain of **Cheetham Close Stone Circle** on Turton Heights. The 50ft (15m) circle is found 1 mile

(2km) north-west of the tower, near the county border. The 55-acre (22 hectares) Jumbles Reservoir is at the centre of **Jumbles Country Park** in the Bradshaw Valley. It is fed by the Bradshaw Brook and opened in 1971. It is both the newest and most southern of three reservoirs. Along with Wayoh and Entwistle reservoirs, water is provided for the Bolton district. From the 17th century the valley was a thriving industrial area. One of the mills, Horrobin, which closed in 1941, had functioned in various forms since the early 18th century. Its remains are now beneath the waters of the reservoir. Coal, paper and cotton were also important industries. Although the area is now rural, it is still possible to trace some of the industrial history of the area by following the Jumbles Trail.

ULNES WALTON [Chorley]
SD5120: 1 mile (2km) SW of Leyland

The base of two ancient crosses are to be seen here. The first is located behind the bridge over the River Lostock. This is on Ulnes Walton Lane, towards the Chorley Road end. The base is situated immediately below the western side of the bridge wall on the south bank of the river. The second, where Ulnes Walton Lane meets the Southport Road, has a legend attached to it. Road widening was due to take place so the stone had to be moved. Every morning, when the workmen came back to the site, it had been moved back to its original position. This continued to happen each day. It only stopped when some local lads dressed up as ghosts and moved the stone to its present position.

UPHOLLAND
[West Lancashire]
SD5205: 6 miles (9km) E of Ormskirk

Tales of highwaymen and their exploits recall the days of the 18th and early 19th centuries, when the inns of the village were a gathering place for these mounted robbers. It is recorded that one, George Lyon, was hanged for such activities at Lancaster Castle in 1815. He is buried is the churchyard, in close proximity to the **White Lion Inn**, which is opposite the church in Church Street. The inn has a history going back six centuries. Lyon is said to have plotted his crimes in the inn. A number of folk have claimed to have seen his ghost, fully dressed in highwayman's livery. There is evidence, centuries before this, of a Roman community in the area. A small statue to a goddess was discovered in the locality in the 19th century. Local records also tell of Celtic settlements. The village is mentioned in the Domesday Book. From the early 13th century, the de Holland family became lords of the manor. Such was their eminence, that in 1380 Thomas Holland was installed as Earl Marshal of England. In 1323 Edward II stayed at the Benedictine Priory founded four years previously by Robert Holland. It was the last one to be started before the Reformation. The dissolution of the monasteries in 1536 meant that all of the buildings were destroyed, except for the church and one remaining wall. Agriculture, coal, quarrying, nail-making, weaving and brick-making have been the main industries over the past two centuries. Since the last century **Dean Wood**, immediately north-east of the village, has been a popular centre of recreation and walking.

Most of the structure of the **church of St Thomas the Martyr**, on the corner of Church Street, at the bottom of the hill, is

14th century. Renovations were made in the early 19th century. St Thomas was the patron saint of the earls of Lancaster. The chancel of the original priory church, from which there is also some stained glass in the south window, is now the nave. The communion rail, a churchwardens' pew and staircase down to the crypt (now the vestry) are late 17th century. A new chancel was built in 1882. In that year the church ceased to be a chapel of ease to Wigan parish church and became a parish in its own right.

The Roman Catholic seminary of **Upholland College**, at the junction of College Road and Stony Brow, north of the village, was founded in 1883, specialising in the training of young vocations. A chapel was added in 1930. In extensive grounds and fronted by a lake, the imposing building is looking for a new lease of life now that it has ceased to train priests.

WADDINGTON [Ribble Valley]

SD7344: 2 miles (3km) NW of Clitheroe

Henry VI had to escape from the village to avoid capture in the 15th century. Since then life has quietened down considerably and now far more visitors than kings come here. The Coronation Gardens, commemorating the coming of Queen Elizabeth II to the throne, are a colourful sight in summer. They are laid out along the banks of the stream which runs alongside the main street. Beyond the village, which derives its name from a Saxon chief named Wada, the moors of Bowland beckon. Wade's Hill, in the grounds of Waddow Hall, is the site of Wada's camp before the Battle of Billangahoh (Billington), where he was defeated. The remains of a mill by the stream, 1 mile (1.5km) outside the vil-

lage, are a reminder that the textile revolution did not completely bypass the locality. Farming is now the predominant occupation.

The 15th-century architectural style disguises the fact that most of the **church of St Helen**, in the centre of the village, was rebuilt in 1901. As with the previous building, stone from Waddington Fell was used. The 1501 tower remains, containing six bells cast from 1774. The west window includes a depiction of St Helen, the patron saint, as well as representations of Wada and Henry VI, who hid at the Old Hall. Some parts of the south wall and the north wall of the Waddow Chapel, on the south side of the chancel, also date from the same period. The interior retains some of the furniture of the earlier building in the form of some medieval glass in the north aisle window and the font, whose bowl is 14th century. The Browsholme chapel, in the north aisle, contains 17th-century pews. Generations of the Parker family of Browsholme were buried here from the early 16th century onwards. In the churchyard, near the porch, is a 17th-century sundial standing on an old millstone. A small garden by the church houses the village stocks.

Henry VI escaped from **Waddington Hall**, which is on the main street opposite the church, after seeking refuge following his defeat at the Battle of Hexham in 1464. First of all, the king had stayed at Bolton Hall. Then, after a year at Waddington, he was betrayed. Henry made his escape down a secret stairway. His freedom did not last long for he was soon captured in Clitheroe Wood. Some parts of the hall, such as the monk's room, are 11th century, whilst the great hall, with its oak panelling, dates from the 13th century. Hidden behind the panelling is the secret staircase which leads to a room above the hall. By the 19th century the hall was being used as a farmhouse. The building eventually fell into a dilapidated state before it was renovated by John Waddington in 1900.

First erected at the beginning of the 18th century, the **Parker Almshouses**, also known as 'Waddington Hospital', were rebuilt at the present site, near the start of West Bradford Road, beyond the Higher Buck pub. On three sides of a square, with an open space in the centre, they were expanded to accommodate twenty-nine widows and spinsters. The inscription over the entrance gate refers to the founder, Robert Parker of Marley Hall, Yorkshire, and has the date of 1706. There is also a small chapel in which a reader took the services every Sunday.

Waddow Hall, by the River Ribble, near Brungerley Bridge on the Clitheroe Road, is a 16th-century structure, with additions a century later. It was built as a dower house for the Tempest family. The oldest part of the building is at the back, which was formerly the front of the house. Some of the oak-beamed bedrooms are from the original Tudor house. The Girl Guide Association bought the hall in 1928.

WALMER BRIDGE
[South Ribble]

SD4824: 5 miles (8km) SW of Preston

Near the Ribble marshes, between Longton and Much Hoole, this rural community had a cotton mill in the 19th century. It was on the Walmer Brook, which flows from the River Douglas. The hamlet is recorded as being part of the estates of Cockersand Abbey in 1251. The bridge from which it takes its name was demolished in 1901.

WALTON-LE-DALE AND
HIGHER WALTON
[South Ribble]

SD5628 and 5827: 2½ miles (4km) SE of Preston

The smaller settlement of Higher Walton stands on higher ground, looking out towards the River Darwen, east of the M6. To the west, Walton-le-dale, the name meaning 'enclosure by a ford', is nearer the meeting place of the Darwen with the River Ribble. It was north of the latter, on the banks of the River Ribble, that ninth-century coins, known as the **Cuerdale Hoard**, were found in 1840. Previous to this, the Roman emperor Julius had sent soldiers as part of his attempt to subdue the north. The area belonged to the de Lacy family until, in the 16th century, the de Hoghtons took their place. Nearby was Ribble Bridge, 100yds/m below the present one, at which the Parliamentary forces defeated the Royalists in 1648. The two villages are divided by the M6 motorway. At Higher Walton, the **church of All Saints**, next to the Swan Inn on the main road, was erected in 1862. Seven years later the tall steeple was added. **Kathleen Ferrier**, the outstanding contralto, was born in the mill village in 1912. She was the daughter of a headmaster and was baptised in the church. Situated between the two communities, **Osbaldeston House** is along a footpath parallel to the west side of the M6, north of Higher Walton Road, and dates from 1661. The **church of St Leonard**, Walton-le-dale, at the top of Church Brow, looking out over the valley of the River Ribble, is referred to in a charter of 1140. Its castellated tower is 16th century, as are the font and chancel. In the tower is an inscription stating, 'This is the body of Samuel Brooke, who was killed on his way to the Assizes.' Obviously someone took the law into his own hands. The wide nave contrasts with the low chancel. Inside there is a priest's door from the early 13th century and memorials to the Hoghton family. A major restoration took place in 1906.

WARTON [Fylde]

SD4129: 8 miles (13km) W of Preston

The village, with the surrounding hamlets of Bryning and Kellamergh, looks out over the estuary of the River Ribble. It is a suburban tourist centre. The **Fort San Antone** theme park, golf driving range and many caravans are testimony to this. The stone **church of St Paul** has a small, conical tower and was built in 1886. Next to the Pickwick Tavern lies the huge **British Aerospace Factory**, which stands on the site of the Second World War airfield, reputed to have the longest runway in the country.

WARTON [Lancaster and Morecambe]

SD4128: 1 mile (1.5km) N of Carnforth

George Washington was the first president of the United States of America. The historical links of the Washington family with the village guarantees a steady flow of American visitors to this community, just beneath Warton Crag.

Warton was an important centre in the Middle Ages, being on the main route from Lancaster to Kendal. Its market charter was granted by King John in 1200.

Every year on Independence Day, 4th July, the Stars and Stripes fly from the tower of the church of St Oswald. As the flags wear out, so others that have flown

on Capitol Hill in Washington are sent over to replace them. Just inside the north door is the Washington family tree, alongside it the descent of Winston Churchill from Robert Kitson of Warton Hall is traced. Above hang two flags, the American flag from the Capitol and that of Great Britain. The arms of the Washington family used to be on the tower but, because of wear, they have been moved inside the church to the wall of the tower room. On the stone are the three mullets and two bars, which were later used for the USA flag. It was Robert Washington who provided the money for the erection of the tower in the 15th century. Thomas Washington, the last of the family in Warton, was vicar early in the 19th century. The major part of the building, which is in an imposing hilly position near the Black Bull Inn on Main Street, is from the 15th and 16th centuries. There was a major renovation in 1892. The oldest part of the church is the south aisle wall from a century earlier. The three bells date from 1577, 1731 and 1782. The barrel font is thought to be 11th century, although it received a new plinth and lead lining in 1661.

Opposite the church, the **Old Rectory** is in ruins, but there is still enough left to reveal what a beautiful building it was. Basically, it is two buildings. One is a smaller dwelling. The other, with its hall, kitchen and storerooms, is said to have been a forerunner of some of the large medieval houses. Besides serving as the incumbent's residence, it was also used as a court of law. First erected in the 14th century, the house was greatly altered in the 18th century. Ancient soot from the fire darkens the walls of the kitchen, which has storerooms on either side. The walls of the great hall still stand. The oldest part is the chimney stack, part of a previous house.

It is not certain that **Washington House**, higher up Main Street from the church, was the Washington family home. The house was erected in the early 17th century, but completely rebuilt a century later.

The **Malt Shovell Inn**, at the bottom end of Main Street, was once a court house, and later a coaching inn.

Built in 1902, the **school** has the foundation stone from the establishment of the original building in 1594. It was endowed by the Bishop of Durham. Now a private residence, it stands back from Main Street, below the church.

Warton Crag is included in the Arnside/Silverdale Area of Outstanding Natural Beauty as well as a Site of Special Scientific Interest. The whole limestone district is rich in flora and fauna. At the top of the crag is **Crag Hill Fort**. The three rings of ramparts of the first-century fort were built by the Brigantes, one of the early British tribes, and cover 15 acres (6 hectares). A beacon of timber was placed on the site as part of the commemoration of the Spanish Armada in 1588. The name Warton is derived from the fort, 'Weardtun' meaning 'town with a look-out'. Articles from Roman times have been discovered in some of the caves.

WATERFOOT [Rossendale]

SD8322: 2 miles (3km) SE of Rawtenstall

If a good place to do the soft shoe shuffle is required, then Waterfoot, in the Rossendale Valley, is it. The manufacture of shoes was once the main occupation of the villagers. This is reflected in the shopping arcade. It was built by a 19th-century mayor of Rawtenstall. The inscription on the main road corner of the arcade reveals that he made his money through the making of slippers. The River Irwell flows under the road by the arcade. The history of shoe manufacture in the area since the middle of the 19th century is demonstrated at the **Footwear Heritage Centre**, on the site of Gaghills Mill, off Burnley Road East. The **church of St James**, on the main road, was built in 1865 in 13th-century style. Just north of the village is **Thrutch Gorge**. Through the side of it runs the 592ft (180m) tunnel of the old Rawtenstall to Bury railway, built in 1852. A two-mile walk across the moors from Cowpe Road leads to **Waugh's Well**, where the Lancashire poet and writer went to gain inspiration for his work. The **Irwell Way Sculpture Trail** ends in Waterfoot. By the **St Michael's Countryside Centre** is the tomb shaped 'Monument of Nature' sculpture. On the other side of the gorge, on the Bacup side of the village, is the 'Weave' sculpture, depicting the hills and valleys of the area.

WEETON WITH PREESE [Fylde]

SD3835: 5 miles (8km) E of Blackpool

A martyred Roman Catholic priest, William Harcourt, was born in the village in 1609. His allegiance to his faith led to his execution in 1679. To the north of the village is the large expanse of Weeton Barracks, surrounded with fences to deter unwelcome visitors. The village itself, adjacent to the hamlets of Preese, Esprick, Greenhalgh, Thistleton and Great and Little Plumpton, is set around a small, well-kept green. The **Eagle and Child Inn** is the focal point, just across the road. Cromwell supposedly stayed at the inn, which has an old halberd from the Cromwellian period just inside the main door. Ghost hunters should look out for a coffin that makes its own way to a meadow every full moon. Church Road leads underneath the M55. Just beyond it is the small, brick **church of St Michael**, built in 1842.

WESHAM [Fylde]

SD4230: 1 mile (2km) NW of Kirkham

Before the 16th century, the neighbourhood was owned by the monks of Cockersand Abbey. The lords of the manor lived at **Mowbreck Hall**. Reached by a narrow road next to the Roman Catholic church, the estate grounds are now used for caravans. Only the hall farm and some outbuildings remain. In the 19th century the village busied itself with cotton and flax weaving. A major employer in the village is the factory of Fox biscuits. The 19th-century **parish church of Christ Church**, on the main road, is a brick structure with a small, conical tower.

WEST BRADFORD [Ribble Valley]

SD7545: 2 miles (3km) N of Clitheroe

The river here has a shallow and wide fording place called the Broadford, and this is likely to have given the settlement its name. At the older end of the village, a stream runs between the road and the cottages. A cotton community in the 19th century, the population is now mainly suburban. The small **church of St Catherine**, on the Waddington road, was erected in 1898. East of it, the **Three Millstones** pub is a reminder of the industrial past of this quiet village. The first floor of the cottages opposite acted as the Anglican mission room before the church was built. The bell from the mission room was put in the new place of worship.

WHALLEY [Ribble Valley]

SD7336: 3½ miles (6km) S of Clitheroe

A village that has the ruins of an abbey and one of the most important historic churches in Lancashire has a lot going for it. The Tudor and Georgian buildings along the main street start to seem comparatively modern. The River Calder flows gently through.

Even monks do not always get on together, as the story of **Whalley Abbey**, at the end of Church Street, proves. When Cistercian monks at Stanlow on the Wir-

Saxon cross, Whalley

ral, the site of the present oil refineries, decided that the bracing sea air there was a bit too much for them, they decided to move to Whalley in 1297. The abbot and staff at Sawley Abbey felt that this was too close to them and so lodged an official complaint with the Pope. Monasteries needed plenty of land around to sustain their occupants. Eventually, however, permission was granted. Building began in 1320. The tea breaks must have been fairly long because the abbey was not finished until 1444. The first part completed was the western outer gatehouse. Over the archway, divided for pedestrian and carriage entrance, is a room which was used by the monks as a school. The eastern gatehouse, close to the railway viaduct, was erected in the 15th century. The Sands, a lane from the western gatehouse, passes through it.

The Victorians were no slouches at building either. This is confirmed by the **rail viaduct** built in 1850. So meticulous were the builders that the three of the forty-eight arches which are in proximity to the abbey are in Gothic style to match the abbey gatehouse. The viaduct, 600yds/m long and a maximum height of 70ft (21m), carries the Blackpool to Clitheroe line across the Ribble Valley. Immediately facing the western gatehouse is the abbot's lodgings. This was converted into a house by the Assheton family in 1605, after it became the owners of the abbey estates. Since 1926 it has been used as a conference centre by the Diocese of Blackburn. Although the property was much altered, the chapel still retains its piscina and aumbry (wall recess). There is little left of the church, except for the foundations giving the outline of the ground plan and a slab of stone marking the position of the altar. In length it was 260ft (79m). An usual fea-

ture is that the choir is placed in the nave rather than the chancel. This is somewhat similar to Westminster Abbey, where Edward the Confessor insisted that there should be no one behind him in the chancel when he was crowned. He obviously had a few enemies. The Whalley choir stalls were over a pit dug in the ground. This acted as a sounding board to enhance the resonance of the singing. Perhaps recalcitrant choirboys were put down there! The remains of the chapter house, refectory and dormitory are more substantial. The last abbot before the dissolution of the monasteries was John Paslew. He was one of the leaders of the Pilgrimage of Grace, a northern uprising against the policies of Henry VIII. He was executed, some think on the banks of the river by the abbey. Stonework from the dismantled abbey appears in a number of the post-13th-century buildings in the immediate area.

If you want to become invisible, then visit the churchyard of the **church of St Mary and All Saints**, on Church Lane, not far from the abbey gatehouse. Apparently, anyone who can decipher the inscription on one of the three Celtic crosses will have the ability not to be seen. The crosses are thought to date from the visit of missionaries from the Scottish west coast island of Iona in the 10th century. The sundial is 18th century. The church itself is an architectural gem. Mainly 13th century, with a 15th-century tower, it is also a good place for those with a sense of humour. The first smile comes from a close look at the magnificent choir stalls. These came from the abbey. The misericords – ledges on the seats which enabled someone to support themselves while standing – have carved on them a whole host of pictures, including dragons, eagles, a lion and a dragon. There are two which are very amusing. One is of a man shooing a goose, and has an inscription underneath. The other is of a woman hitting a man with a frying pan. This speaks for itself. Then there is a 1515 brass memorial on the north wall which pictures the Catterall family. Behind father are nine sons, and behind his wife nine daughters. The Cage Pew, immediately in front of the chancel on the south side, reflects a story of uncharitable Christianity. Roger Nowell of Read Hall is the magistrate who arrested the Pendle witches and committed them to Lancaster in 1612. He had this large pew made for his own use in the church. He must have forgotten to ask the vicar first, for he was refused permission to put it in. Lengthy and unproductive law suits followed, and the pew languished in a barn. A compromise of dividing the pew, so that both parties in the dispute had a share, was to no avail. It was 70 years later that the pew was eventually placed in its present position. By then, Roger Nowell was not in a position to use it. The interior of the church overflows with other antique items. The chancel screen is 15th century and the screens in the two old chantry chapels 14th century. St Nicholas's or the Soldier's Chapel, on the north side, is thought to contain the grave of the last abbot at Whalley. A bookcase in St Mary's Chapel, on the south side of the chancel, contains a chained Bible, as well as a collection of brasses. In the days before William Caxton and his printing press, books were so rare that measures had to be taken to ensure that they were not stolen. Security was tight even in those days.

The font dates from the 15th century, but the cover from two hundred years later. There is a churchwardens' pew of 1690 and a constable's pew of 1714. The chandelier is 18th century. The chest which held the church valuables is from 1684. The idea behind the three locks is that the vicar and two churchwardens had to be present before the chest was opened. The organ, in the 19th-century gallery, was made in 1728. Resident in the church porch are part of a Roman stone and two 13th-century coffins.

Cricket lovers will want to take a look at the **Old Grammar School**, at the junction of Station Road and King Street. On its playing field, the first Yorkshire and Lancashire cricket match was played. The present 1725 building is on the site of the original one of 1547.

The remains of **Porterfield Camp**, an ancient fortification, are 1 mile (1.5km) south-east of the village.

WHEELTON [Chorley]
SD6021: 2½ miles (4km) NE of Chorley

One of the most impressive war memorials for miles around stands by the crossroads in Lower Wheelton. It is a clock tower, built as a memorial to those who died in the First World War. Both Lower and Higher Wheelton – the latter a mile away up the Blackburn Road – prospered with the arrival of the Leeds and Liverpool Canal nearby. The first mill was erected in 1856. It was easy for the raw material for the mills to be brought in and then shipped on as manufactured goods. The Denham Mill building still remains, close to **Top Lock**, at the summit of a quick succession of seven locks. The bargemen would certainly have needed the services of the adjacent pub by the time they reached Top Lock. Another of the local industries is remembered by the name of the **Dressers' Arms** pub, on Briers Brow, near the main road. The dressers were slate workers from the quarry. Bell towers are usually found on the roofs of churches, but the cupola from the Heapey church of 1776 lay for many years in the grounds of Prospect House, which is near the canal on the old Blackburn Road, north of Lower Wheelton. It was placed there when it was deemed unsafe to stay in its proper position. It is now in the graveyard of the present **church of St Barnabas**, Heapey, which lies in an isolated position on Chapel Lane. The transepts and chancel of the large, towerless, brick church were erected in 1865. Previous buildings had been enlarged in 1740 and 1829. The churchyard is full of large and varied monuments.

WHITE COPPICE [Chorley]

SD6219: 2 miles (3km) E of Chorley

This hamlet could make a strong claim to have the most attractive setting in the county for a cricket ground. Just beyond the cluster of cottages by a stream, the ground is overlooked by the hills of Anglezarke on one side, with a couple of white-faced houses on the other. The name of the hamlet is said to come from the time that all the cottages were painted white, as some still are. The man-made Goit stream runs past the ground on its way to Anglezarke Reservoir. Most of the cottages were built for workers at the mill. The last remains of the mill – its chimney – were taken down in 1950. It was powered by water coming down from the reservoir behind the cricket field, which nestles beneath the surrounding hills. This is one of five small reservoirs around the hamlet. The nearest church was at St Barnabas, Heapey. The church ran a school, now closed, at White Coppice. There was also formerly a place

of worship which was started by the wife of the local squire when she fell out with the vicar.

WHITECHAPEL [Preston]

SD5659: 6½ miles (10km) NE of Preston

Threlfall was the original name of this small village. The lands were owned by the Knights Hospitaller in the 12th century, and later by the de Mitton and de Caterall families. A track leads from Button Street to the moss which was used by the turf cutters.

A small chapel called Threlfall New Chapel preceded the small **church of St James**, with its tiny bellcot. The building of local stone stands on the road through the village. Originally part of Goosnargh, the parish became independent in 1846. The chancel was replaced in 1818, and most of the interior is 19th century. An interesting feature is the fold-down seats along the front of the choir pews. There is a sundial in the churchyard.

Almost opposite the church is the **Cross Keys Inn,** which was a 16th-century coaching inn and also a working farm. Further east along the village road is **Ashes Farm**, which was the home of the Threlfall family. One of their number, Edmund, was a Jacobite sympathiser at the time of the rebellion. He hid in the house. When eventually he ventured outside, he was killed in a fight whilst being arrested in 1690. **Bullsnape Hall**, 1 mile (1.5km) south-east, was originally a 16th-century house, some of which survives.

The 185 acres (75 hectares) of the **Beacon Fell Country Park** lie within the Forest of Bowland Area of Outstanding Natural Beauty. It includes moorland and woodland on the millstone grit hill.

On the 873ft (266m) summit is a stone on the site of an earlier beacon, part of a chain across the country. Besides being lit to warn of possible invasion, it was also fired to celebrate the pagan feast of Tenalaes on Midsummer and All Saints' Days.

WHITEWELL [Ribble Valley]

SD6647: 6½ miles (10km) NW of Clitheroe

There may or may not be fairies at the bottom of your garden, but there were some living in caves at Whitewell. The River Hodder sweeps through the wooded valley below New Laund Hill, known as 'Little Switzerland'. On the other side from the village are the **Fairy Caves**. Excavations carried out earlier in the 20th century revealed not fairies, but evidence of occupation in Neolithic times. The tiny village itself is on a bend in the river. The **church of St Michael** replaced an earlier building in 1817. Of interest inside is a Flemish tapestry depicting the descent of Christ from the cross and an early 17th-century pulpit. The rendered structure has no tower, but possesses a quaint little bellcot. Next to the church, **The Inn At Whitewell** has had a varied career. In the 14th century it was erected as a home for the lord of the manor. It also served as a court house. The area in front of the inn was a busy market to which people came from the surrounding area to sell their wares. Near Burholme Bridge, 1 mile (1.5km) north of the village, is the 14th-century **Burholme Farm**.

To the east of the village is evidence of the historic importance of limestone. The **limestone quarry and kiln** are examples of many in the area. The product was used for mortar and for putting on the land to improve the soil.

WHITTINGHAM [Preston]

SD5636: 4 miles (6km) NE of Preston

Cows' ribs are very prominent in the village. At **Old Rib Farm**, built in 1612 on Halfpenny Lane, a rib is to be found over the doorway. The story goes that an old dun cow which grazed the moors was the only one in the locality still producing milk at the time of a severe drought. A witch milked her dry with a sieve and the cow died. The skeleton was preserved and one of the ribs was placed over the doorway of the farm as a memorial of the event. **Halfpenny Lane** is so called because it was the old toll road and that was the price incurred by those who travelled along it. It is found north of the main road, on the western edge of Longridge.

The Whittingham family, who lived at **Whittingham Hall**, were lords of the manor for six centuries. Although it has suffered fire damage, some of the timbers are from a 14th-century chapel at Broughton. There was also a moat, until it was filled in 1865. Opposite Stump Cross Farm, on a minor road to the north of Cumeragh village, is the ancient **stump cross**, which was found in a ditch in 1931. There were a number of such crosses in the parish until an extreme Protestant, 19th-century vicar had them removed. It is on Eaves Green Lane, just after the junction with Ashley Lane and Camforth Hall Lane. Continuing along the lane and turning left down a farm track after Pointer Villa, a large cross base stands in the hedge opposite the first house.

WHITTINGTON [Lancaster and Morecambe]

SD6076: 2 miles (3km) SW of Kirkby Londsdale

The visitor may be in for a shock for William Sturgeon, the inventor of the electromagnet, was born here in 1783. The **church of St Michael and All Angels** has been on its site on Church Street since at least the late 13th century. The tower is 15th century, but most of the building dates from 1875. It looks down over the village of stone, terraced cottages. Fragments of stone in the doorway date from the 11th century. Two of the six bells are 18th century.

Adjacent to the church is the mound of a Norse moothill (meeting place). On the summit is a sundial placed on the base of five steps of an ancient cross. The 1678 doorway of an older building is built into a wall of **Newton Hall**, 1 mile (1.5km) south of the village. It was rebuilt in Jacobean style in 1880.

The **Tobilane Designs Workshop**, also at Newton, makes traditional wooden toys in an old, converted barn.

WHITTLE-LE-WOODS [Chorley]

SD5822: 3 miles (5km) N of Chorley

Bath, Leamington and Droitwich may be the names of spa towns that spring immediately to mind, but in the mid-19th century Whittle Springs was in the premier league of places people went to for the healing properties of the water. During mining excavations in 1836, a spring was discovered. Consequently, a spa was built. By 1852 there were more than 30,000 visitors arriving each year. The hotel is now called the Howards' Arms Hotel, and is off Dark Lane, near the B6229 junction. A brewery which made use of the spring water was also built by the canal. The other main industry was not importing people, but exporting stone from the quarries. There had been quarrying in Roman times. Further evidence of their occupation was a find of Roman coins on the canal bank in the 19th century. In the 17th century, a number of lead mines were worked. The area was the scene of a canal race in the late 18th century. The Leeds and Liverpool and the Lancaster canal companies wanted to get to Wigan first. The Lancaster Canal won, and the Leeds and Liverpool was forced to make a sharp turn through the seven locks above Johnson's Hillocks. It then used the Lancaster Canal to Wigan. Ironically, this is now part of the Leeds and Liverpool and most of the Lancaster canal below Preston has gone. There is a short section left just below the seven locks and the tunnels which were made through the quarries on Whittle Hills. The quarries can be seen by following Mill Lane and Hill Top Lane to the east, off the A6. They produced millstone grit. Further along the road, towards Hill Foot Farm, are the Whittle Hills tunnels. Although there are now two tunnels because of the collapse of one section, it was all originally one. The Duke of York pub on Chorley Old Road is adjacent to the basin of the old canal. Millstones which were found in the canal can be seen by the pub. One section of the old canal, immediately to the east, is part of a nature trail.

The new part of Whittle has grown up around the **church of St John the Evangelist**, on the west side of the A6. This large building, looking out over the fields at the rear, was erected in 1882, replacing a previous one erected in 1830. **Shaw Hill**, immediately south of the

B5248 and A6 junction, is now part of the golf club. The two-storey, stone building was erected in 1807 and is distinguished by its Roman-style columns. The Crook family lived in the house. In the park is a memorial to one of the racehorses owned by the family. There is a lodge at the entrance.

Formerly known as Crook Hall, **Lisieux Hall**, at the end of a long drive off Dawson Lane, is early 19th century, but has some 17th-century mullioned windows at the back. The Crook family lived here from the 17th century.

WINMARLEIGH [Wyre]

SD4647: 8½ miles (14km) SW of Lancaster

Watch where you put your feet on a visit to this neighbourhood. To the west of the village are the Cockerham and Winmarleigh Mosses. This tract of land has remained unchanged for thousands of years and is now an Area of Special Scientific Interest. The bumpy car journey along the subsiding roads is warning enough. To the east lies the Lancaster Canal. On the western edge of the village, **Winmarleigh Hall**, originally built 1871, suffered a disastrous fire early in 1927 and was completely rebuilt. The area had been bought by John Wilson Patten, who later became Lord Winmarleigh, in the early 18th century. It belonged to the Lancashire College of Agriculture and Horticulture until the opening of Myerscough College. Just east of the hall is the turreted **church of St Luke**. In the churchyard is the grand family vault of the Reddaway family, owners of the hall for over a century. The vault is guarded by a large, stone angel, with the inscription 'Rock of Ages'.

WITHNELL FOLD AND VILLAGE [Chorley]

SD6123: 4½ miles (7km) NE of Chorley

Love of money may be the root of all evil, but the little hamlet of Withnell Fold, meaning 'wooded hill', produced most of the paper for the world's banknotes in the 19th century. The local landlords, the Parke family, built the paper mill on the banks of the canal in 1840. Two brothers owned the Whithnell area. They not only built the mill, but also erected a small village as a model community. It consisted of 35 workers' cottages round the square. Spiritual and educational needs were provided for by a chapel, a school and a reading room. The hamlet is now a conservation area. The mill production was at its peak from 1890, when Wiggins, Teape and Company took control of it. The chimney of the mill remains. A memorial garden has been added in the hamlet and there are also some old stocks on display. Across the canal bridge, where the infant River Lostock runs through the woods, is a nature reserve. Withnell village is 2 miles (3km) away, to the east of the Fold. The unusual shape of the small spire distinguishes the **church of St Paul**, at the top of the steep street of mill cottages. In the churchyard is a memorial to James Miller, who was awarded the Victoria Cross for gallantry in the First World War.

WOODPLUMPTON [Preston]

SD5035: 4½ miles (7km) NW of Preston

'You can't keep a good man down,' is the saying. This was also true of Meg Shelton, a witch buried in the churchyard. The boulder placed over her grave is to prevent her getting out and there is good reason for this. Apparently, she got out three times after burial in the 17th century. The final answer was to bury her face down with the large stone on top. Good luck is guaranteed to anyone who walks round the grave three times. Her grave, with a descriptive plaque, is to the west of the church. She should not be allowed to draw attention away from the splendours of the **church of St Anne**. St Anne was the mother of the Virgin Mary. A memorial to Henry Foster, an explorer, who drowned in the Gulf of Mexico in 1831, is inside. The tower, with its distinctive lantern-shaped summit, dates from the 15th century, but has undergone a number of restorations. The castellated, low aisles were erected in 1748. The roofs were raised to a higher level in 1639. Most of the north aisle is from the 14th and 15th centuries, whilst the remainder is from the following century. During restoration work in 1900, stones and tracery from the old church were discovered. Although the one bell is modern, its predecessor from 1596 is kept in the tower. Here also is a 17th-century table. The trefoil window near the north door is 13th century. Near the small gate entrance to the churchyard are a 1637 sundial, and a 1689 gravestone on which the mason has had to run the surname 'Carter' on to two lines. Outside the main lych-gate are stocks in front of a mounting block. The sides of the smaller gate to the west look as if they have previously been used as stocks.

In the Domesday Book the settlement is referred to as Plunpton. Later it was called 'Plumpton', with 'Wood', being added to distinguish it from a number of nearby places of the same name.

Next to the school, at the side of a footpath, is the 17th-century **Cuckstool Farm.** A black roof covers earlier thatch. To the right of the main door is a smaller one, now blocked up. This was once the entrance to a weaver's shop.

WHITWORTH [Rossendale]
SD8820: 3½ miles (6km) S of Bacup

If a man wanted to sell his wife, **Whitworth Square** was the place to do it. It is recorded that in the early 19th century, a man auctioned his spouse for the princely sum of two shillings and sixpence. The square, up the hill from the main road, is at the heart of the old village. Fortunately, it became more famous locally for the work of the Whitworth Doctors. **Whitworth House** was the home of the Taylor family, who practised medicine here for over 100 years from the middle of the 18th century. The earliest of the 26 doctors in the family, of whom James Taylor was the first in 1764, treated both humans and animals. The latter took preference. Even so eminent a patient as the Bishop of Durham was left waiting when a horse arrived for treatment. People came from all over the country for consultation and remedy. This enabled the **Red Lion** next door to do the best trade it had ever done since it opened in 1674. At the top end of the square is the churchyard, which was handily placed to bury the doctors' mistakes. Leading left out of the graveyard is the lane known as Cripples' Walk. This is where patients were directed to take exercise. Inside the graveyard is the Taylor monument and also the village stocks.

The large **church of St Bartholomew**, standing high above the steep graveyard, was built in 1847 on a piece of land which may have been levelled when a previous building was erected in the early 16th century. Sadly, the present structure suffered severe fire damage in

1984. Stone from the local quarries has travelled far and wide. In London, it helped with the laying out of Trafalgar Square, and in Paris, with the erection of the Eiffel Tower. As well as quarries, sheep, weaving and coal mining were important in the 19th-century life of the village. The museum of the **Whitworth Historical Society**, in North Street, has documents and information about the life and history of the community. At nearby Facit, which along with Whitworth and Healey forms one continuous community along the valley, the large 1871 **church of St John the Evangelist**, standing high above the main road, looks out across the valley.

Fairies can be found at **Healey Dell Nature Reserve,** which is sited on land to the west of the A671 and B6377, below Whitworth. In a gorge by the River Spodden are the rock shapes which have led to tales of witches and fairies. Steps lead down to the Fairies' Chapel. Nearby is Station Road, a reminder of the railway history of the valley. The Lancashire and Yorkshire Railway Company opened a line from Rochdale to Facit in 1870, extending it to Bacup in 1881. Closure took place in 1967. Now the Healey Dell section has been converted into a walkway. The remains of Broadley Station are evident at Station Road. Further south is the 111ft (34m) high and 200ft (61m) long, eight-arched viaduct. Made of local stone, it was constructed to carry the railway line over the valley of the River Spodden. Near this are the remains of the **'Owd Mill i't Thrush**, built in the 17th century. The area is now a nature reserve. Just where the B6377 leaves the A671 is **Healey Hall**. The present building is 18th century, on the site of earlier halls. These were owned by the de Heleya family, from which name Healey is derived.

WISWELL [Ribble Valley]

SD7538: 2½ miles (4km) S of Clitheroe

Storie sof murder, secret rooms and ghosts makes the village of Wiswell (locally pronounced 'wizell') a somewhat mysterious place. This belies its rural solitude, narrow lanes and stone houses.

The murder took place at **Cold Coates Farm**, a stone farmhouse on the right-hand side of the road to Pendleton. One day a maid found a traveller loitering in the dairy. She hit him so hard that he died.

The secret rooms are at the medieval **Old Vicarage**, opposite the phone box and Coronation Gardens. Here priests hid away during times of persecution.

The ghost is of Abbot John of Whalley Abbey, owner of the local lands, who haunts the grounds of **Wiswell Old Hall**, where he used to live. He is said to walk the lane from Shay Cross to the hall.

Before the hamlet became part of the Whalley Abbey estates, it had been granted to the de Arches family by the lords of Clitheroe in 1193. The hall has been rebuilt, only a porch remaining of the original building. Next to it is **Wiswell Hall Farm.** To reach them go down the road from Coronation Gardens, before the junction with Old Back Lane. Just over the stone wall at the junction is **Shay Cross**, a well-preserved Celtic cross. Part of the road that legions of Roman centurions marched lies between the village and Lamb Roe, on the other side of the A59.

The small hamlet of **Wymondhouses**, 1 mile (1.5km) north of Wiswell, off the Pendleton Road, is the remote spot where Thomas Jollie started a Congregational church in 1667, after he had been ejected as vicar of St James's church, Altham. This was because of his refusal to accept the Act of Conformity, requiring him to use the I662 Prayer Book. When attitudes became more tolerant, he moved to Barrow, where the **Jollie Memorial Chapel** still stands.

WORSTHORNE [Burnley]

SD8733: 2 miles (3km) E of Burnley

When Jesus spoke of the life of the Spirit, he probably did not mean the bar in the tower of the village church. The **church of St John**, built in the early 19th century by the Thursby family, is the church in question. It claims to be the first to have located a bar in the church building. Standing at the centre of the village, it is more well known for the high quality wrought-iron work. The central square is spacious, with a small green in the middle. The village is a pleasing mix of what used to be millworkers' cottages and 16th-century houses. It has an agricultural, weaving and coal mining industrial history.

The village derives its name from Wordestorn, meaning 'homestead'. In the early 13th century a man named Henry de Wordst was the main land owner. In the Brun valley to the west, the Anglo-Saxons defeated the Danes in the battle of Brunenburk in the 10th century. Linked to Burnley to the west, away to the east of the village, the moorlands of Hemeldon soar towards the county border. North of Swinden Reservoir, 1 mile (1.5km) north-east of the village, are a number of ancient stone circles and earthworks, These include the remnant of **Noggarth Cross**, near Roggerham Gate Inn on the Worsthorne to Haggate road. Legend has it that it holds down a witch, although it is more likely to have acted as a waymarker across the moors.

WORSTON [Ribble Valley]

SD7742: 1 mile (1.5km) E of Clitheroe

The speeding traffic of the A59 is forgotten in the few seconds it takes to enter the peaceful world of stone cottages on either side of the narrow street through the hamlet. East of the Calf's Arms Inn, the white-fronted **hall**, is believed to contain stonework taken from the demolished Sawley Abbey.

WRAY [Lancaster and Morecambe]

SD6067: 7 miles (11km) E of Carnforth

In its heyday in the 17th and 18th centuries, Wray was a scene of busy activity. Along the main street, the dates of the stone cottages are to be seen by the doors. They housed the workers employed in the mill. The initials of one of the occupants, along with the date 1820, can be seen in the cobbles outside one of the cottages. The local mill has been converted into a private residence. The Quaker meeting room and graveyard from 1704 stand at the north end of the village, alongside the chapel, near the New Inn.

The church of **Holy Trinity**, halfway along the main street, has a double bellcot. It was built in 1840 and the chancel added 40 years later.

The annual fair and Scarecrow Festival is held in early May.

Wennington Hall is to the north-west of the many-greened village of **Wennington**, 2 miles (3km) north of Wray. It was first built in the 14th century and altered in the middle of the 19th. It is now a school.

WREA GREEN [Fylde]

SD3932: 7 miles (11 km) SW of Blackpool

The large green and duck pond, surrounded by houses, make this village very attractive. At one corner stand the Grapes Inn and the church, opposite a row of thatched cottages. **Cookson's Farm** was built in the early 17th century, but has been much restored since that time.

An unusual Italian reredos behind the altar is the centre of attraction in the **church of St Nicholas**. Whereas most have a carving of the last supper, this dwells on the subject of the Epiphany. Built in 1849, St Nicholas's is the parish church of Ribby-cum-Wrea. East of the adjoining community of Ribby, on the B5259, **Ribby Hall**, a Georgian house, was built by the Hornby family in 1776.

WRIGHTINGTON [West Lancashire]

SD5312: 2 miles (3km) E of Parbold

The large parish stretches from Hilldale in the west, to Mossy Lea in the east. Now part of a hospital, the stone **Wrighting-ton Hall**, on the A5029, was home to the Dicconson family. The 1742 building, reordered in the mid-19th century, contains remnants of earlier structures. Further east the road goes over a 1778 bridge with balustrades. This was built across the lake which was in the grounds of the hall.

To the west of the hospital, **Boars Den Tumulus**, on the opposite side of the road from Fairy Glen, dates from the Bronze age. The battlemented **Harrock Hall**, 1 mile (1.5km) north-west of this, was the home of the Rigbye family. It was built in the late 17th century and added to 200 years later. Set in extensive grounds, a good view of the house can be gained by

following the public footpath that starts from the Low Moor Restaurant. The Banastre family lived at the predecessor of the two-storey, 18th-century **Fairhurst Hall**, at the corner of the junction of the Common and Chorley Lane, north of Parbold. At Mossy Lea, the stone **Tunley Presbyterian church** was founded in 1662 and built in 1691. It stands in the fields, opposite Manse Avenue and near the Hinds Head Inn. When Jonathan Schofield was removed from the incumbency at Douglas Chapel at Parbold because of his refusal to adhere to the Act of Conformity, he and his followers at first worshipped in secret and then built a church.

WYCOLLER [Pendle]

SD9339: 3 miles (5km) E of Colne

A once-deserted village and a derelict hall give an air of mystery and excitement. Two thousand years ago or more, the village was known as Wicair, meaning 'dairy farm among the alders'. Until the 18th century it remained a farming area. The type of soil made it unsuitable for anything but sheep and cattle grazing. Vaccaries, or cattle farms, were separated by walls of stone slabs. Remains of these are visible up the old coach road from the visitor centre. Sheep became more important as the woollen industry began to expand in the 18th century, and the women of the farming families became weavers. To drain water off the yarn, a process called 'wuzzing' took place. The wet yarn was put in a basket on the end of a stick then placed in a hole in the wall. The basket was then spun round until the yarn was dry. Some of the old wuzzing holes can be seen in the wall of **Pierson's Farm**. At the height of its

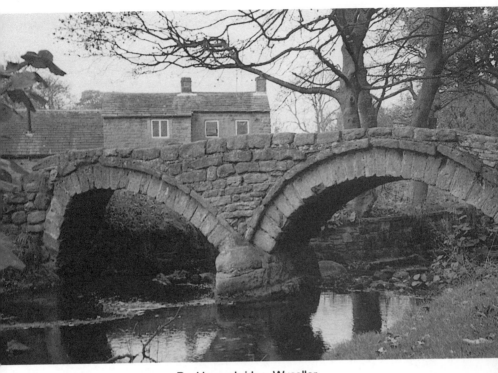

Packhorse bridge, Wycoller

prosperity, the village population was 350. The invention of the power looms brought an end to family weaving, as it did in many other villages. Workers had to move to Colne or Nelson, where the new mills were being built. The last of the weavers left the village in 1871. There were plans to flood the valley for reservoir use. However, in 1973 the County Council bought the village and 350 acres (142 hectares) of the surrounding land from the water authority. It is now a country park. Out on the moors, the grouse, plovers, curlew, wheatear, sparrowhawks and kestrel lord the skies, while stoats and weasels inhabit the ground.

Charlotte Brontë knew the area well. **Wycoller Hall**, next to the visitor centre, is thought to be the Ferndean Manor of her novel *Jane Eyre*. Built at the end of the 16th century, the hall was extended 200 years later. The grand new fireplace was the centrepiece. The keyhole-shaped space next to the fireplace is thought to be the entrance to a wig-powdering cupboard. The extension to the hall proved to be so costly that the owner, Henry Cunliffe, was, at his death in 1818, almost bankrupt. During the subsequent years of neglect, raids were made on it to take away whatever was transportable. It was only in 1850 that restoration began. Others cottages in the village have been finely restored as residential accommodation.

The **Pump House** is reached by following the beck downstream, along the footpath towards Laneshaw Bridge. It was built above a borehole and the blue water tank is still visible at roof level on the nearside of the house. Between the house and the visitor centre is **Pepper Hill Barn**, now used as a study centre by Lancashire County Council.

Clam bridge, Wycoller

The **Country Park Visitor Centre** is in one of the best buildings of its type in the county. The aisled barn was built in the early 17th century from the material of a cruck-frame barn. It has had various uses over the years – storage of grain and crops, housing cattle and as a coach house. The arched door allowed coaches to pass through.

Of the seven bridges over the Wycoller Beck, three are historically outstanding. The **Clam Bridge**, upstream from the visitor centre, is over 1000 years old. It consists of a single slab across the beck. The holes in the side used to be for a hand-rail. Damage occurred after floods in 1989 and 1990, but the bridge has been well restored. The **clapper bridge**, opposite the old hall, used to resound to the clatter of the clogs of the 19th-century weavers taking their cloth to the tenter fields. It is made up of a number of slabs, with stone supports. Originally there was just one supporting pier in the centre, but after a tree fall, this was replaced by three. It is said that ruts caused by the weavers' clogs could be seen until it was made flat after a fatal accident on the bridge. The narrow **packhorse bridge**, with two arches, may be 13th century. It is called 'Sally's Bridge', after the mother of the last squire. The reason it looks as if it is tilting is because it has been built straight out of the bedrock. Over the years, the bridge has been repaired and adapted many times.

Wycoller has its own resident ghost. One of the squires murdered his wife. He rides through the village and her anguished cries are said to echo from the hall.

YEALAND CONYERS AND REDMAYNE [Lancaster and Morecambe]

SD5074 and SD7076: 2½ miles (4km) N of Carnforth

'What's in a name?'. In this case quite a lot. One owner of the Yeland lands, on the slopes of Warton Crag, had no sons to inherit the estate so it passed to his two daughters. Each had a share in the land. When they married, each half of the estate was known by the name of each husband – Conyers and Redmayne. Yeland is from a word meaning 'high land'. Looking out over Ingleborough, the historic industries of the area have been farming, quarrying, lime production and weaving. Both villages are linear. The stone houses have many connections with the Quaker movement.

The **church of St John**, east of the road through Yeland Conyers, was built in 1838 and the chancel added in 1882. The small tower looks out of proportion to the rest of the building, which clings to the edge of the hillside. The **Friends' Meeting House**, on the main street in the village of Yeland Conyers, looks at first sight like an ordinary, old cottage. The graveyard around it suggests that it was something more. The porch and mounting stone date from 1692, when the place of worship was founded, but it was restored after a fire in the 18th century. It claims to be not only the oldest Quaker place of worship, but the most venerable of any of the free churches in England. Its interior panellings are original. When George Fox, the Quaker leader, came to the village in 1652, it is recorded that a Puritan clergyman appeared, armed with a pistol. He wielded the weapon as he asked for a light for his pipe. Fortunately,

his intentions were thwarted. The house next door to the meeting house is the old Quaker school.

Built in 1805, **Yeland Manor**, almost opposite the Friends' Meeting House, was designed in Grecian style. It was the home of the Ford family. To the west is the site of the Neolithic settlement of **Storrs Moss**.

The Gillow family, of Waring and Gillow furniture manufacturers' fame, still live at **Leighton Hall**, on the western outskirts of Yeland Conyers. It is a beautiful country house, standing where a house has stood since medieval times. In 1173 land was granted by William de Lancaster to Adam d'Avranches, who constructed a fortified manor not long after. It was destroyed by government troops in 1715 as they returned from chasing Jacobite rebels northwards. It was rebuilt in Adams style by George Towneley in 1763. In 1786 the estate was sold to a Lancaster banker, Alexander Worswick, whose mother was Alice Gillow. It was he who was responsible for adding, in 1825, the neo-Gothic façade we see today. Inside the house, the old bell pulls to summon the servants are still in place, plus the ledgers of how life was lived downstairs in the last century. Gillow furniture is much in evidence, in particular the Daisy Table, a table with eight wings. There are also collections of clocks, paintings and silver. The hills of Lakeland form a backdrop to the extensive grounds, which contain a rose garden and 1647 sundial. An added attraction is the aviary. Some of its birds of prey give displays.

Index

Also of interest from:

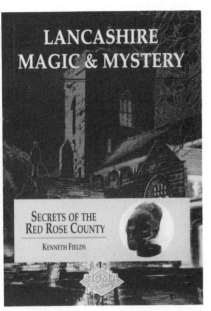

Lancashire Magic & Mystery: secrets of the Red Rose County

Covering all of Lancashire, including Merseyside and Greater Manchester, Ken Field's book guides you to places of mystery and curiosity. 'It's a smashing read!' ALAN BESWICK-GREATER MANCHESTER RADIO

£6.95

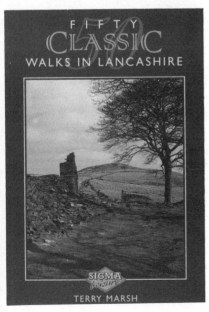

50 CLASSIC WALKS IN LANCASHIRE

"The walking country of Lancashire ranks amongst the finest in the British Isles" says Terry Marsh.
Terry writes with the determined aim of enlightening those whose image of the county is unfavourable. He reveals Lancashire at its diverse best - from wild woodland expanses and witch country, to tranquil river valleys.

£7.95

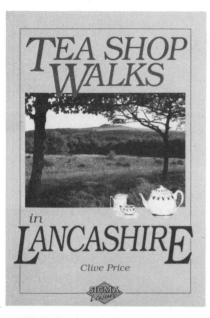

BEST TEA SHOP WALKS IN LANCASHIRE

Walk with Clive Price through breathtaking upland scenery, lush river valleys and along impressive coastal paths.

Complete your day by indulging in the celebrated English pastime of afternoon tea. This refreshing blend of walks and tea shops reveals the delights of the Lancashire countryside and its culinary specialities!

£6.95

BY-WAY BIKING IN LANCASHIRE

From Morecambe Bay to Bolton and from Blackpool to Burnley, Henry Tindell reveals Lancashire's outstanding potential as a destination for mountain bikers. 27 routes explore a fine variety of off-road tracks leading you to a wealth of countryside and villages within easy reach of towns and cities. As well as routes for the hardened off-roader, Henry has includes some safe riding and easy trails suitable for the young and old.

£7.95